WORDS

IN TIME AND PLACE

WORDS

IN TIME AND PLACE

EXPLORING LANGUAGE THROUGH *THE HISTORICAL THESAURUS OF THE OXFORD ENGLISH DICTIONARY*

DAVID CRYSTAL

OXFORD
UNIVERSITY PRESS

OXFORD
UNIVERSITY PRESS

Great Clarendon Street, Oxford, OX2 6DP,
United Kingdom

Oxford University Press is a department of the University of Oxford.
It furthers the University's objective of excellence in research, scholarship,
and education by publishing worldwide. Oxford is a registered trade mark of
Oxford University Press in the UK and in certain other countries

© David Crystal 2014

The moral rights of the author have been asserted

First Edition published in 2014

Impression: 1

Published in the United States of America by Oxford University Press
198 Madison Avenue, New York, NY 10016, United States of America

British Library Cataloguing in Publication Data
Data available

Library of Congress Control Number: 2014932092

ISBN 978-0-19-968047-4

Printed in Great Britain by
Clays Ltd, St Ives plc

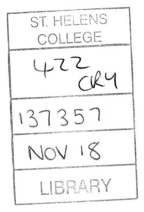

Contents

Symbols and abbreviations

†	The dagger is used to identify words no longer used in English. It is not used for words and senses whose first recorded usage is in the twentieth century.
>	develops into
c.	*circa* – used to identify an approximate date
|	shows a line break between lines of poetry
ch.	chapter
eOE	early Old English
HTOED	*The Historical Thesaurus of the Oxford English Dictionary*
lOE	late Old English
OE	Old English (see Glossary)
OED	*The Oxford English Dictionary*
Plays	A single numeral refers to an Act; a sequence of two numerals to Act-Scene; a sequence of three numerals to Act-Scene-Line. (Shakespeare line references and play chronology follow David and Ben Crystal, *Shakespeare's Words* (Penguin, 2002), also online at www.shakespeareswords.com.)
vs	versus

General introduction

Welcome to the *Historical Thesaurus of the Oxford English Dictionary* (*HTOED*) – or, rather, a tiny part of it. This huge two-volume work was published in 2009, with an online version viewable on the main *OED* website (http://www.oed.com). It was nothing short of a breakthrough in the historical study of English. I had been waiting for such a work for almost the whole of my linguistic life. I was in the audience at the Philological Society in 1965 when its originator, Michael Samuels, made public his proposal. His ambitious plan – to chart the semantic development of the entire language over a thousand years – was received with a mixture of incredulity and anticipation. Not only would it be the first historical thesaurus for any language, it would be dealing with a language whose vocabulary was known to be especially large. Expectation grew as articles and books began to be published on aspects of its content, and when it appeared, over 40 years later, it was widely acclaimed by readers for its breadth and depth of coverage. Since then, historians, linguists, philologists, and language enthusiasts in general have been working out the best ways of exploring and exploiting this unique resource. *Words in Time and Place* is an introduction to its treasures. My aim is to illustrate the way the *HTOED* is organized, to show the synergy between the thesaurus and its lexicographical parent, and to explore some of the linguistic and social insights that emerge from this interaction.

Thesaurus vs dictionary

The title *HTOED* contains two terms, *thesaurus* and *dictionary*, that are not usually seen in such a close relationship, as they deal with the study of vocabulary from opposite points of view. We use a dictionary when we encounter a word and want to find out its meaning (or some other aspect of its use). We use a thesaurus when we encounter a meaning and want to find out the words that best express it. Bringing the two approaches together always presents a challenge.

The traditional approach is that of the dictionary. Here the words are organized alphabetically, a principle first made explicit in the history of English by Robert Cawdrey in his *Table Alphabeticall* (1604), who finds it necessary to tell his readers how to use his book (I have modernized his spelling):

> If thou be desirous (gentle Reader) rightly and readily to understand, and to profit by this Table, and such like, then thou must learn the Alphabet, to wit, the order of the Letters as they stand, perfectly without book, and where every Letter standeth: as (b) near the beginning, (n) about the middest, and (t) toward the end. Now if the word, which thou art desirous to find, begin with (a) then look in the beginning of this Table, but if with (v) look towards the end. Again, if thy word begin with (ca) look in the beginning of the letter (c) but if with (cu) then look toward the end of that letter. And so of all the rest.

The alphabetical principle is an enormous convenience (once one has learned to spell), but it is a semantic irrelevance. Words which belong together are separated: *aunt* under A, *uncle* under U. We do not learn words in alphabetical order, either as children or adults. Rather, we learn them in a meaningful relation to each other as we develop our understanding of areas of experience. From the earliest years, vocabulary is presented to children thematically: they learn to distinguish *aunts* from *uncles*, *cats* from *dogs*, and *hot taps* from *cold taps*. In short, they learn the way the world is organized, lexically, into semantic fields.

The thesaurus – a genre that actually pre-dates alphabetical dictionaries – solved this problem. Roget's *Thesaurus* of 1852 is probably the best-known exemplar, and its full title summarizes its purpose: 'Thesaurus of English Words and Phrases Classified and Arranged so as to Facilitate the Expression of Ideas and Assist in Literary Composition'. There had been books of synonyms before Roget, organized alphabetically, like a dictionary. What Roget did was group these thematically, and organize his themes into a hierarchy that covered all areas of meaning. An index at the back of the book lists all the words in alphabetical order, so that a user can find the places in the thesaurus where they appear. But there are no definitions. A thesaurus assumes that you know what the words mean – or, if you do not, that you will look them up in a dictionary.

We might think that the ideal lexical product would be to combine the strengths of a dictionary with those of a thesaurus into a single book, but it takes only a moment's reflection to see how impossibly large and unwieldy such a conflation would be. *Words in Time and Place* illustrates the point on the smallest of scales. It contains only 1,240 entries representing just fifteen semantic fields, but even with minimal definition and illustration we are still dealing with over 90,000 words. Online solutions are more practicable, as we see with the *OED* website, where it is possible to display a semantic field from the thesaurus and link directly to the associated entries in the dictionary. It is this combinatorial approach which provides the most illuminating results, and which the present book illustrates.

Why time *and* place?

A thesaurus brings together all the words and phrases that belong to a particular semantic field. But how do we choose which item to use? If the English language gives us over a hundred synonymous expressions in a particular field, as we see illustrated in several chapters of this book, how do we decide which one is appropriate for the meaning we have in mind? Or, if we are faced with someone else's use of vocabulary, how do we establish the factors which explain why that person chooses one word rather than another?

The *Historical* element in the *HTOED* provides one answer: we need first to establish *when* the item appears. Words and meanings change over time, so it is crucial to know what period we are dealing with before we are able to interpret someone's lexical use. This is the challenge facing all writers of historical fiction: they need to put words into their characters' mouths that suit the time in which they lived. It would be singularly inappropriate to have eighteenth-century characters using twentieth-century slang. And one of the commonest criticisms of historical films comes from the failure of the writers to carry out the required chronological checks. For example, in Episode 5 of the television series *Downton Abbey*, Thomas the footman says 'our lot always get shafted' (meaning 'treated unfairly') – a usage that is attested only from the 1950s, and certainly not contemporary to the time when the series was set, the 1910s. The *HTOED* helps prevent such lexical anachronisms.

But a historical perspective is not enough, for in any one period there are still choices to be made. We know from present-day experience that our ability to select an appropriate word depends on our awareness of such factors as *where* the word is used – by which sections of society, on which social occasions, in which part of the country or of the English-speaking world. In modern English, we know that some words have a regional dialect background (American, British, Australian, Scottish...), some are stylistically distinctive (technical, formal, colloquial, slang...), and some are simply idiosyncratic, being used by an individual speaker or writer for special effect (often, on just a single occasion). It was ever thus. It may be more difficult to establish what these nuances are in older vocabulary, but one thing we can be sure of: they will definitely have been there. The citations collected by the *OED* over the years provide the best means I know to establish the historical contexts of use that give us a sense of a word's place in the society of the time.

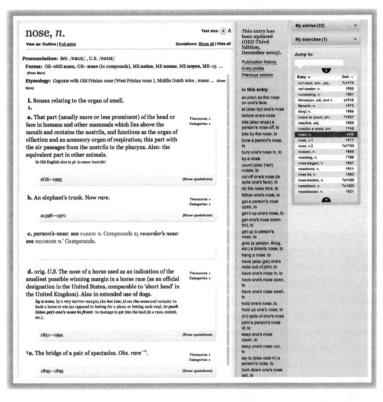

The opening of the online entry for *nose* (*n.*) in the *OED*, showing sense 1 and its subdivisions in outline mode. To see the lists of supporting quotations one clicks on *Quotations: Show all* at the top of the entry. The alphabetical character of the organization is evident in the listings on the right, showing related words in the *nose* entry and the location of *nose* in relation to the dictionary as a whole. To see the corresponding *HTOED* treatment, one clicks on the *Thesaurus* button to the right of the definition.

Words in Time and Place illustrates this double perspective for the set of semantic fields it contains. The coverage within a field is chronological, reflecting the way the items in the chosen field are organized in the thesaurus; but the treatment is lexicographic, reflecting the way these items are handled in the dictionary, and I rely on the unabridged *OED* for the definitions.

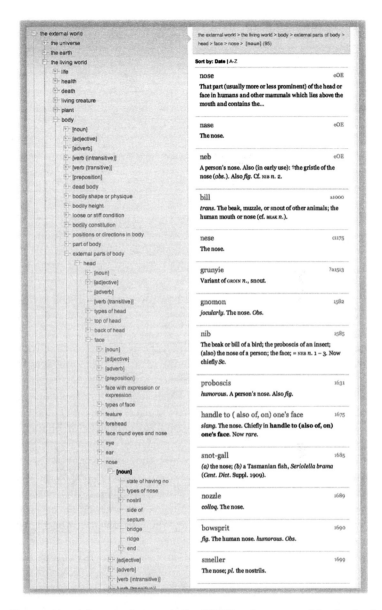

The opening of the entry for *nose* in the *HTOED* – the source of the timeline in Chapter 2 of this book. On the left one sees the path through the thesaurus taxonomy, summarized in Wordmap 2 (see Chapter 2): the initial heading (the external world) > the living world > body > external parts of body > head > face > nose > noun. Clicking on an item in red takes one immediately to the corresponding entry in the *OED*. The number of items in the category is shown at the top of the right-hand column (95). These totals will not always correspond exactly to the number of items in the corresponding chapter of this book, as I have conflated words with closely related forms, and sometimes added words from adjoining categories, as explained in the General Introduction and the Introductions to Chapter 5 and Chapter 6.

Which semantic fields?

So, faced with the vast amount of data contained in both the *HTOED* and *OED*, how does one make a selection from the thousands of semantic fields to illustrate the explanatory power of a historical thesaurus? I used several criteria in choosing the fifteen fields presented in this book, bearing in mind that the primary aim is to convey the content of the *HTOED* in such a way that readers can see how it works and how best it can be used.

My first criterion was to ensure that the choice of fields would reflect the general balance of those found in the thesaurus. At the topmost level of the *HTOED* classification, we see the whole of experience divided into three categories: 'The External World', 'Mind' (in the print edition, 'The Mental World'), and 'Society' (in the print edition, 'The Social World'). In the print edition, 905 pages are devoted to the first of these (51%), 302 pages to the second (17%), and 560 pages to the third (32%). I have therefore reflected this ratio by choosing seven, three, and five fields respectively.

My second criterion was pragmatic. The English language is now a global phenomenon, and reflects a wide range of settings, each of which has vocabulary that expresses local identity. The distinctiveness is not so much regional (though this is one of the most rapidly growing areas of the lexicon) as technological and cultural. Fields such as fauna and flora, science, education, religion, and the arts are lexically prolific, and tend very quickly to break down into sub-fields that are specialized in character, with the words requiring a great deal of semantic explanation before it becomes possible to appreciate the way they relate to each other. Chemistry and Catholicism need a thesaural treatment just as much as any other subject, but their arcane terminology would present a barrier if used in an introduction for the general reader. For this book I have chosen themes which are part of everyday life, wherever one might live in the world: (in the order in which they appear) death, parts of the body, drink, food, hygiene, mental capacity, love, language, travel, morality, money, weather, age, pop music, and space exploration (both fictional and factual).

My third criterion was linguistic: to represent the types of word-class (part of speech) and word-formation found in English. The *HTOED* routinely distinguishes words that are nouns, verbs, adjectives, and so on, and as nouns always form the bulk of a semantic classification, that grammatical bias is reflected here, in eleven of my fifteen chapters. The remaining four show a verb (Chapter 1: Dying), two adjectives (Chapter 3: Drunk and Chapter 12: Calm and stormy weather), and an interjection

(Chapter 8: Oaths). In relation to word-formation, it seemed sensible to choose semantic fields that illustrate the range of possibilities in English. There are some semantic fields where little of lexical interest happens: under the heading of 'town', for example, there are long lists of nouns (*twin town, county town, port town, fishing town, mining town*, and so on) where all one can do is note the real-world diversity. By contrast, the fields I have chosen for the present book represent most of the ways in which words are created in English.

Fourth, I have selected fields which show how the *HTOED* taxonomy operates. Most of the chapters (1: Dying, 2: Nose, 3: Drunk, 6: Fool, 7: Endearment, 10: Prostitute, 11: Money) show single semantic categories of varying constituency (ranging from the 33 entries in Chapter 2 to the 151 entries in Chapter 3). Chapter 4: Meal and Chapter 5: Privy illustrate a field where there is a main category and one subcategory. Chapter 8: Oaths, Chapter 14: Pop Music, and Chapter 15: Spacecraft illustrate a category that has several subcategories. Chapter 9: Inns illustrates two vertically related categories; Chapter 12: Weather illustrates two horizontally related categories (opposites); and Chapter 13: Old Person a combination of vertical and horizontal categories.

At the end of each chapter I have devised a Wordmap showing how the chosen category or categories relate to other categories in the online thesaurus taxonomy. Categories comprising the focus of the chapter are shown in boldface. Above this focal item is shown the path that relates it, through various superordinate categories, to one of the three major divisions of the *HTOED*. Below it are shown any subcategories. To its sides are shown the categories operating at the same level of classification. Users of the print edition should note that there are some minor differences in headings between online and print versions of the taxonomy. My Wordmaps do not display the numerical codes used for navigation in the print edition.

It is very important to appreciate that the range of items included in an *HTOED* category – and thus, the ones dealt with in my chapters – is totally dependent on the application of the taxonomy. In this respect, we need to acknowledge that there is no such thing as a universal taxonomy. Taxonomies always reflect the mindset of their devisers, as the comparison of any two quickly illustrates. The taxonomy found in the Dewey decimal classification system, for example, widely used in libraries, differs in many ways from that used in the *HTOED*. Dewey's 'top ten' categories (general works, philosophy, religion, social sciences, language, pure science, technology, the arts, literature, history) very much reflect the interests of its author. And as one looks at lower-level categories, differences multiply. To take just one example: in Dewey, Central America is listed as part of North America; in *HTOED* it is grouped along with South America.

What this means is that users of a thesaurus must always be prepared to look upwards, downwards, and sideways when exploring a semantic field. There are several cases in this book where I noted the omission of an expected word only to find it in an associated category. I discuss problems of this kind in the introductions to Chapter 5: Privy and Chapter 6: Fool. In a few cases, it is helpful to 'borrow' a word from an adjacent field to act as a source for later coinages. For example, in Chapter 3: Drunk, we find *bene-bowsie* (1637) and *boozed* (1850), which are clearly part of a semantic thread that should lead us back to *bousie* (1529) – but this last item is found not in the category I am expounding ('Drunk'), but in a co-ordinate category ('Affected by drink'). The moral is plain: read (or at least, skim) through the whole of a semantic field before deciding to focus on a part of it.

Another point to note is that, in a thesaurus, words may appear in more than one semantic category – a point not immediately obvious in the present book, where I have chosen single categories for illustration. For example, *lunch* is listed in the 'Light meal' category in Chapter 4, but in *HTOED* it is also found in a category reflecting its modern usage, 'Midday meal/lunch'. In the printed book, the comprehensive index to the *HTOED* is the place to go to find out which categories include a particular item. Online, clicking on the Thesaurus button attached to a sense will take you directly to the related locations.

Coverage and treatment

Having chosen a semantic field, I expected that the question of coverage would be decided for me: I would simply include in this book every item in the relevant *HTOED* list. In practice, there is a difficulty due to the ongoing revision process of the *OED*. The point is often missed by the general reader, who tends to think of a dictionary as a fixed and unchanging resource. In fact, all dictionaries need to be kept up to date, as new words enter the language, old words die out, and new discoveries are made about existing words. Traditionally, this was never a great problem, as new editions of dictionaries would appear only at intervals. But with online lexicography, everything has changed. As research continues, the latest findings are uploaded to the online *OED* every three months (latest revision dates are now carefully recorded at the website). This means that there is inevitably an increasing gap between the presentation of the lexicon in the last paper printing and what will be seen online. The *HTOED* was published in book form in 2009, so its electronic incarnation now differs in many small ways from what can be read there. Those who wish to relate my listings to those found in the book will therefore note several differences, as I followed the online version whenever I encountered a discrepancy.

The same point applies to treatment. Because of the intimate relationship between the *HTOED* and the *OED*, I took pains to use the definitions of the latter and to relate usage to the citations listed there. All the dates in *Words in Time and Place* reflect what is known about a word, in our current state of knowledge. I frequently talk about 'a first *OED* citation' or 'a single *OED* citation', in my entries. Always, this means: as far as we now know (i.e. in 2014). One of the most exciting things about the Internet is that it is allowing lexicographers to search for words in texts that previously have never been explored from their point of view. The gaps left by the first *OED* editors, with their limited human resources, are slowly being filled. The present editorial team is steadily working through the whole dictionary, but of course it will be many years before that task is completed. As I write, roughly a third of the entire work has been fully revised – and even the revised entries are often updated as new material arrives. Any 'first recorded usage' is thus subject to change, and by the time *Words in Time and Place* appears it will inevitably be a little out of date in this respect. Similarly, a word considered obsolete (marked by †) might easily be reborn, if someone decides to use it and the usage catches on. None of this is a reason to withhold publication, of course, for there is never a terminus when it comes to dictionary revision. The notion that a dictionary will one day be fully revised is a chimera. But it is wise to remember these methodological caveats whenever we cite a 'fact' from a historical dictionary.

A noticeable example of the way different periods of *OED* history are conflated online is in the treatment of the earliest period of the language. The *OED* included only those words in Old English that continued to be used in the language after 1150. By contrast, the *HTOED* included the entire vocabulary of Old English as recorded in *A Thesaurus of Old English*. The date-display also varies: earlier editions of the *OED* gave year-dates for occurrence (insofar as these could be established, and often qualifying them by a *circa* ('around') convention); whereas the *HTOED* labels all items in Old English as 'OE', giving no year-dates at all. The latest edition of the *OED* is in transition between the two systems, now further distinguishing early ('eOE') and late ('lOE') stages. My listings reflect the current trend, with all Anglo-Saxon citations showing simply as 'OE'.

A timeline organizes the entries within each chapter; but chronological listing can obscure linguistic relationships. After its first recorded use, a word can reappear, with only a slight modification, decades or centuries later; or it can be the trigger for a set of closely related compounds. It makes sense, in these circumstances, to cluster the related words within a single entry. For example, in Chapter 7: Endearment, I have placed in the entry on *honey* (1375) all later *honey*-related words, whose dates of first recorded use range from 1405 to 1978. They do not, therefore, appear in the timeline in their chronological place; but they are all, of course, listed separately in the Word Index.

I have departed from *OED* practice in just one respect: in citations from old periods of the language, I often modernize the spelling and punctuation to make the text easy to assimilate for those who are unused to reading early orthographic conventions. I don't do this when the example needs the original form to make its point (such as when recording Scots dialect expressions), or where a respelling would detract from the expressive impact of the text. But in cases where little is lost (such as in quotations from Shakespeare), I have gone down the modern route. Readers who want to see a citation in its original orthography can of course easily find it in the relevant online *OED* entry.

Although my treatment of individual entries relies on the *OED*, it is not restricted to it. In particular, I frequently refer to regional usage as recorded in Joseph Wright's *English Dialect Dictionary* and to the fuller account of colloquial usage found in Eric Partridge's *Dictionary of Slang and Unconventional English* – works listed in the 'Further reading and sources'. Whenever I have used an *OED* citation I have added some literary or cultural background so that the example can be fully understood – for example, saying who the speaker is in a quotation from a play. And in my introductions to individual chapters, I have summarized the salient features of the semantic field from both a linguistic and (where relevant) a sociolinguistic or cultural point of view. One of the main functions of the *HTOED* is to provide a window onto the social and cultural history of English-speaking peoples. *Words in Time and Place* also provides a window – into what the *HTOED* has to offer – as well as acting as a homage to one of the most significant lexicological projects ever.

1

From *swelt* to *zonk*

WORDS FOR DYING

A remarkable creativity surrounds the vocabulary of death. The words and expressions range from the solemn and dignified to the jocular and mischievous. And there is no better example of the latter than the 'parrot' sketch in the BBC television series, *Monty Python*. A customer returns to a pet-shop where he had earlier bought a supposedly living parrot. The owner refuses to accept that the bird is dead, and the confrontation leads to a glorious outburst of deathy lexicon (quoted here without the accents of the characters shown in the spelling):

Customer: He's bleeding demised!
Owner: No no! He's pining!
Customer: He's not pining! He's passed on! This parrot is no more! He has ceased to be! He's expired and gone to meet his maker! He's a stiff! Bereft of life, he rests in peace! If you hadn't nailed him to the perch he'd be pushing up the daisies! His metabolic processes are now history! He's off the twig! He's kicked the bucket! He's shuffled off his mortal coil, run down the curtain, and joined the bleeding choir invisible! This is an ex-parrot!!

This profusion of defunctive synonymy is not solely a modern phenomenon. An Anglo-Saxon equivalent to the *Monty Python* scriptwriters would have had over 40 expressions in Old English to choose from. His customer could have described his parrot as gone (*gegan*), departed (*leoran*), fallen (*gefeallan*), died away (*acwelan*), parted from life (*linnan ealdre*), gone on a journey (*geferan*), totally died off (*becwelan*), with its spirit sent forth (*gast onsendan*), completely scattered (*tostencan*), or glided away (*glidan*). We can't be sure about the nuances of meaning differentiating all of the verbs, but it's plain that the Anglo-Saxons were as concerned about finding different ways to talk about death as we are today.

There's a world of difference, though, between the tone of those Anglo-Saxon expressions and those often encountered now, and this is reflected in the opening entries of the intransitive verbs for 'die'. The early verbs are rather mundane and literal notions of 'leaving', such as *wend, go out of this world, fare, leave*, and *part*. Only later do we get a sense of where one is going to, with an initial focus on ancestors evolving into the notion of a divine presence: *be gathered to one's fathers, go over to the majority, go home, pass to one's reward, launch into eternity, go to glory, meet one's Maker, get one's call*.

The list displays a remarkable inventiveness, as people struggle to find fresh forms of expression. The language of death is inevitably euphemistic, but few of the verbs or idioms shown here are elaborate or opaque. In fact the history of verbs for dying displays a remarkable simplicity: 86 of the 121 entries (over 70%) consist of only one syllable, and monosyllables figure largely in the multi-word entries (such as *pay one's debt to nature*). Only sixteen verbs are disyllabic, and only three are trisyllabic (*determine, disperish, miscarry*), loanwords from French, and along with *expire, trespass*, and *decease* showing the arrival of a more scholarly vocabulary in the fourteenth and fifteenth centuries. Even the euphemisms of later centuries have a markedly monosyllabic character (such as *slip one's cable, kick the bucket, meet one's Maker*).

Influences

Words for death in all the semantic and grammatical categories represented in *HTOED* are numerous (over 1100), as people search for ways of renewing their stock of apt metaphors, and they display a variety of sources. The Bible is one influence on the list below, as seen in Wycliffe's *disperish*, Tyndale's *depart*, Coverdale's *die the death*, and the King James Bible's *give up the ghost* and *the silver cord is loosed*. Classical texts are another: Greek mythology is the source of *take the ferry*; Latin, the source of *pay one's debt to nature* and *go over to the majority*. Shipping provides *slip one's cable*; the livestock industry, *kick the bucket*; pastimes, *peg out* and *cash in one's checks*; mining, *go up the flume*; finance, *hand in one's accounts*. Wartime produces a wide range of slang expressions (e.g. *pack up, cop it, conk, stop one, buy it*) as well as more solemn idioms (e.g. *shed one's blood, fall a victim*). Regional variation is very limited, but we do see some Australianisms in the list (*pass in, go bung*), and some words are clearly favoured in certain parts of the English-speaking world (e.g. *succumb* in India).

Another reason for the length of the list is that a large number of coinages are known from just a single citation. People seem to be quite discerning, when it comes to judging the acceptable terminology of death, and several innovations simply never catch on. Some periods were clearly more inventive than others, reflecting times of major English lexical expansion, notably the end of the sixteenth century (e.g. *relent, unbreathe, transpass, lose one's breath*) and the euphemism-conscious nineteenth century, where a fifth of the items in the list appear for the first time (e.g. *stiffen, drop short, step out, walk, knock over*). A significant strand also originates in individual authors and texts, such as Gower (*shut*), Cursor Mundi (*flee*), Thomas More (*galp*), Shakespeare (*shuffle off*), and Pope (*vent*).

There is a great deal of stylistic variation. We see class division operating: at one extreme, upper-class slang (e.g. *walk* and *pip*); at the other, the language of the underworld (e.g. *croak, kiss off, perch*). There are signs of journalese (e.g. *succumb*), because finding an appropriate way to report a death is a perpetual challenge. Formality and solemnity contrast with colloquialism and slang: *yield the ghost, expire,* and *pass away* vs *go off the hooks, kick the bucket,* and *zonk*. Some constructions evidently have permanent appeal because of their succinct and enigmatic character, such as the popularity of ' – it' (whatever the 'it' is): *snuff it, peg it, buy it, cop it, off it, crease it, have had it*. It's possible to see changes in fashion, such as the vogue for colloquial usages in *off* in the middle of the eighteenth century (*move off, pop off, pack off, hop off*). And styles change: we no longer feel that *pass out* would be appropriate on a tombstone.

But some things don't change. *Pass away* has been with us since the fourteenth century. And, in a usage that dates back to the twelfth, we still do say that people, simply, *died*.

Timeline

swelt/ forswelt † OE	King Alfred is the first recorded user of these two verbs meaning 'die, perish', with the prefix adding a nuance of 'off' or 'away'; *forswelt* passed away in early Middle English, as did other prefixed forms, such as *aswelt* and *to-swelt*, but *swelt* survived; Joseph Wright's *English Dialect Dictionary* shows widespread use at the end of the nineteenth century from Scotland to Sussex; in standard English, still remembered in *sweltering* – said of weather that is so hot it could kill you.
give up the ghost OE	This is *ghost* in the sense of 'soul' or 'spirit'; first used as *give the ghost*, later *give away the ghost* and *yield up the ghost*, with a pronoun often replacing *the* (as in *gave up his ghost*); the *up* usage is first recorded in late Middle English, and became the norm after its repeated use in the King James Bible.

dead † OE	*To dead* is totally ungrammatical today, but in its sense of 'become dead' it is in the Lindisfarne Gospels, and continued until at least the fifteenth century, sometimes with a prefix (*adead*). Chaucer talks about the body being *deaded* – a usage heard today only among young children struggling with irregular verbs.
i-wite † OE	*Witan* in Old English meant 'see'. With the prefix *ge-* or *i-* it developed the sense of 'look in a certain direction before taking that direction' – so, to 'set out' or 'depart', and thus to 'pass away'. The hermit Layamon used it in his chronicle of Britain (*c.*1200), and there are examples without the prefix until the sixteenth century.
wend OE	Now only used poetically, or in the expression *wend one's way*, but in Middle English a very common verb, with a wide range of meanings to do with movement, including *wend from life, wend out of this world, wend into heaven,* and *wend to death.*
forworth † OE	Literally 'become away', used in Old English and until the fourteenth century in the sense of 'perish'; *worth* also appears in *to-worth*, literally 'come to nought', used by Layamon in his thirteenth-century chronicle.
go out of this world OE	*World* has been used with a wide range of verbs (such as *depart, leave, wend, pass from*) since Old English to describe the notion of going from one state of being to another. Probably often shortened to *go out*, though examples are only attested from the eighteenth and nineteenth centuries. It remains a popular euphemism.
quele † OE	The French *qu* spelling replaced an earlier *cw*. In its sense of 'die', it is recorded from Old English until the end of the fourteenth century, often with a prefix, as in *becwelan*. Related meanings appear in *quail* and *quell*.
starve OE	Today, of course, it typically means 'be very hungry'; but the notion of 'starving to death' captures the original use of *starve*, which meant simply 'die'. Chaucer in *Troilus and Criseyde* (*c.*1374) has Christ 'first starf, and ros' – he died and rose again. Regional usage (starving from the cold, as well as from hunger) has kept the sense going into modern times in several British and US dialects.
die *c.*1135	The default term for 'cease to live'. Old English records several verbs for dying, but *die* is not one of them. It could have emerged out of a local English dialect, not recorded in writing, or perhaps it arrived as a borrowing from Old Norse.

fare † *c.*1175	The basic meaning of 'journey, travel' was common in Old English, and by the twelfth century had developed the sense of 'journey from life'. The idea of 'moving away' could be emphasized by prefixes, as in *forthfare* and *forfere*. None of these usages outlived Middle English.
end † *c.*1200	'Farewell, friends: thus Thisbe ends', says Flute as Thisbe in the play performed at the end of Shakespeare's *A Midsummer Night's Dream* (*c.*1595, 5.1.338). The usage is recorded until the late nineteenth century, when *end up* began to replace it, and later, *end up dead*. Don't leave hospital against the doctor's wishes, says an online health site, with the header: 'Stay in that bed, or end up dead'.
let † *c.*1200	The original sense of *let*, meaning 'leave', naturally developed a meaning of 'leave life behind', in such phrases as *let one's life*. The chronicler Holinshed (1587) talks of someone making his will and testament 'not long before he let his life'. *Lose one's life*, also recorded from around this time, became the standard expression.
shed (one's own) blood *c.*1200	One of the earliest of the vivid substitutes for *die*, when someone has undergone a violent death for a cause. Christ is often described as 'shedding his blood for mankind'. The expression becomes more elaborate over time, as when people say they are prepared to 'shed the last drop of their blood'.
yield (up) the ghost *c.*1290	*Yield* developed a sense of 'surrender, give up' in the thirteenth century, and became a popular alternative to the earlier *give up* expression, coming to be used with other nouns, such as *soul*, *breath*, *life*, and *spirit*; Jesus 'yielded up his spirit' in several present-day Bible translations.
take the way of death † 1297	The use of *way* to mean a specific direction of travel led to this expression; the Porter in Shakespeare's *Macbeth* (1606, 2.3.18) produces a more flowery alternative, as he describes the professions 'that go the primrose way to the everlasting bonfire'.
die up † *c.*1300	An early way of saying that a group of people or animals died, perhaps because of hunger or disease, *up* adding the sense of 'entirely', as in *eat up*. The husbandmen 'died up with the famine and pestilence', says a sixteenth-century source. *Die off* and *die out* were later replacements.
fall *c.*1300	A natural extension of the everyday meaning of this verb in the context of sudden death, where one 'falls (down) dead', especially as a result of violence. It is still used as a solemn way of referring to death in wartime: 'those who have fallen in battle'.

fine † *c.*1300	When the Old French word for 'to end, finish' (*finer*, modern *finir*) came into English, it was almost immediately applied to dying: 'Now that I've found what I had lost', says the author of the medieval poem, *Pearl* (*c.*1400, line 328) 'Schal I efte forgo hit er ever I fyne?' – 'Shall I lose it again before ever I die?'
leave † *c.*1300	'To leave one's life' was quite a common expression in Middle and early Modern English: 'Sexburga...left her life at the door of Milton church', says a sixteenth-century source.
spill † *c.*1300	*Spillan* meant 'to kill' in Old English (the modern sense of 'flowing over an edge' is much later, seventeenth century), and a weaker sense of 'perish' was often used in Middle English. In the fourteenth-century *Romance of William of Palerne* (line 1535), Melior begs the ill William to speak to her quickly 'or i spille sone' – 'or I shall die straightway'.
tine *c.*1300	An Old Norse word meaning 'lose', which later developed the sense of 'perish'; can still be heard in this sense in the Shetland Isles and parts of eastern Scotland. The idiom *tine the sweat* – 'lose life-blood' – is also recorded in the fourteenth century.
leese one's life-days † *c.*1325	*Leese* is an early form of *lose* (also related to *lease*, *less*, and *loose*), and *life-days* was a popular and succinct way of talking about 'all the days of one's life'. The combination of the two to mean 'die' was a natural outcome, though few instances have been recorded. *End one's days*, recorded first in 1533, proved to be the long-term usage.
part *c.*1330	In Shakespeare's *Henry V* (1599, 2.3.12), Mistress Quickly reports Falstaff's death: 'a parted e'en just between twelve and one'. The verb was often complemented by *from this life*, hence, *in peace*, or suchlike, and is still used in this way, especially in formal obituaries.
flit † *c.*1340	Today, *flit* has developed the sense of light and rapid movement, often secretive: butterflies flit, as do people who want to avoid paying for something. The medieval use was far more serious, emphasizing a change in state, including the change from life to death. 'When a man fra this world sal [shall] flitte', writes the fourteenth-century hermit Richard Rolle. Nobody would use it today in relation to dying.
trance † 1340	Today we know this word as a noun, associated with hypnotism; but it came originally from French *transir* 'pass away' – literally (from Latin) to 'go across'. Few examples have been recorded.

pass 1340	An important verb of death, which gave rise to many later phrases. 'Vex not his ghost, O let him pass', says Kent of the dead king at the end of Shakespeare's *King Lear* (*c.*1608, 5.3.312). Today, the noun *passing* is globally used, but to say that someone has *passed* is common chiefly in North America. It has also become a favoured usage by spiritualists, along with *pass over* (first recorded use 1897), *pass to the other side*, and other such expressions.
determine † *c.*1374	The original meaning was 'come to an end' or 'cease to exist', so an extension to the end of life was very natural. Chaucer has Troilus telling Pandarus he would 'rather deye…and determyne…in prisoun' than lie to him – 'end his days in a prison' (*Troilus and Criseyde*, *c.*1374, 3.379).
disperish † *c.*1382	The word is known (also spelled *dispersh*) only in Wycliffe's early translation of the Bible, as in Judith (6: 3): 'All Israel with thee shall dispershen' – 'perish utterly'.
be gathered to one's fathers † 1382	One of the earliest idioms capturing the idea of being buried with one's ancestors, made popular by the use of *gather* in Bible translations, starting with Wycliffe. In later usage one could also be gathered *to one's people* or *to the saints*.
miscarry *c.*1387	If you miscarried, in earlier English, you came to some sort of harm, which at its worst could mean death. The fatal sense has carried over into modern English only in relation to babies within the womb.
go 1390	This unpretentious replacement for 'die' is one of the most common colloquial expressions used when observing a death ('she's gone'), and has achieved proverbial status ('Here today and gone tomorrow'). But it also introduces many other expressions, some religious in origin (e.g. *go the way of all flesh, go to glory, go to a better world*), some jocular (e.g. *go aloft, go west*).
shut † 1390	In *Confessio Amantis*, by poet John Gower, there is a single recorded instance of *shut* meaning 'close one's life': Pope Nicholas 'Hath schet as to the worldes ye' (2.2808) – 'shut to mortal eyes'.
expire *c.*1400	A French word (*expirer*) ultimately from Latin, meaning 'breathe out', and soon adapted to mean 'breathe one's last'. Printer William Caxton used it several times in his translations. A somewhat affected usage in modern times, the TV comedy series *Monty Python* gave it a new lease of life as one of the verbs describing a dead parrot: 'He's expired and gone to meet his maker!'

flee † c.1400	A single recorded instance, in the religious poem *Cursor Mundi* (translation: 'How shall we live when you will flee?') illustrates the sense of 'depart this life'. It never became popular, probably because people shied away from the sense of haste involved in other uses of the word.
pass away c.1400	The most popular of all the euphemisms for 'die', beloved of undertakers. In its earliest use, people talked about the 'life' or the 'soul' passing away. Today it is the named person. Related phrases, such as *go away*, never caught on.
seek out of life † c.1400	A rare use of seek to mean 'go in a particular direction', used in the alliterative poem *The Destruction of Troy*, when King Remys kills one of the Greeks: 'that he seyt [sank] to the soil, & sought out of life'. It's an unusual construction, probably prompted by the need to find a word beginning with *s* to complete the alliterative pattern.
sye † c.1400	Old English *sigen*, meaning 'sink, fall', developed a general sense of 'go, proceed', and turns up briefly in Middle English in the expressions *sye of life* ('depart from life') and *sye hethen* ('go hence') – the latter in the poem *Sir Gawain and the Green Knight*: Gawain prays that his soul should be saved 'when he schuld [should] seye heþen' (line 1879).
trespass † c.1400	A strange, rare usage – a borrowing from French *trespasser* 'to pass beyond' (the origin of modern French *trépasser*, 'pass away'), occurring also in the form *trepass*. In a sixteenth-century translation of a French chronicle, people are said to have 'trespassed', or to have 'trespassed out of this uncertain world' and 'trespassed this life'.
decease 1439	In earlier centuries, such usages as *The king deceased at his palace*, *If she deceases of the plague*, and *He deceased this world* were commonplace, but today we rarely use the word as a verb. Rather, we encounter *deceased* as a noun (*the deceased*) or an adjective (*her deceased husband*, *he's deceased*), invariably in official and legal settings.
ungo † c.1450	This intriguingly simple construction has a single recorded instance, in a religious anthology: 'They schalle se heuyn ungo' – 'they shall see heaven not go', that is, 'pass away' or 'perish'. It deserved a longer life.
have the death † 1488	Today, people *meet* their death; in the fifteenth century they could *have* or *take the death*, or even *catch* it. This last is still heard in colloquial speech: 'If you go out without a coat you'll catch your death (of cold)!'

vade † 1495	A variant form of *fade*, found until the end of the seventeenth century, when it went out of use. Many notions could *vade* – flowers, grass, beauty, health – and life itself.
depart 1501	William Tyndale's translation of the Bible in 1526 popularized the use of *depart* alone to mean 'die': 'Now lettest thou thy servant depart in peace'. People soon expanded it, as in *depart to God*. The later development of the verb, especially followed by *from* (as in *The train will depart from platform 1*), led to the form which is the modern expression: *depart (from) this life*.
pay one's debt to nature c.1513	The notion of life as a loan from 'nature' which has to be repaid was known in the Middle Ages but came to its full flower of expression during the sixteenth-century classical revival in a variety of forms: *pay the debt of nature, pay nature's debt*. The source lies in classical Latin. An index in one of the works of the Roman biographer Cornelius Nepos (first century BC) contains *debitum naturae reddere*, glossed simply as *mori* ('die'). A century later, the idiom took a new direction: *pay nature her due*.
galp † 1529	There is just one recorded instance (by St Thomas More) of *galp up the ghost* – a word which seems to relate to *gape* and *gawp*. The notion of having your mouth open led to a sense of 'vomit forth', and thus this vivid (but rather surprising) figure of speech for having your spirit leave you.
go west c.1532	Today, when things have 'gone west' we usually mean they've come to grief in some way; but the idiom was widespread during the First World War in the sense of 'died'. Why 'west'? Probably because it was the place of the setting sun, and in Celtic tradition the abode of the dead. And the nineteenth-century US usage ('Go west, young man') may have contributed to its popularity, given the association with the pioneering unknown.
pick over the perch † 1532	The origin is obscure, but presumably has something to do with the sight of a pet bird dead on the floor of its cage, having fallen from its perch. *Pick* (meaning 'fall') is the earliest expression, but usage must have been uncertain, for we find it alternating with the phonetically similar *peck* and *peak*. Over the next 200 years, a range of other verbs came to be used: one could *hop, drop off, pitch over*, and *tip over the perch*, and at least one of these is still heard today. In the *Daily Mail* in 1995 we read 'So many of my old contemporaries have been dropping off the perch recently.'

die the death 1535	The apparently tautologous expression appears first in Coverdale's Bible, and is picked up by many writers, including Shakespeare: in the opening scene of *A Midsummer Night's Dream* (c.1595, 1.1.65), Hermia is told she must 'die the death' or enter a nunnery if she does not do her father's bidding. Dr Johnson concluded it was 'a solemn phrase for death inflicted by law'.
change one's life † 1546	The expression never caught on: only one *OED* citation has so far been recorded.
jet † 1546	Another rare usage: a single *OED* citation, from a husband and wife rhyming dialogue in a collection of proverbial expressions by John Heywood (Part 2, ch. 4). 'God forbid, wife, ye shall first jet'. 'I will not jet yet', she replies. The sense derives from *jet* meaning 'go, walk, stroll'.
play tapple up tail † 1573	*Play* or *turn topple-tail* is an early version of *turn topsy-turvy* or *turn a somersault* – an expression that seems to have been used colloquially to mean 'die'. We see a similar idea in *topple up one's heels* and later versions where the heels are *turned up, kicked up, laid up*, and *tipped up*. The nineteenth century adapted the notion: an 1860 source talks about people who 'turned their toes up'.
inlaik † 1575	*Laik* is a Scottish form of *lack*, and *inlaik* (also spelled *enlaik*) was used until the nineteenth century to mean 'be wanting' or 'failing' – and thus 'failing through death'. 'I sall [shall] enlaike of my present disease', writes the Scots historian David Calderwood in the 1650s.
finish † 1578	A rare sixteenth-century usage, which never caught on – though there is an instance in Shakespeare's *Cymbeline* (c.1611, 5.5.36). Cornelius reports the death of the Queen, and how there were wet cheeks among the observers 'when she finished'.
relent † 1587	A single *OED* citation shows how the notion of finally yielding to a request (the most common sense today) prompted the application of this verb to the giving up of life. The writer talks about his father who 'must by sickness last relent'.
unbreathe † 1589	The widespread sixteenth-century practice of coining new verbs with the *un-* prefix is found in this rather pedestrian innovation. It has only one recorded usage to date.
transpass † 1592	A similar derivation to earlier *trespass*, from French *transpasser* 'to pass over'. A single poetic citation by Samuel Daniel shows its use in English to mean 'pass away'.

lose one's breath 1596	*Lose* has always been used with a range of anatomical or physiological objects: one can lose one's heart, head, mind, nerve, sleep, voice, senses, life ... – and, in a single sixteenth-century *OED* citation, breath. Today, if we *lose our breath*, we are simply having difficulty breathing. But when Bartholomew Griffin writes, in his sixth sonnet to Fidessa, 'Oh better were I loose ten thousand breath | Then ever live ...' he is thinking of something much more serious.
go off 1605	Some of our friends 'must go off', says Seyward after the battle in Shakespeare's *Macbeth* (1606, 5.6.75). The usage continued into the nineteenth century, but other senses of the verb, such as 'lose quality' and 'explode' have come to dominate modern usage, making a sense of 'pass away' less attractive.
make a die (of it) 1611	A slang phrase, sporadically recorded, and still occasionally heard in regional dialect. 'Your time just hadn't come to make a die of it', says a character in Marjorie Kinnan Rawlings' *The Yearling* (1938).
fail † 1613	'Had the king in his last sickness failed', says Buckingham's surveyor in Shakespeare and Fletcher's *Henry VIII* (1613, 1.2.184). This usage died out as other senses of *fail* came to the fore, but it was still being used in some regional dialects, such as Cumbria, at the end of the nineteenth century.
go home 1618	The operative word is *home*, meaning 'a place which welcomes you after death'. The verb varies: *go* is common, but one can also be *called* or *brought* home, or simply (in an *OED* citation from the 1990s) *get* home.
drop 1654	To *drop*, and a few decades later, *drop off* (1699), meaning 'suddenly die' or 'fall down dead', has always carried a certain colloquial appeal. The association with the word *dead* can be traced back to the fifteenth century, but it was only in 1930s America that this emerged in its strongest form, as a strong expression of dislike or scorn: *drop dead!*
knock off † *c.*1657	The sense of 'leaving one's work behind' seems to have prompted this slang usage, found mainly in the seventeenth and eighteenth centuries. In one of Thomas Brown's letters, we read of 'perverse people ... that would not knock off in any reasonable time, on purpose to spite their relations'. The transitive use remains in use: people are *knocked off*, especially in crime novels.
ghost † 1666	This abbreviated version of *give up the ghost* is known only from the seventeenth century, with two citations in the *OED* from the physician Gideon Harvey.

go over to the majority † 1687	To *go over* was usually a political expression (to change one's party) or a religious term (to convert to Roman Catholicism), but here it seems to have been influenced by a Latin phrase, *abire ad plures*. *The majority* became a popular euphemism for 'the dead' during the eighteenth and nineteenth centuries. One could also *join* and *pass over*, or simply *go* to the majority.
march off † 1693	An isolated seventeenth-century *OED* citation illustrates the use of this expression to mean 'die'. The military associations of the verb, along with its suggestion of being in total control (walking 'with regular and measured tread', says the *OED*'s opening sense) and the accompanying connotations of pride and display, must have combined to make people feel this was not an appropriate way to describe the process of dying.
bite the ground †/ **sand** †/**dust** 1697	By contrast, people liked the dramatic metaphor of falling down in death during battle and thus 'biting' *the ground* (as used by Dryden), *the sand* (by Pope, 1716), or (by Smollett, 1749, and later by innumerable American writers) *the dust*. There have been many figurative applications of the latter: politicians bite the dust when they lose an election, as does anyone who suffers a serious defeat in a competition. Even inanimate entities can be so described: 'Anti-Independence Scare Stories Bite the Dust' read a news headline in 2013 about the campaign for political independence in Scotland.
die off 1697	Another attempt, after *die up*, to capture the notion of a group being 'carried off' by death. Today it's plants and animals that *die off*, following disease, cold, and suchlike; groups of people are usually said to *die out* (1865).
pike † 1697	This is an unusual application of the verb *to pike*, meaning 'hurry away' or 'make off with oneself' – itself an unusual extension of the meaning 'provide oneself with a pike or pilgrim's staff'. It also appears in the form *pike off*. In the north of England, until the nineteenth century, the staves used for carrying a bier at a funeral were called *pike-handles*.
pass to one's reward 1703	The implication is that the deceased has *gone* (*passed*, *been called*) to heaven, but people have never been slow to point to an alternative possibility. Mark Twain was one who used the expression ironically, in *Life on the Mississippi* (1883, ch. 51). Talking about an old friend, he comments: 'He went to his reward, whatever it was, two years ago.'

sink † 1718	Like earlier *sye* and *fail*, this was a natural extension of the sense of *sink* meaning 'decline, fail in health'. 'The patient sunk under this last complaint', reports a doctor in 1804.
vent † 1718	Liquids and gases are the entities usually vented ('poured out, discharged'), and not life; but this did not stop Alexander Pope from writing, in his translation of the *Iliad* (Book 4), that Maris 'vents his Soul effus'd with gushing Gore'. It was a favourite word of Pope's: he uses it seventeen times in the work, in various senses.
demise 1727	The word is still used as a solemn noun, but is hardly ever heard as a verb (*When Shaw demised . . .*), apart from in some legal contexts.
slip one's cable 1751	An early nautical expression, meaning 'to leave an anchorage in haste'. Tobias Smollett, in *Peregrine Pickle* (1751, ch. 73) has the dying Commodore Trunnion consoling Peregrine with a storm of nautical metaphors and a caustic remark about his doctor: 'Swab the spray from your bowsprit, my good lad, and coil up your spirits. You must not let the toplifts of your heart give way, because you see me ready to go down at these years. . . . Those fellows come alongside of dying men, like the messengers of the Admiralty with sailing orders; but I told him as how I could slip my cable without his direction or assistance . . .'
turf † 1763	The use of *turf* as a verb, meaning 'to cover with turf', is known from Middle English, and was probably used regionally as slang for 'die' long before its first recorded use by poet William Cowper: 'That you may not think I have turfed it . . . I send you this letter'. He is aware that the usage is restricted, adding, after *turfed it,* 'to speak in the Newmarket phrase'.
move off † 1764	Occasional *OED* citations show that there was a vogue for colloquial usages in *off* in the middle of the eighteenth century: *move off* and *pop off* first recorded in 1764, *pack off* in 1766, *hop off* in 1797. *Hop* and *pop* were also used on their own, especially in the north of England. *Pop off* is still heard, usually in a comedy setting referring to a rich relative. Albert Chevalier's music-hall hit 'Knocked 'em in the Old Kent Road' (1892) includes the lines 'Your rich Uncle Tom of Camberwell | Popped off recent, which it ain't a sell [i.e. mistake]', and this was reprised in the film *Ziegfeld Follies* (1945).

kick the bucket 1785	Joseph Wright lists several expressions for 'die' under *kick* in his *English Dialect Dictionary*, such as *kick one's clog*, *kick stiff*, and *kick up the heels*, but not *kick the bucket*, perhaps because by the end of the nineteenth century it had become so widely used in general colloquial English. *Bucket* here refers to the beam on which a slaughtered pig was suspended by its heels – a recorded usage in Norfolk, and probably known elsewhere.
pass on 1805	A genteel euphemism, based on the core sense of the verb, 'proceed from one existence or activity to another'. A poem in the *Ladies' Repository* of 1860 reflects on 'the dear ones who passed on before'.
exit 1806	The theatrical use of *exit*, 'leave the stage', made this verb an obvious candidate for 'die', and was an especially popular choice in newspapers reporting the death of an actor. It still is. When John Candy died in 1994, one headline ran: 'Exit Laughing'.
launch into eternity 1812	A favourite word of journalists when the event is sudden. One is not *born*, but *launched into the world*; and someone sentenced to death by hanging, as in an *Examiner* report of 1812, does not do anything as boring as *die*.
go to glory 1814	The most celebratory of all the religious expressions. Tom uses it on his deathbed in Harriet Beecher Stowe's *Uncle Tom's Cabin* (1852, ch. 41): 'I'm right in the door, going into glory!'
sough † 1816	A development, pronounced 'suff', of the Old English onomatopoeic verb, *swogan*, 'to make a rushing sound'. A widely used dialect word, it captured the notion of 'breathing one's last', especially popular in Scotland, in the form *sough away*.
hand in one's accounts † 1817	Not long after *account* came into English in the fourteenth century, it was used for the Day of Judgement: the *last* or *final account*. But it is not until the seventeenth century that we find such expressions as *go to one's account* and *make one's account*, and then in the USA, during the nineteenth century, the undeniably final *hand in one's accounts*.
croak 1819	One of the most widely known London slang words for 'die', which travelled the world, thanks (among others) to swindler James Hardy Vaux, transported to Australia for his crimes on no less than three separate occasions. He includes it in a vocabulary of 'flash language' at the end of his *Memoirs* (1819).

slip one's breath † 1819	This is *slip* in the sense of 'lose hold of', also seen in the slightly later *slip one's wind*, another well-travelled cant expression. In Frederick Marryat's *Peter Simple* (1834, ch. 37) Captain Kearney defies his doctor by not dying, and remarks: 'he thinks I'm slipping my wind now'. In Australian writer Henry Lawson's short story 'The Bush Undertaker' (1896), a shepherd talks to a corpse he discovers in the bush: 'it must be three good months since yer slipped yer wind'.
stiffen † 1820	An unusual – but, given the profession of the speaker, understandable – clinical usage, illustrated by a single *OED* citation. 'I wish you'd stiffen', says Hatband the undertaker to King Tims, in John Hamilton Reynolds's *The Fancy*.
buy it 1825	Readers of Second World War novels will be very familiar with the report that an airman has 'bought it' – been shot down. In fact the expression was used not just of airmen but of any serviceman killed in battle, and the first recorded slang usage of *buy* meaning 'suffer a serious reverse' is in relation to a naval battle. It feels somewhat dated today.
drop short † 1826	A single *OED* citation from a sporting magazine shows a further slang development of *drop*: 'One of these days he must drop short.'
fall a sacrifice to 1839	A trend to increase the level of solemnity by moving away from the potential abruptness of short single words: 'Brave men have fallen a sacrifice to this kind of daring.' Alternatives to *sacrifice* were *victim* and *prey*.
go off the hooks 1840	Hooks keep things attached, so they are a prime candidate for a colloquial adaptation for death, attracting several verbs. After *go off* we find *be off* (1862), *slip off* (1886), *pop off* (1887), and *drop off* (1894) *the hooks*. The expressions all still have some life in them.
succumb 1849	This verb is usually accompanied by a stated cause – one succumbs to a disease or injuries. The usage today is often encountered in newspaper headlines: 'Five-month-old succumbs to swine flu' (*The Times of India*); 'Tiny Tim, Houston's fat cat, succumbs to cancer' (*Houston Chronicle*), both from March 2013.
step out † 1851	It is surprising to see this usage referring to death, given that the commonest sense of the phrasal verb in the nineteenth century was 'to leave a place usually for a short distance or short time'. The single *OED* citation, from 'The last bloody duel fought in Ohio' by the US short-story writer Thomas A. Burke, describes a man lying under a table as 'dead – stepped out'. However, as the speaker is drunk, it is perhaps no more than a piece of personal slang.

walk (forth) † 1858	A piece of upper-class slang, with just a single *OED* citation. In Anthony Trollope's *Doctor Thorne* (ch. 4), the Honourable John suggests that if Frank Gresham's father were to die ('if the governor were to walk'), Frank would benefit greatly.
snuff out 1864	The notion of snuffing ('extinguishing') the flame on a candle proved an apt analogy for death, so we find both *snuff out* and *snuff* widely used in slang, as well as *snuff it*. The automatic nature of the everyday act promoted its use in casual contexts, where the speaker lacks any feeling of emotion or personal involvement.
go/be up the flume 1865	The earliest sense of *flume* ('stream, river') morphed in the USA into an industrial sense ('artificial water-carrying channel'), and ended up as mining slang. The flume was usually carried on tall trestles, hence the 'up'. One has to ignore the modern sense of an amusement park water-chute.
pass out c.1867	Yet another attempt to capitalize on the 'steady movement' connotations of *pass*, but overtaken by modern uses, such as 'complete a course of instruction' and 'lose consciousness'. Most people would find the first recorded use, a tombstone inscription, incongruous today ('Caroline wife of E J Langston born on 23 March 1833 Passed out 18 December 1867'), though the usage remains alive in some American dialects.
cash in one's checks 1869	One of the meanings of *check* was a counter representing a particular value, used in card games such as poker, and in the USA this proved an apt way of concluding the metaphor of life as a game. The most vivid of the expressions was *cash in one's checks*, later shortened to *cash in* or simply *cash*; but one could also *throw in*, *pass in*, *send in*, and *hand in* one's checks – or, later, *chips*. The usage transferred to Britain in the twentieth century, in the form of *to have had one's chips*.
peg out 1870	Two games compete for theories of origin: cribbage, where pegs are used to keep the score, and the winner is the first to finish the game, or *peg out*; or croquet, where hitting the peg is to finish a round and thus to *peg out*. Eric Partridge, in his *Dictionary of Slang*, felt that the former theory, 'from lower down the social scale', was the more likely source of the phrase when used in the context of death. Other twentieth-century slang uses include *peg*, without a particle, and *peg it*.
go bung 1882	*Bung* or *bong* is an Australian aboriginal word for 'dead'. In Australian and New Zealand English, *go bung* is 'to die', used both of humans and equipment. 'The telly's gone bung' is an example in the *New Zealand Oxford Dictionary*.

get one's call 1884	*Call* has had the sense of 'summons' since the fifteenth century, but it was not until the nineteenth century that it came to be used, especially in regional dialect, for a 'divine summons' as death approaches. The first recorded usage (as *get the call*) is from Scotland.
perch † 1886	The many earlier phrases referring to a *perch* (such as *drop off the perch*) eventually simplified into the stand-alone verb. A single *OED* citation from *Sporting Times* illustrates a slang usage: 'S'pose I perched first?'
off it † 1890	A slang use of a particle as a verb, first recorded in the pages of *Punch* in a story about a young man who gave £1,000 to some sportsmen 'to see some stock which they said belonged to them – of course he found out after they'd off'd it that they didn't own a white mouse among 'em'.
knock over † 1892	A single *OED* citation from the *Illustrated London News* captures the notion of dying after an unexpected event: 'Captain Randall knocked over with some kind of a fit.' This is *knock over* in the sense of 'cause to fall down'.
pass in 1904	The abbreviated form of *pass in one's checks* or *chips*, or (in Australia and New Zealand) *pass in one's marble*. 'I want to breathe American air again before I pass in', from a New York paper, is the only citation in the *OED*. The expression may need its full idiomatic form in order to be clear.
the silver cord is loosed 1911	A biblical allusion: in the King James Bible translation, 'Or ever the silver cord be loosed' (Ecclesiastes 12: 6), referring to the dissolution of life at death. Given the widespread influence of the KJB on English idiom, it's surprising that there are no earlier examples.
pip (out) 1913	The two *OED* citations, both from this decade, indicate a youthful upper-class slang usage of the time. 'His mother's pipped', says a character in Arnold Lunn's *The Harrovians: A Tale of Public School Life*. And in *Potterism* (1920), Rose Macaulay describes a 17-year-old Jane as saying 'in her school-girl slang … "I think it's simply rotten pipping out"' (Part 3, ch. 4).
cop it 1915	From the seventeenth century on, *cop* developed a range of dialect and slang uses to do with taking and receiving. To *cop it* was to get into trouble. Army slang in the First World War is chiefly responsible for its application to sudden death. If you *copped a packet* you were wounded, probably severely; but if you *copped it* you were dead.

stop one 1916	Army slang from the First World War: 'to be hit by a bullet', which might be fatal. Only subsequent context would say whether a soldier was wounded or dead if he had *stopped one*.
conk (out) 1918	The etymology of *conk* in this sense is obscure, but probably an onomatopoeic word from the noise made by an engine when it breaks down. It is first listed in E. M. Roberts's Appendix to his war memoir, *A Flying Fighter*: 'A new word which is taken from the Russian language and which means stopped or killed.' The reference to Russian is inexplicable.
cross over 1920	A variant of *go over* and *pass over*, attested by only two *OED* citations from the 1930s, but probably still in use.
kick off 1921	US slang, first recorded in a John Dos Passos novel, *The Three Soldiers* (Part 2.1): the soldiers, worrying about the dangers of sickness, have heard about someone who has 'kicked off' with meningitis. In *The Drum* (1959), lexicographer Sidney Baker finds the same usage in Australia.
shuffle off 1922	Probably the most famous of all the literary alternatives to 'die' is Shakespeare's 'when we have shuffled off this mortal coil' (*Hamlet*, *c*.1600, 3.1.69), so it's not surprising to find writers tempted to use it. In 2011 it actually became the title of a novel: *Shuffled Off: A Ghost's Memoir*, by Robert McCarter. The verb actually means 'get rid of', which is included in a different category of *HTOED*.
pack up 1925	Various senses of the phrasal verb ('depart for good', 'cease to function', 'retire') combined to produce this (chiefly British) colloquial usage. The first recorded usage is in a dictionary of army and navy slang, compiled soon after the end of the First World War.
step off 1926	Just one *OED* citation illustrates this clearly self-conscious slang usage, in Edgar Wallace's *The Man from Morocco*: 'There will only be the bit of money I have when I – er – step off.' *Step out* (above) seems similarly idiosyncratic.
take the ferry 1928	A literary allusion to the boat which in Greek and Latin mythology takes the shades of the departed across the River Styx. John Galsworthy heads his chapter on the death of Soames Forsyte: 'Soames takes the ferry' (*Swan Song*, 1928, Part 3, ch. 15). The allusion remains available to writers.

meet one's Maker 1933	*Maker,* referring to God as creator of all things, has been used since the fourteenth century, but the notion of *meeting one's Maker* is, surprisingly, not recorded until the twentieth century. It first turns up in one of Dorothy L. Sayers' novels, *Murder must Advertise* (ch. 15). Chief-Inspector Parker is annoyed that there are so few clues on the dead man's body: 'In fact, the wretched man had gone to meet his Maker in Farley's Footwear, thus upholding to the last the brave assertion that, however distinguished the occasion, Farley's Footwear will carry you through.'
kiss off 1945	A favourite slang expression with American crime writers. A typical example is John Evans, the pen-name of Howard Browne, who has his private eye say: 'I've got a customer who wants to know who kissed off Marlin . . . and why' (*Halo in Blood,* 1946, ch. 11).
have had it 1952	An idiom that causes maximum confusion to foreign learners, due to its meaning being apparently opposite to what it is saying. As a 1943 *OED* citation from *Time* succinctly put it: '"You've had it," in R.A.F. vernacular, means "You haven't got it and you won't get it."' The notion easily extended to loss of life, especially death through a sudden event. 'One slip and you've had it', says a writer about walking a tightrope.
crease it 1959	*Crease it* is the latest in a long line of *it* slang constructions for dying. The sense development is somewhat cryptic: 'cut a furrow in something' > 'stun an animal by a shot in the neck' > 'stun a person' > 'kill'. A character in John Braine's novel, *The Vodi* (1959), knows 'who's going to crease it before even the doctors do'.
zonk 1968	Originally an onomatopoeic word echoing the sound of a heavy blow, suggestive of finality. Two *OED* citations within a decade illustrate its slang use as a verb in the context of dying: 'If Johnny zonked, it would be bad'; 'she zonked and went rigid'. The phonetic appeal of the word has motivated a wide range of urban slang uses, mainly to do with being overcome by events, so *zonk* is unlikely to have much of a future in the context of mortality. If Johnny zonked these days, it's more likely to be the result of playing dice-games, drink, or drugs.

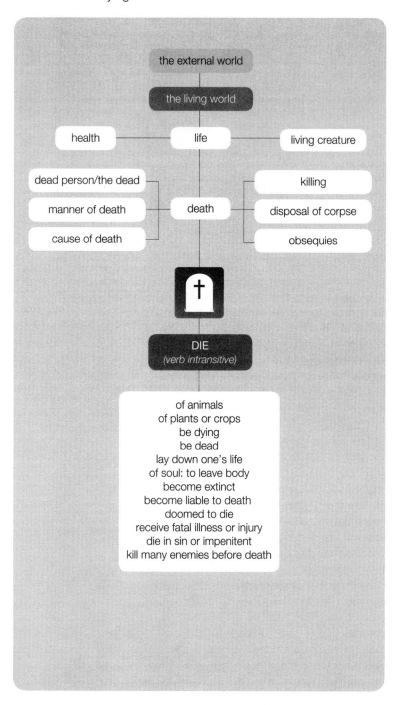

the external world

the living world

health — life — living creature

dead person/the dead

manner of death — death — killing

cause of death — disposal of corpse

obsequies

DIE
(verb intransitive)

of animals
of plants or crops
be dying
be dead
lay down one's life
of soul: to leave body
become extinct
become liable to death
doomed to die
receive fatal illness or injury
die in sin or impenitent
kill many enemies before death

2

From *neb* to *hooter*

WORDS FOR NOSE

Comments about the size of someone's nose are not just a modern phenomenon. In ch. 11 of King Alfred's translation of St Gregory's *Pastoral Care*, made at the end of the ninth century, we see the nose interpreted as one of the measures for judging the capability of a ruler. In the section headed 'What manner of man is not to come to rule', the writer reflects on the function of different parts of the body. The nose is the means whereby 'we discern sweet odours and smells, and so by the nose is properly expressed discernment, through which we choose virtues and avoid sins'. A contrast is drawn between someone who has 'too large a nose or too small', both of which evidently could cause political problems.

There is little lexical development in the early centuries, but we do see the beginnings of what would be the later story of noses: the search for descriptions that are apposite, jocular, or downright rude. In Old English we see the first animal allusions, *neb* and *bill*, alongside the various dialect forms of *nose*, and the animal theme continues into Middle English with *snout* and *grunyie*, into Early Modern English with *trunk*, and into Modern English with *beak* and *snoot*. At the end of the sixteenth century, we see a sign of what might have become a new fashion, with the first synonym from a classical language, *gnomon*; but apart from *proboscis*, a few years later, English speakers looked for their analogies elsewhere.

Shape was the dominant motivation for colloquial and slang coinages. Anything with a prominent point would suggest itself as nose-like (*nib, bowsprit, handle, index*), and some have retained their popularity over the centuries (*nozzle, conk*). Perhaps unsurprisingly, the liquid that the nose exudes never prompted much by way of coinage (apart from *snot-gall* and *vessel*), but the function of the nose was more attractive (*smeller, scent-box, snuff-box, spectacles-seat*). In the nineteenth century the noise made by the nose became a recurrent theme (*sneezer, snorter, sniffer, snorer*), and this carried through into the twentieth, with new industries providing new auditory analogies (*horn, honker, hooter*).

This is a lexical field dominated by slang. Almost all of the items in the listing below have a strongly colloquial tone, used by fraternities across the social range – at one extreme, by lawbreaking hooligans and smugglers; at the other, by upper-class sets. Sporting slang turns up several times, especially prize-fighting, where the nose is of special significance (*scent-box, snuff-box, boko, beezer*). But, as is so often the case with slang usage, the etymologies are sometimes unclear or unknown. We can speculate about such words as *boko* and *conk*, but with little hope of reaching a firm conclusion.

The ingenuity that we find in the nineteenth century largely disappeared in the twentieth. If it hadn't been for Jimmy 'Schnozzle' Durante, the pre-eminent popularizer of a Yiddish family of nose-words, there would have been hardly anything of interest to report. If I were to move on to the related categories in this semantic field, the listings would begin to display a certain predictability. Nouns for types of nose? *Hawk-nose, bottle-nose, hook-nose, Roman nose* . . . Adjectives? *Bottle-nosed, sharp-nosed, button-nosed, beaky-nosed* . . . It's been over half a century since the last ingenious lexical innovation (*hooter*, 1958). We seem content with our noseological legacy.

Timeline

nose eOE	The contrast between a large and a small nose (see the above introduction) in King Alfred's translation of St Gregory's *Pastoral Care* is given as the first recorded use of the word in English. The usual form was *nosu*, but we see the modern spelling in the compound word *nosegristle*.
nase eOE	A dialect form of *nose*, well attested in the north of England and in Scotland. *OED* citations go all the way through to the early twentieth century.
neb eOE	The first animal allusion, a *neb* being the beak or bill of a bird. It came to be widely used in regional dialects all over Britain, but today is mainly heard in Scotland, Northern Ireland, and the North of England. The *English Dialect Dictionary* has a fine collection of idioms using the word, such as *keep a man's neb at the grunestane* ('keep him hard at work') and *poke the neb into other folk's porridge* ('pry into other people's affairs').

bill eOE	Another bird allusion, used especially for a bird whose beak is slender or flattened. Shakespeare uses *bill*, along with *neb*, in *The Winter's Tale* (c.1610, 1.2.183), when the jealous Leontes observes his wife talking to Polixenes: 'How she holds up the neb, the bill, to him!' The usage diminished as other senses of *bill* developed and more ingenious ways of describing the nose became available.
nese c.1175	Another early dialect variant of *nose*, known especially in Scotland, and still heard there. Diverse spellings, such as *niz, neis, nees*, and *nease*, suggest considerable variation in local pronunciation.
snout c.1300	*Snout* originally had a wide range of applications, including elephants, insects, and birds, but it was probably animals such as pigs that led to the first strongly contemptuous description of the human nose. The adjectives in the *OED* citations provide the connotations: snouts are *colmie* ('dirty'), *filthy, foul*, and *false*. Snouts snivel. Enemies, such as Saracens, have snouts. And the negative associations continue today. Nogood Boyo in Dylan Thomas's *Under Milk Wood* (1954) is 'too lazy to wipe his snout'.
grunyie † c.1513	A variant of *groin*, 'snout of a pig' – an ideal barb for anyone wanting to be rude, such as the Scots poet William Dunbar, who provides the first recorded usage in one of his 'flyting' (ritual insult) poems. He attacks his opponent (Kennedy) by comparing his ugly nose to that of the executioner of St Lawrence, who was roasted on a gridiron: 'For he that roasted Lawrence had thy grunie'.
gnomon † 1582	The classical revival of the sixteenth century was a hard-nosed affair, with fierce debates between those who welcomed the arrival in English of scholarly borrowings ('inkhorn words') from Latin and Greek and those who opposed them. There was little sign of a sense of humour. *Gnomon* – the pillar or rod that casts a shadow on a sun-dial, thereby showing the time – is an exception. In Ben Jonson's *Cynthia's Revels* (1616), Crites describes Hedon's nose as 'the gnomon of Loves dial'.
nib 1585	A development of *neb*, mainly found in Scotland. It came to be used for a wide range of items with a pointed or tapered end (such as the end of a pen) – including noses.
proboscis 1631	A sixteenth-century Latin borrowing for an elephant's trunk or the elongated snout of certain other animals proved attractive to later writers as a humorous description of a human nose. The Australian magazine *Heartbalm* (1993) describes Cyrano de Bergerac as having 'a naughty nose, a penile proboscis'.

snot-gall † 1685	*Snot*, the everyday word for mucus from the nose, was unremarkable in the seventeenth and eighteenth centuries. Dr Johnson includes it in his *Dictionary* without comment. If it had had its present-day associations, he would certainly have labelled it as vulgar. So when we encounter *snot-gall* as a label for the nose, we need to disregard its modern inelegant connotations. It could even be used in a romantic context: one of the signs of fair weather, says the writer in *Poor Robin's Almanac* (1763) is when a lass allows a lad to 'salute her under the snot gall'.
nozzle 1689	Originally a candlestick socket, then a spout or pipe which discharges liquid or gas. With shape and function both offering an analogy, the colloquial application to the nose was inevitable, especially when the intention is to suggest its size. In Tobias Smollett's *Humphrey Clinker* (letter of 18 April), medical treatment for a wart on a nose goes wrong, resulting in inflammation and swelling, and a face 'overshadowed by this tremendous nozzle'. The appeal of the word has continued to the present day.
bowsprit † 1690	The similarity between a nose and the long boom running out from the bow of a sailing ship evidently struck playwright Thomas Shadwell. In *The Amorous Bigotte* (1690), he has a character describe a nose as 'that bolt-sprit of thy face', and he uses the word again in *The Scowrers* (1691). He seems to have been alone in his predilection, for no other citations have (yet) been recorded in the *OED*.
smeller 1699	A *smeller* is 'one who smells'; but in street slang it came to be used for the 'thing that smells'. It was popular in portrayals of low-life dialogue in nineteenth-century novels and periodicals. In *The Further Adventures of Mr Verdant Green* (1854, Part 2, ch. 4) by Cuthbert Bede (pen name of Edward Bradley), Verdant is protected from a group of belligerent townspeople by a prizefighter, the Putney Pet, who threatens them with 'let me have a rap at your smellers'.
snitch 1699	As with *snot*, *snivel*, *sneeze*, *snipe* (the bird), and several other nosey words, this is a sound-symbolic slang adaptation of (presumably) *snout*. It's difficult to resist the speculation that, aeons ago, the *sn-* onset was a linguistic reflection of a sneeze.
trunk 1699	The distinctive proboscis of the elephant has proved to be a popular analogy for a nose, especially if it's a large one. In twentieth-century sailors' slang, anyone with a large nose would be called a *trunky*.

handle 1708	A jocular description, capturing the close link between the nose and the hands (for scratching, rubbing, picking, tweaking . . .). It turns up especially in the phrase *handle of the face*.
vessel † 1813	A slang usage, attested by a single *OED* citation from a sporting magazine – 'I've tapped your vessel'. The motivation probably comes directly from the general use of the word to mean 'a receptacle for a liquid', though we can't rule out an association with blood vessels and other fluid-carrying parts of the body.
index † 1817	The image of the face as a clock (as in *dial*) had several slang spin-offs, including this one. Like earlier *gnomon*, it comes from the pointing function of the hand on a clock or watch.
conk 1819	'Oh there's a conk', says Lily Smalls, one of the characters in Dylan Thomas's *Under Milk Wood* (1954), as she looks at her face in a mirror. The etymology is uncertain – possibly a figurative use of *conch*, the shell – but its phonetic punch has made it one of the most popular slang words for a nose. If you have a large nose, you might well be nicknamed *Conky*; and you would have illustrious predecessors. The first Duke of Wellington was often called 'Old Conky' in the satirical press – though doubtless never to his face.
sneezer 1820	The nineteenth century seemed to go in for slang expressions based on the sound a nose makes, especially popular in the sporting world. A little later we have *snorter* (1829), and then *sniffer* (1858) and *snorer* (1891). Any of them might still be heard today.
scent-box † 1826	A nice example of the way people choose the most incongruous expressions to produce a piece of slang. Where would you least expect the description of the nose as a 'scent-box' to appear? As the *OED* citation sedately puts it: in 'pugilistic slang'. Boxing, to you and me.
snuff-box † 1829	The practice of carrying snuff in a box provided an irresistible analogy, especially in relation to boxing, where people were always looking for fresh ways of describing the fate of the nose. The Putney Pet (see *smeller* above) is one who used it: 'There's a crack on your snuff-box!' As the writer Cuthbert Bede comments: Pet was 'a skilful adept in those figures of speech . . . in which the admirers of the fistic art so much delight'.

beak 1854	This is quite a late date for the first recorded use of a nose being compared to the beak of a bird. The *English Dialect Dictionary* has an 1815 citation from Northumberland. Eric Partridge found examples coming from smugglers in 1822. And the *OED* has a reference to a *beake-nose* dating from 1598. All the signs suggest that the usage has been around a very long time.
boko 1859	Another boxing word for the nose, according to Hotten's *Slang Dictionary* of 1874. 'Origin unknown', says the *OED*. But there have been plenty of theories. It could be a phonetic adaptation of *beak*. It could be a further development of *boke*, meaning 'point', common in British dialects, and probably coming from *poke* (as in *poke one's nose* into something). It might be from French *beaucoup* ('much, a great deal'), applied to a large nose. At least one Victorian commentator (James Redding Ware) thought it came from the way Grimaldi the clown tapped his nose while saying 'C'est beaucoup!'
snoot 1861	Originally a dialect variant of *snout*, *snoot* seems to have entered general slang, both regionally (on both sides of the Atlantic) and socially. *OED* citations show the full social range, from the low 'I'll bash you on the snoot' (in a US magazine, 1866) to 'busting the fellow one on the snoot' (in P. G. Wodehouse, 1924). The word is still with us. 'We love her snoot', says a proud mother of her cute little girl, in a blog post of January 2013.
horn 1893	A unique case where two distinct senses, of shape and sound, reinforce each other. On the one hand, we have a traditional animal allusion, this time to the curved and pointed growth seen on the head of such species as cattle and reindeer. On the other hand, we have the warning instrument in motor-cars, which, in its earliest incarnation as a bulb-horn in the early 1900s, readily evoked the noisy blowing of a nose. Today, in the age of the automobile, any slang reference to the nose as a horn would most likely relate to the loud noise it makes.
spectacles-seat 1895	A literary novelty, from an account of a fight in George Meredith's *The Amazing Marriage* (1895, ch. 16): 'Ben received a second spanking cracker on the spectacles-seat.'
razzo 1899	London slang for someone with a red nose, sometimes spelled *rarzo*. It is a shortened form of *raspberry*, with an *-o* suffix (like *aggro* and *combo*). The earliest recorded usage is by Clarence Rook in *The Hooligan Nights*. The subtitle indicates the stylistic level: 'Being the Life and Opinions of a Young and Impertinent Criminal Recounted by Himself'.

beezer 1915	In Scotland, anything larger than normal has long been called a *beezer*, so we might expect the word to be used as slang for noses sooner or later. The first recorded use in the *OED* is from boxing, but later examples from P. G. Wodehouse and others show that it had an upper-class usage too. In *Jeeves in the Offing* (1960), we are introduced to a writer with an ink spot on her nose. Wodehouse comments: 'It is virtually impossible to write a novel of suspense without getting a certain amount of ink on the beezer.'
schnozzle 1930	A modification of a Yiddish word, *shnoitsl*, which in turn is a diminutive form of *shnoits* 'snout', which in turn is from German *Schnauze*. The coincidence of sound with *nozzle* (see above) gave it extra popular appeal, and we see it used in a variety of slang forms, such as *schnozzola* and *shnozzola*, as well as in an Anglicized form, *snozzle* (also 1930). The context is invariably jocular, and indeed its first wave of popularity stems from its use as a nickname by the large-nosed American entertainer, Jimmy 'Schnozzle' Durante. It had a second lease of life in a shortened form, *schnozz* (1940).
honker 1948	This term for a motor-vehicle horn was already recorded in a dictionary (*Funk and Wagnalls*) by 1928, so it will have been around for a while before that. Its application to noses could also date from around that time: Eric Partridge in his *Dictionary of Slang* claims it was in Australia from as early as 1910. The first recorded use in the *OED* is from an Australian writer, Ruth Park, in *The Harp in the South*: Mr Diamond makes an erratic attempt to light a cigarette butt in Hughie's mouth, burns his nose, and responds to the howl of pain with: 'It's yer own fault for having such a God-forgotten honker.'
hooter 1958	Several things hooted during the twentieth century, such as factory sirens, steam whistles on ships, motor vehicles, and toy trumpets. It's impossible to say which of them most contributed to the rise of *hooter* as jocular slang for a nose, but it became very popular in British comedy shows. It figures prominently in an episode of *Hancock's Half Hour* in 1959, 'The New Nose', where Tony Hancock gets a plastic surgeon to do something about his 'hideous hooter'.

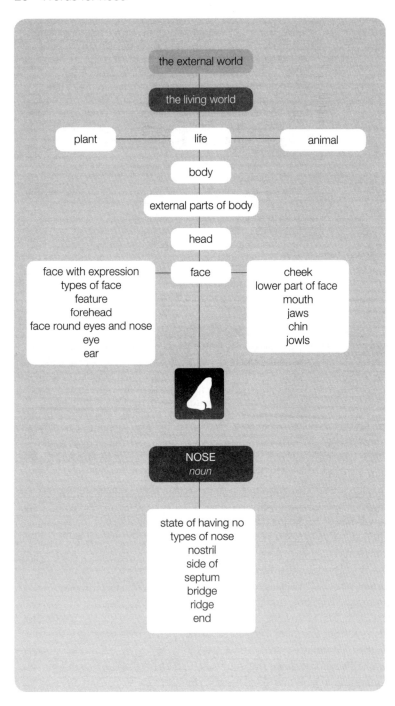

the external world

the living world

plant — life — animal

body

external parts of body

head

face with expression
types of face
feature
forehead
face round eyes and nose
eye
ear

face

cheek
lower part of face
mouth
jaws
chin
jowls

NOSE
noun

state of having no
types of nose
nostril
side of
septum
bridge
ridge
end

3

From *cup-shot* to *rat-arsed*

WORDS FOR BEING DRUNK

In the beginning, one was simply *drunken* or *fordrunken* ('very drunk'). But already the Anglo-Saxons had begun to develop a more sophisticated vocabulary. One could be *oferdrunken* ('overdrunk') or *indruncen* ('saturated with drink'), *symbelgal* ('wanton with drink-feasting') or *symbelwlonc* ('elated with drink-feasting'), or simply *dryncwerig* ('drink-weary'). But nothing in Old English vocabulary anticipates the extraordinary growth of alcoholic lexicon over the next thousand years. The adjectives for being drunk provide one of the longest lists in the thesaurus, with over 150 items in the section illustrated below, and many more in the associated subcategories.

The history of drinking vocabulary is an exercise in semantics rather than sociolinguistics. Terms for being drunk can't usually be explained by referring to such variables as age, gender, social class, occupation, or regional background. Being drunk cuts across barriers. The list below shows only the occasional indication of a class preference (such as genteel *whiffled* vs thieves' cant *suckey*), and occupational origins are seen only in some nautical expressions (*three sheets, oversparred, up the pole, tin hat, honkers*), though the etymology is not always definite. There are very few formal terms in the list, apart from a few expressions fostered by the law (*intoxicated, over the limit*), and some early scholarly words (*inebriate(d), temulent, ebrious*). Local regional variations are sometimes apparent, such as from Scotland (*fou, strut, swash, blootered, swacked*), England (*bottled, pissed, rat-arsed*), and Australia (*blue, rotten, shickery, plonked, on one's ear*); and since the eighteenth century most new words in this semantic field have started out in the USA. But it's rare to find a word that stays in one country for long, and these days online slang dictionaries have largely broken down geographical boundaries.

Semantic themes

It's the semantic analysis which is most interesting. Why has this field developed to the extent that writers regularly make a special collection of these words? We see it early on in John Ray's collection of proverbs (1678) or Benjamin Franklin's *Drinker's Dictionary* (1737), and artful classifications of degrees of drunkenness antedate these (see *fox-drunk*, 1592). It's tempting to think that the linguistic innovation is a direct result of the uninhibited behaviour which follows a bout of drinking. Certainly there are some highly idiosyncratic (and often inexplicable) coinages in the list, such as *pepst, pottical, fap, paid, muckibus, stocious,* and *schnockered.* Many words are represented by just a single citation. And several seem to be motivated by the sound of the word as much as by any meaning it might have: *jingled, whift, whiffled, squiffy, whittled, spiflicated, zonked.* The etymology is often unclear, though in a few cases a linguistic source is known, as with Hindi *poggled* or Yiddish *shickery* and *plotzed.*

There seems to be a universal trend to avoid stating the obvious. To describe someone as simply *drunk, in drink,* or *in liquor* is accurate but evidently uninspiring. One fruitful vein is to find terms that characterize drunken appearance (*owl-eyed, pie-eyed, cock-eyed, lumpy, blue, lit*) or behaviour, especially erratic movement (*slewed, bumpsy, reeling ripe, tow-row, rocky, on one's ear, zigzag, tipped, looped*) or lack of any movement at all (*stiff, paralytic*). Another is mental state, such as being muddled (*fuddled, muzzed, queer, woozy*), elated (*high-flown, wired, pixilated*), or worn down (*whittled, half-shaved, rotten, crocked, the worse for wear*).

Some of the earliest descriptive terms come from the containers used by drinkers: the fourteenth-century *cup-shotten* is the first, but later centuries have given us such words as *pot-shotten, jug-bitten, tap-shackled, flagonal, tanked, canned, potted,* and *bottled,* as well as the more genteel *in one's cups.* The contents of the container are also productive, as with *sack-sopped, groggy, lushy, malty, rummy, swizzled, skimished, plonked,* and *bevvied.* And the fact that the drinks are, by definition, liquid, has resulted in several more, such as *soaken, wet, swilled, swash, sozzled, blotto,* and *liquefied.* At the other extreme, euphemisms bear witness to the desire to avoid making any direct allusion at all to the drinking situation: *concerned, disguised, under the influence, tired and emotional.*

Some of the most interesting terms are those where drinkers exaggerate their state during or after a drinking session, usually by suggesting the thoroughness of their achievement. The notion of being 'completely filled' is one theme: *topped, loaded, overseen, overflown, overshot, well-lubricated, well-oiled, drink-drowned*. The notion of reaching a maximum is reinforced by the frequent use of the particle *up* (*boozed up, tanked up,* etc.). By comparison, there are relatively few words for being mildly drunk (such as *tight* and *squiffy*), though attempts at quantification can be made (as in *half-tanked* and *half-cut*). Cooking is another theme, especially since the eighteenth century: *stewed, boiled, pickled, soused, fried, steamed*. And hurtful danger provides a third theme, especially in the twentieth century: *hit under the wing, shot in the neck, scratched, cut, shot, stung, stunned, toxed, polluted, gassed, bombed*. The lexicon of drink can at times be very dark.

These days, though, the leading question for the lexicologist has to be: what exactly *is* the lexicon of drink? Many of the words formerly associated with drinking are now associated with drugs, such as *high, loaded, pie-eyed, piped, potted, wasted,* and *blasted*. Often it is simply unclear, without further context, what state a person is in. Indeed, sometimes there is a three-way ambiguity, as a further meaning has emerged that is to do with neither alcohol nor drugs. If someone says they are *zonked*, are they drunk, high, or just tired out?

Timeline

fordrunken † OE	First recorded in one of King Alfred's translations, it remained through Middle English; in the prologue to *The Miller's Tale* (c.1386), Chaucer describes his character as so *fordrunken* that he could hardly sit on his horse.
drunken OE	Similar to *fordrunken*, but without the intensifying force of the *for-* prefix; in continuous use ever since before nouns (as in *a drunken sailor*), and thus complements *drunk*, used after verbs (*the sailor was drunk*).
cup-shotten † c.1330	One is 'overcome with liquor'. This is *shotten* in the sense of 'discharged' or 'emptied': everything is gone from the cup. A form *cup-shot* is also recorded, but much later, in 1593. There's a link with the noun, as in *a shot of brandy*. We will meet the adjectival use of *shot* again in later centuries.
drunk c.1340	The default term, a development of *drunken*, and still the commonest usage. It readily cohabits with adverbs, such as *dead* and *blind*, and similes, such as *drunk as a lord*. The adverbs change with the years: in the sixteenth century one could be *beastly drunk*; a few years later we find *mad* and *raging drunk*. So do the similes: OED citations show *drunk as a rat* (1553), *a beggar* (1622), *a wheelbarrow* (1709), and *a fiddler* (1832).

inebriate † 1497	The first of the scholarly expressions, from Latin *inebriatus* 'intoxicated', and used both literally and figuratively. The earliest *OED* citation is in fact about someone 'inebriate in the love of God'. The first recorded use of *inebriated* is much later (1615). In an 1839 essay by Henry Rogers, we see a summary of the way a semantic distinction would later evolve: 'To be "drunk" is vulgar; but if a man be simply "intoxicated" or "inebriated", it is comparatively venial.'
overseen † c. 1500	A quotation from Sir Thomas Elyot (1532) captures the essence of the word: 'Men calleth him overseen, that is drunk, whan he neither knoweth what he doeth, nor what he ought to do.' This is an extension of *oversee* in the sense of 'go beyond a certain point', 'act in an unbecoming manner', and it was often stated explicitly what the source of the problem was: *overseen with drink, overseen with wine*. It was a genteel usage until the seventeenth century, but then became increasingly colloquial, and was eventually heard only in regional dialects.
in liquor 1509	*Liquor*, meaning 'a liquid for drinking', had been in English for a while before it developed its sense of a drink produced by fermentation or distillation. Various adjectival uses for the intoxicating effect quickly developed: one could be *in liquor* or *the worse for liquor* – or, in the seventeenth century, simply *liquored*.
bousy 1529	The first instance of *boozy*, spelled with *ou* or *ow* until the eighteenth century. An early use of a verb *bouse* is recorded in c. 1300, from Dutch (where it was originally the name of a drinking vessel), but it doesn't become common until the sixteenth century, along with the adjective, at first chiefly in the cant of thieves and beggars. 'Up rose the bowzy Sire', writes Alexander Pope in the *New Dunciad* (1742, line 485), one of a long line of poets to be attracted to the word.
fou 1535	A Scots word, derived from *full*. Robert Burns uses it in his poem 'Death and Dr Hornbook' (1787): the poet meets Death on the road, and reflects on how much he'd had to drink: 'I was na [not] fou, but just had plenty.' It is still used in parts of Scotland, especially in such phrases as *blin fou* ('blind drunk'), *roarin fou*, and *fou as a puggie* ('monkey').
nase † 1536	The word turns up in various spellings, such as *nace* and *naze*, and later with a suffix, as *nazzy*. 'Origin unknown', says the *OED*, but some writers have derived it from German *nass*, in its sense of 'liquid'. It seems to have died out in the seventeenth century.

tippled 1564	A *tippler* was a retailer of ale – a tavern-keeper. (The word may be related to *tap*.) It is first recorded in 1396 – curiously, long before the associated verb (to *tipple* – to sell liquor), which is known only from the early sixteenth century. At around that time, a habitual drinker also came to be called a *tippler*, especially when the nuance was a regular drinker of small quantities. The adjective *tippled* soon followed, but isn't recorded after the seventeenth century. The noun is still with us, though: *going for a tipple?*
intoxicated 1576	The verb *intoxicate* arrived as one of the classical (or 'inkhorn') borrowings in the early sixteenth century, meaning 'to poison', used for objects as well as people. A sword, for example could be described as *intoxicated* if it was tipped with a poison. Both verb and adjective were soon applied to the stupefying effects of alcoholic drink, with *intoxicate* a variant form. The formal tone continues to the present day, and is especially encountered as part of law enforcement. A legal distinction is drawn between being drunk (where someone nonetheless has an intention to commit a crime) and being intoxicated (where the person is incapable of having such an intent).
pepst † 1577	A single *OED* citation suggests that this word meant 'drunk'. The writer was evidently looking for a rhyme to go with *slepst* ('sleepest'), and came up with *pepst*, so it may be a personal coinage. Its origin remains a mystery.
overflown † 1579	The notion is one of being overwhelmed with alcohol. In Thomas Middleton's *The Phoenix* (1607), the prince is attacked for his exaggerations, but defends himself by blaming drink: 'I was over-flown when I spoke it, I could ne'er have said it else.'
whip-cat † 1582	*Whip the cat* has long been used as an idiom with a wide range of meanings, such as 'shirk work' or 'play a practical joke', and 'get drunk' was one of the earliest. Presumably the drunkard comes home in a bad mood and takes it out on the cat – and noisily, judging by an entry in John Florio's Italian/English dictionary of 1611. *Parlare brianzesco* is glossed as 'to speake tipple, drunken or whip-cat language'. To *jerk*, *shoot*, or *whip the cat* also meant 'vomit', especially from too much drink – a usage recorded by the *OED* under *cat*.
pottical † 1586	This is an adaptation of *pot* (as in modern *pint pot*), to refer to a poet who has been 'inspired by alcohol'. It is a pun on *poetical*, and seems to have had a brief vogue at the end of the sixteenth century.

fox-drunk † 1592	This is the last in a sequence by Thomas Nashe in his pamphlet *Pierce Pennilesse: His Supplication to the Devil* (1592). There are eight kinds of drunkenness: *ape-drunk* (leaping about); *lion-drunk* (quarrelsome); *swine-drunk* (sleepy); *sheep-drunk* (incoherent); *maudlin-drunk* (weeping); *martin-drunk* (drinking oneself sober); *goat-drunk* (becoming lecherous); and *fox-drunk* (becoming crafty). Some of the allusions date from medieval times.
nappy † 1592	*Nap* has a long association with drinking. In Old English the word could refer to a drinking cup, and in late Middle English *nappy* began to be used to describe beer with a foaming head. It was applied to people by the end of the sixteenth century: to be *nappy* was to be slightly drunk, 'merry'. Usage was mainly in northern dialects of England and in Scotland. Scots poet Charles Gray sums it up (in his 'Epistle to P A H', 1811): 'When bousin', carousin', | Man gies [gives] his mind to mirth; | While nappy, he's happy, | As onie [any] King on earth.'
sack-sopped † 1593	The word is recorded only in a poem 'The Ass's Fig' by writer and scholar Gabriel Harvey. It is part of his diatribe against Thomas Nashe, whom he describes as having a 'claret spirit' and displaying 'sack-sopt miseries'. (*Sack* was a general name for a type of Spanish white wine.)
fap † 1597	Scholars have not known what to make of this word, first appearing in Shakespeare's *The Merry Wives of Windsor* (1597, 1.1.164): Bardolph refers to someone who has 'drunk himself out of his five sentences [*i.e.* senses]' as being *fap*. Some editors conclude it is a typesetter's error. But Elizabethan scholar C. J. Sisson found another example of it, meaning 'drunk', in seventeenth-century church-wardens' accounts in the West Midlands. And Joseph Wright records a south-west England dialect word referring to beer-froth, spelled *fob*, which may be related.
in drink 1598	The use of *drink* to mean 'intoxicating alcoholic beverage' can be traced back to Anglo-Saxon times, but it is Shakespeare's Falstaff who has the first recorded use of the phrase *in drink*. In *Henry IV Part 1* (c.1597, 2.4.407), while play-acting the role of Henry IV, he tells Prince Hal: 'I do not speak to thee in drink, but in tears.'
disguised † c.1600	John Dryden makes the meaning clear, in his comedy *The Wild Gallant* (1669). Failer offers Bibber some ale, who demurs: 'I had too much of that last night; I was a little disguised, as they say.' Failer isn't sure what he means, so Bibber explains: 'Well, in short, I was drunk; damnably drunk with ale.' The other meanings of *disguised* led to more explicit expressions, such as *disguised in liquor*.

drink-drowned † 1600	The expression is recorded just once, in an epigram (No. 22) by the pamphleteer Samuel Rowlands about a 'mad drunk fool'.
pot-shotten † 1604	A parallel development to medieval *cup-shotten*. It also appears in the form *pot-shot* (1627).
tap-shackled † 1604	A different view of the drunkard: fettered to the tap of the beer barrel. In his translation of Bishop Hall's *The Discovery of a New World* (c. 1609), John Healey tells of a man who, 'being truly tap-shackled, mistook the window for the door'.
dagged † c. 1605	*Dag* has long been used dialectally in many parts of England and Scotland for 'dew', and as a verb 'to bedew', so it was a short step to an adjective meaning 'bedewed' and thus 'soaked'. The slang use to mean 'soaked with drink' then travelled the world. Benjamin Franklin includes it in the *Drinker's Dictionary* he compiled for the *Pennsylvania Gazette* in 1736/7: 'He's dagg'd'.
bumpsy † 1611	The staggering gait of someone drunk doubtless motivated this coinage. But it also appears in the spelling *bumsie*, where there may be a different origin. *Bum* is used in Langland's *Piers Plowman* (1362) meaning 'to drink' – a usage which may be onomatopoeic, imitating the motion of the lips while drinking. During the sixteenth century, *bum* was a child's word for a drink, and in *Tom Tytler and his Wife* (1598) we read of Tipple arriving with liquor and saying 'here is good bum'.
foxed † 1611	A common expression around the year 1600 was *to catch the fox* or *hunt the fox*, meaning 'to get drunk'. The association is the notion of craftiness, which is one of the stages of drunkenness (see *fox-drunk* above). *Foxed* as an adjective gradually became colloquial, and then dialectal, and fell out of use as other meanings of the verb arose. Today, anyone who is 'foxed' is puzzled, not drunk.
in one's cups 1611	The King James Bible gave this expression a popular boost, which has lasted to the present day. In the first book of Esdras (3: 22), a young man writes about what wine does to people: 'And when they are in their cups, they forget their love both to friends and brethren, and a little after draw out swords.' A parallel usage is *in one's pots*, or *in the pots*, first recorded in 1618, and also still encountered today, though not with such frequency.
love-pot † 1611	Another expression (see *whip-cat* above) found in John Florio's Italian/English dictionary: *berghinellare* is glossed as 'to gad abrode a gossoping as a pratling love-pot woman'. He seems to have liked coinages in *pot*: *brianzesco* is glossed as 'tipsy, drunken, pot-sick'.

whift †
1611

One of the senses of the verb *whiff* was to 'imbibe' (liquor), and it seems (from the solitary *OED* citation) that the associated adjective developed a slang usage meaning 'drunk'. Randle Cotgrave, in his French/English dictionary (1611), glosses *entrebeu* as 'halfe drunke, almost whift'. A similar form resurfaces some 300 years later in society slang, as *whiffled* (1927).

reeling ripe
*c.*1611

The widely used expression is *reeling drunk* – so drunk that one staggers around. But in Shakespeare's *The Tempest* (*c.*1611, 5.1.279) Trinculo is described as *reeling ripe*, and the bard's influence seems to have kept the idiom alive. Tennyson is one who used it, in 'Will Waterproof's Lyrical Monologue' (1842). It was reinforced in the nineteenth century by the slang use of *ripe* (from 1823) and a dialect use of *reeling*, both meaning 'drunk'.

owl-eyed †
1613

If you are *drunk as an owl*, you are 'dead drunk' – a nineteenth-century usage Joseph Wright found in Somerset (reported in his *English Dialect Dictionary*). The explanation probably lies in this seventeenth-century usage, where the glazed eyes of the drunk echo the unblinking stare of the owl.

scratched
1622

In *The Water-Cormorant his Complaint*, the pamphleteer John Taylor observes about a drunken man that 'some say hee's...scratched'. This indicates a wider usage, but to date his quotation is the only one supporting this sense in the *OED*.

high †
1627

The use of *high* to mean 'elated, merry' (as in *high spirits*) made it a natural description of someone drunk. People were described as 'high with wine' or 'high in their cups', and in the twentieth century people talked about being *high as a kite*, meaning 'very drunk'. But drugs have since overtaken drink. In 1846, the historian James Taylor writes: 'I met three gentlemen...and they were all high.' That could not mean 'drunk' today.

temulent †
1628

A Latin borrowing, which had some popularity in the mid-seventeenth century, typically used with behavioural nouns (*temulent rage, frenzy, rapture*). Some writers preferred *temulentive*; others *temulentious* (1652). The word was picked up by the medical profession, along with *temulency* ('drunkenness'), and retained its appeal into the nineteenth century.

ebrious 1629	Several words based on Latin *ebrius* 'drunk' came into English in the sixteenth and seventeenth centuries, such as *ebriety* ('drunkenness'), *ebrious*, and *ebriously*. In the nineteenth century, the root seems to have caught the eye of magazine writers, who use it jocularly. In an issue of *Blackwood's Magazine* (1847), a youth is described as having 'ebriate eyes'. A Cassell's publication (1858) talks about 'those young sots with the ebrious faces'. *Atlantic Monthly* (1871) refers to a 'copiously ebriose' cabman. The words are still occasionally seen in literary circles, and attract those who like to search out unusual words.
jug-bitten † 1630	The pamphleteer John Taylor brought together all the receptacles to describe people who have 'lost all reasonable faculties of the minde' through drink. They are 'pot-shot, jug-bitten, or cup-shaken'. The expressions seem not to have outlasted the seventeenth century.
topped † 1632	The notion of *topping up* ('fill to the brim') is attested from the end of the sixteenth century. It was a short step from there to an adjectival use meaning drunk, though there are no *OED* citations after 1637.
toxed † 1635	An abbreviation of *intoxicated*, also spelled *toxt*. *Tox*, *toxed*, and *toxting* were favourite usages of author Thomas Heywood, whose anti-drinking tract, *Philocothonista*, uses them all. There are as yet no citations in the *OED* from other authors, but in the nineteenth century Joseph Wright found *toxie* and *toxified* in Scotland, and Eric Partridge found *toxy* in a 1913 dictionary of slang by A. H. Dawson.
bene-bowsie † *c.*1637	'Well-boozed', in the cant of thieves. The *bowsie* part is a continued use of a word for 'drunk' that had been in English for over a century (see *bousy* above). The *bene* part is probably an Anglicized version of French *bien* or Latin *bene* 'well'. The first recorded usage is from Ben Jonson, in his *Masque of Gypsies*: 'You must be bene-bowsie, | And sleepy and drowsy'.
swilled † 1637	The verb *swill* has always had associations with liquid, with one of its senses emphasizing the notion of drinking greedily and excessively. A single *OED* citation from John Milton illustrates an adjectival use: in *Comus* (line 178). A lady hears the noise of merriment, and worries about meeting at night 'the rudeness and swilled insolence | Of such late wassailers'.

paid † 1638	Another single quotation, this time from poet and playwright James Shirley. In *The Royal Master* (2.1), Domitilla's secretary, Bombo, drinks numerous cups of wine. A servant Iacomo observes 'He'll be drunk presently', and a few lines later his fellow-servant Pietro confirms: 'He's paid.'
soaken † 1651	The notion of saturation implicit in the verb *soak* led naturally to a sense of 'drenched with drink', first as *soaken* and later (1737) as *soaked*. The latter is still encountered today, but usually as the second element of a compound such as *gin-soaked* and *rum-soaked*, to avoid ambiguity with *soaked* meaning simply 'wet through'.
flagonal † 1653	A literary coinage, by Sir Thomas Urquhart in his translation of Rabelais's *Gargantua and his Son Pantagruel*: 'a cup of dissimulation or flagonal hypocrisy' occurs in the 'Discourse of the drinkers' (1653, ch. 1.5).
fuddled 1656	The verb *fuddle*, 'to have a drinking bout', is known from the late sixteenth century, and led to several idioms, such as *to fuddle one's cap* or *nose* – 'to get drunk'. The rhyme with *muddle* brought a later blurring of the two meanings, so that, when we read (in an 1830 publication) 'I was not drunk, I was only fuddled', it isn't clear whether the sense is 'slightly drunk' or 'not drunk at all'. Modern usage of *fuddle* tends to go for the 'confused' sense (as with *befuddled*).
high-flown † 1656	Today, *high-flown* is used chiefly with reference to an elevated style of language, but in earlier centuries it could be used with reference to any kind of elation – including that which comes through drinking. The usage is illustrated by a quotation from James Ussher's chronology, *The Annals of the World* (1656): 'The king, being somewhat high flown with drink'.
cut 1673	Slang idioms such as *cut in the leg* and *cut in the back* hint at how the adjective *cut* developed its sense of 'drunk'. We find *a little cut over the head*, 'slightly drunk', in the late eighteenth century. The meaning is usually reinforced by a modifier of some kind, such as *deep cut*, *completely cut*, and (1893) *half-cut*.
nazzy 1673	A development of *nase* (above), found also in other spellings, such as *nasie* and *nazy*. It is still used in parts of northern England, especially Yorkshire. There is even a gender distinction: a drunken man is a *nazy-cove*; a drunken woman a *nazy-mort*. And a drunken fool is a *nazy-nab*.

concerned † 1687	This euphemism became really popular in the eighteenth and nineteenth centuries. In 'Mary the Cook-Maid's Letter to Dr Sheridan' (1723), Jonathan Swift gives a good account of himself through the rhyming persona of Mary. He was never drunk, she asserts: 'Not that I know his reverence was ever concern'd to my knowledge, | Tho' you and your come-rogues keep him out so late in your wicked college'. The usage is an ingenious development of *concerned* meaning 'actively involved', but the possible ambiguity led to the context usually being made explicit: *concerned with drink, concerned in liquor*.
whittled † 1694	A single example, from a translation of Rabelais, shows the adjectival use; but the use of *whittled* as a verb dates from the 1530s. The link with the original sense of *whittle* ('cut thin slices or shavings from a surface') isn't immediately obvious, but there is clearly some sort of analogy between wearing away a stick and being worn down with drink. Or perhaps it is the movement which motivated the link: to be *on the whittle* is to be in a state of fidgety unease (recorded in Joseph Wright's *English Dialect Dictionary*). Wright also found *whittled* 'drunk' in some north country dialects of England, but thought the usage was already obsolete.
suckey † 1699	A canting dictionary glosses this word as 'drunkish, maudlin'. *Suck* was also slang at this time for any strong drink.
oiled 1701	*Oiled* must at first have meant 'mildly drunk', for otherwise there would have been no reason to coin the very frequent *well-oiled* (which is in fact the first recorded use). A twentieth-century oft-repeated pun describes the drunken narrator as telling *the oiled oiled story* (for *the old old story*).
wet † 1704	The usage captures the idea of being kept primed with liquor, as seen in a later quotation from Samuel Taylor Coleridge (1834): 'Some men are like musical glasses; to produce their finest tones, you must keep them wet.' Thackeray (1849) talks of a drinking session resulting in a 'wet night' (in 'On Some Old Customs of the Dinner Table'). The adjective is no longer used in this way, but modern idioms continue the verb usage, as in *wet the baby's head* and *wet one's whistle*.
tipped † 1708	The basic sense ('tilted, overturned') was an obvious source of a slang usage for 'drunk'. A single *OED* citation records 'songs obscene and tipt discourse'.

tow-row † 1709	This rhyming reduplication of *row* ('noisy argument') was popular in the nineteenth century in the sense of 'uproar', but a single *OED* citation from the *Tatler* periodical indicates a much earlier slang usage. The implication is probably one of being 'drunk and disorderly'.
swash † 1711	An onomatopoeic dialect word, found especially in Scotland during the eighteenth and nineteenth centuries. We were 'right swash', says Allan Ramsay, in his Scots dialect poem, 'Elegy for Maggy Johnstoun' (1711).
strut † 1718	Another Scots word, often spelled *strute* or *stroot*, meaning 'crammed full' – of either food or drink. Allan Ramsay again provides an example: in 'Christ's Kirk on the Green' (1718, Canto 2), two sturdy lads hold the 'strute' Tam Lutter up to stop him falling over.
jagged 1737	*Jag* was an English dialect word which travelled to America. John Ray, in his collection of English proverbs (1678), includes it as a description of someone who has had a 'load' of drink. But the adjectival use seems not to have developed in Britain. All the citations in the *OED* are from the USA or Canada. It's still in use: an *Urban Dictionary* citation from 2005 talks about being 'soooo jagged last night'.
rocky 1737	The tottering gait of a drunk led to this colloquial adaptation. 'He's rocky…lost his rudder', says the first *OED* citation, from the *Pennsylvania Gazette*. Joseph Wright found it in Yorkshire and Nottinghamshire, and it was probably much more widespread.
stewed 1737	This is the first of the cooking-related slang substitutes for 'drunk', where the notion of food being slowly and thoroughly boiled in a closed vessel is seen as analogous to the way a drinking session can steadily reduce someone to a state of total inebriation. (Later terms include *corned*, *salted*, and *pickled*.) Additional reference to the top part of the body reinforce the extent of the drunkenness: one is *stewed to the ears, eyebrows, hat*, or (to those who 'drink like a fish') *gills*.
stiff 1737	After the drunken fall, the rigid body. From the sixteenth century, hardened imbibers were being called *stiff drinkers*; and since the nineteenth century, strong spirits have been described in the same way (*I need a stiff drink*). The use caught on in the USA: if you're *stiff*, you are very drunk indeed.

muckibus †
1756

A jocular usage reported in an anecdote of Horace Walpole (in a letter to George Montagu, 20 April): at a supper, he hears Lady Coventry say that 'if she drank any more, she should be muckibus'. Lady Mary Coke enquired what this meant, and was told that it was 'Irish for sentimental'. The mock-Latin ending is known from other facetious eighteenth-century slang formations, such as *stinkibus*, but there's no obvious connection with *muck*. Lady Coventry came from Ireland. The likelihood is that Walpole misheard a genuine Irish word, perhaps *maoithneach* 'sentimental'.

groggy †
1770

The nautical mixture of rum and water known as *grog* has come down to us through many a pirate story – most famously in Robert Louis Stevenson's *Treasure Island* (1883) – and having too much grog made one *groggy* or (1842) *grogged*. The sense of 'drunk' died out in the nineteenth century as the modern meaning of 'tottering, unsteady' emerged.

muzzed
c.1788

The eighteenth century saw the arrival of a group of *muzz*-words, all to do with being confused: *muzz, muzzle, muzzy,* and *muzzed* – the last two especially associated with the befuddled state arising from too much alcohol. *Muzzy* (from 1795) now has a wide range of colloquial application, referring to anything that is hazy or indistinct, so when used with reference to drink it is usually qualified in some way, as in a 1956 quotation which refers to a woman 'whose head was muzzy with champagne'.

slewed
1801

The nautical verb *slew* (first recorded in 1769) refers to the way an object swings round without shifting from its place – an apt description of the uncertain oscillations observed when drunks try to stand up. The earliest use is by an American writer, but by the mid-nineteenth century it was being used by writers such as Charles Dickens. A twentieth-century intensification is to be *slewed out of one's skull*.

blootered
1805

Blooter – spelled also as *bluiter* and *bloother* – is a sixteenth-century Scots word for a noisy fool or clumsy oaf. It had developed a verb use by the nineteenth century, and *blootered* 'very drunk' was one of the consequences. It's still used in Scotland, as well as in Northern Ireland and parts of the north of England. In the twentieth century, it turns up again in Ireland as a jocular colloquialism, *peloothered* (1914).

lumpy †
1810

Punch in 1845, commenting on the lyrics of a song, refers to *lumpy* as 'modern parlance', and suggests it could replace *boosey*, but it didn't survive much beyond the end of the nineteenth century. The earliest recorded use is a curious simile: *as lumpy as an ass*.

lushy 1811	The noun *lush* arrived as low slang at the end of the eighteenth century, referring to any kind of beer or liquor. Fifty years later, a bout of drinking was being called a *lush*, and by 1900 the word was being used for a drunkard. *Lushy* fell into this pattern: we find 'they were both pretty lushy' in an 1821 quotation. The word is now most widely used in the USA, where it functions both as adjective and noun.
pissed 1812	The word is chiefly British, along with *pissed up, get pissed*, and various intensified expressions. The most common simile is *pissed as a newt*, but it's by no means the only one. Among the more decent examples, one can also be *pissed as a rat* or *a coot*, and in Australia also as *a parrot*.
blue 1813	It was probably the bluish colour of the skin, a consequence of reduced blood circulation, that led to *blue* being used in the fifteenth century for the accompanying dejected mood, and thus as an adjective for low spirits of any kind. This may in turn have led to an association with drunken melancholy. On the other hand, there's a sixteenth-century idiom *till all the ground looks blue*, referring to the effect on the eyes of a prolonged bout of drinking. Whatever the origin, we find *blue* meaning 'drunk' first in the USA and later around the English-speaking world, especially in Australia and New Zealand, along with the more explicit *blue blind* and *blue drunk*.
half-shaved † 1818	American slang for 'half drunk', popular until the mid decades of the nineteenth century. The semantic development may be similar to that seen in *whittled* (above).
malty † 1819	The medieval proverb *the malt is above the meal* was said of a person who was drunk. In the first half of the nineteenth century, *malty* came to be used – usually with a light-hearted tone – for anyone made tipsy from drinking malt beer.
three sheets (in the wind) 1821	Nautical slang, which became one of the most widespread euphemisms for drunkenness. The *sheets* are ropes attached to the lower corners of a sail, to keep it steady, so if three of them come loose, the flapping sails will cause the ship to move erratically – like a drunken sailor. The popularity of the expression brought several adaptations. If you were *two sheets in the wind*, you were not so drunk; if *a sheet or so in the wind*, even less so; and if *a sheet in the wind's eye*, less still. A further colloquial adaptation abbreviated the expression to *three sheets* – now the name (since 2008) of a US television pub-crawl travel show.

mixed 1825	A halfway house between being drunk and being sober, but including the notion of being mentally 'mixed up' because of the effects of alcohol. It was chiefly used in Scotland, where it can still be heard.
sprung † 1826	The usage is recorded in several dialects of England and Scotland, but the link with other senses of *spring* is obscure. In some places, *sprung* was used to describe sheets moistened and shaken before ironing. But the most likely association is nautical: masts and planks can *spring* ('split') and thus be shaken about.
queer † 1826	A short-lived usage, related to the general use of *queer* to mean 'unwell, faint, giddy'. These other meanings were always more dominant, even in the nineteenth century, and in the twentieth the primary association with homosexuality vitiated any further use of the word in the sense of 'drunk'.
shot in the neck 1830	An American slang idiom, reflecting the use of *neck* to mean 'throat', as in *pour a drink down one's neck*. If you take too many shots (e.g. of whisky) in the neck, you end up being *shot in the neck*.
tight 1830	It is first recorded as *tightish* – 'somewhat drunk', and seems to have taken a while to settle down as a recognized usage, for *OED* citations even into the 1880s were still in inverted commas. English journalist George Augustus Sala uses the word three times in his *America Revisited* (1882), and highlights it on each occasion, such as when he talks about 'a rough American who is wholly or partially "tight", and proportionately fractious'. At around the time we see *screwed* emerge as a further synonym – from *screwed tight*.
rummy 1834	Another American usage – an extension of the use of *rummy* to mean 'relating to rum' (as in a *rummy flavour*). A 2005 *OED* citation talks about 'rummy men drowsing by the fire'. It didn't develop this sense in Britain, probably because *rummy* was already well established as a slang expression meaning 'odd' or 'singular'.
inebrious 1837	A euphemistic development of *inebriated*. The *OED* citations suggest it was used when referring to the social elite – an *inebrious pontiff*, an *inebrious surgeon*. Times have changed. A Sydney punk rock group goes by the name of *Inebrious Bastard*.
pickled 1842	The traditional process of *pickling* (the verb is first recorded in the sixteenth century) involves steeping something in a preserving liquid (including alcohol), so it was an easy semantic jump to drunkenness. The only surprise is that it happened so late. It follows in the figurative tradition begun with *stewed* and to be followed by *soused* and others.

paralytic 1843	An apt description of those who are so drunk that they are unable to do anything. The first recorded use is Australian, but it may have travelled from Ireland, where it is recorded (from 1877) in an adapted colloquial form as *parlatic* or *palatic*. I've often heard it in Liverpool and other parts of north-west England, again probably influenced by Irish English.
swizzled 1843	In the eighteenth and early nineteenth centuries, *switchel* and *swizzle* were slang names for drinks made of various mixes, such as molasses and water. A *green swizzle* was popular in the West Indies, acknowledged by P. G. Wodehouse in *The Rummy Affair of Old Biffy* (1925): Bertie Wooster observes, 'if ever I marry and have a son, Green Swizzle Wooster is the name that will go down in the register'. The origins are unclear. Eric Partridge thought *swizzle* could be a blend of *swig* and *guzzle*. There's a dialect background too: a *swizzler* was a name for a drunkard in Yorkshire. A *New York Times* article in 1910 explains it by saying that *swizzled* means 'beaten, as with an egg-beater, into a froth'. Whatever the origin, *swizzled* 'totally drunk' had a vogue which lasted into the twentieth century.
hit under the wing † 1844	The analogy is with a bird shot under the wing, and thus disabled. An earlier usage about a night out in London, reported in the first volume of *Punch* (1841, p. 278), makes it clear that the degree of drunkenness is somewhat less than total: 'I got rascally screwed: not exactly sewed up, you know, but hit under the wing, so that I could not very well fly.'
pixilated 1848	A combination of *pixie* and the *-ated* suffix (as in *opinionated*), with an *l* added to provide an easy-to-pronounce link. There may also be an echo of earlier *pixie-led* ('lost, bewildered') and *elated*, as the first recorded usage (in the USA) spells the word *pix-e-lated*. *OED* citations are almost entirely American, but its use in films (notably, in *Mr Deeds Goes to Town*, 1936) brought it before a wider audience.
boozed 1850	The verb *booze* has been in continuous colloquial use since the Middle Ages, with *boozy* the earliest adjective (see *bousy* above). *Boozed* provided an alternative with extra impact, thanks to the option of using an intensifying particle, as in an 1886 *OED* citation: 'This fortune teller gets boozed up.'

ploughed
1853

The action of a plough, turning over ground so that it is deeply and roughly cut up, must have made this an attractive analogy for someone seriously affected by drink, and it became popular in the USA. An *OED* citation from the periodical *American Speech* in 1963 finds the word used for those 'in the more extreme states of drunkenness'.

squiffy
1855

This description of someone slightly inebriated became popular among the upper classes. One of P. G. Wodehouse's characters is called Squiffy (in *Indiscretions of Archie*, 1921, ch. 8), who trashes a hotel while 'completely intoxicated', though without showing it. Archie is impressed. 'It's a gift. However woozled he might be, it was impossible to detect it with the naked eye.' The word is probably a jocular adaptation of *skew-whiff* ('blown askew'). *Squiffed* was a later adaptation (1890).

buffy †
1858

The origin is unknown. It could be connected with *beverage*, via the abbreviation *bevvy*, slang for a public house in the mid-nineteenth century, but the different vowel is a puzzle. Perhaps, as with *blue* (above), the source is a facial colour change – brownish-yellow (*buff*), this time. And *buff* appears in some dialects (especially in Scotland) to mean 'foolish talk'.

elephant trunk
1859

Cockney rhyming slang for *drunk*, also in the form *elephant's trunk*. As with all such slang, used chiefly in abbreviated form: 'He's elephant's'.

scammered †
1859

Another piece of slang with an unclear origin. Several English dialects have words that could be related, such as *scamble* 'walk awkwardly' in the Midlands or *scammish* 'awkward, untidy' in the South-West. There is an *OED* citation as late as 1940, but the 'drunk' meaning is probably obsolete now, and the present-day use of *scammered* ('taken in by a scam [i.e. swindle]') makes it unlikely to have a come-back (though, with slang, one can never be sure).

shickery
1859

An early instance of a group of colloquial words all deriving from Yiddish *shiker* 'drunk', later found as *shicker* (1892) and *shickered* (1911), and abbreviated as *shick* (1916). The words came to be used chiefly in Australia and New Zealand, where *on the shicker* also meant 'drunk'. In the days when pubs closed in New Zealand at six o'clock, the first tram, bus, or train running after that time was called the *shicker express*.

gassed 1863	This slang usage arrived at around the same time as the more familiar modern meaning of 'affected or killed by poisonous gas'. It became especially known through army slang in the First World War. The link is physical: one falls down when one is gassed, in either sense.
rotten 1864	The idiom is usually *to get rotten*, suggesting 'totally drunk', and seems to have originated in Australia. The technical definition ('in a state of decomposition or disintegration') has an obvious figurative application, but the usage could have been reinforced by *rotten* as an intensifier, meaning 'terribly, awfully' – as in *rotten luck, rotten shame*, and thus a shortened form of *rotten drunk*.
shot 1864	Although *shoot* (a projectile) dates from Anglo-Saxon times, the adjectival use of *shot* ('hit, wounded, or killed by a projectile') is attested only from 1837, and the slang application to drunkenness is not long following. As with *gassed* (above), the link is physical: if one is shot, one falls down. The usage is chiefly heard in the USA, Australia, and New Zealand.
under the influence 1879	An abbreviation of *under the influence of drink* or *alcohol*, a favoured expression in formal legal situations, and a genteel euphemism. The 'official' sound of the expression motivated its humorous adaptation as a spoonerism: *under the affluence of incohol*.
boiled † 1886	Another example of 'cooking' slang, which goes back to *stewed* (above). There is also an echo of *owl-eyed* (above), for an idiom emerged, *as drunk as a boiled owl*. The *Daily Telegraph* in 1892 disapproved, calling the expression 'a gross libel on a highly respectable teetotal bird'.
sozzled 1886	The *English Dialect Dictionary* shows several regions using *soss*, an onomatopoeic word reflecting the sound of water being sloshed about. If you were *sossy*, you liked a lot to drink; a *soss-pot* was a drunkard; and an early spelling of *sozzled* was *sosselled*. The word usually refers to a point well up any scale of drunkenness, but not at the top: one is still capable of carrying out some actions, albeit not perfectly, as illustrated by such *OED* citations as 'The voice gave a sozzled chuckle' (1951) and 'With a sozzled smile he began to sing' (1972).

loaded 1890	One of the basic meanings of the verb *load* is 'supply in excess or abundance', so its application to drink was predictable. It became popular in the USA, especially among the beat generation in the 1950s, along with its application to drugs, but it has since been largely overtaken by *loaded* in the sense of 'extremely wealthy'. An unusual expression is *to be loaded for bear* or *bears* ('be ready for anything'), sometimes used as a jocular way of saying that people are sufficiently drunk to make them feel they can deal with any kind of danger.
oversparred † 1890	A nautical word, from a ship that has too many spars, thus making it top-heavy and unsteady in the water. It is an apt description of a drunk, but only one *OED* citation so far supports it.
tanked 1893	*Tank*, meaning an 'artificial storage place for water', dates from the seventeenth century, so the notion of 'filling up' provided a clear parallel to drinking. The degree of tankedness has since often been specified: *tanked to the wide* (1917), *tanked up to the eyebrows* (1968), and the excellent *tanked to the uvula* (P. G. Wodehouse, *Frozen Assets* (1964, ch. 4). One can also be *half-tanked* (1977).
up the pole † 1897	The earliest *OED* reference is to a newspaper report in which a judge has to ask a plaintiff what *up the pole* meant, and is told by the High Bailiff that it is 'slang ... for being intoxicated'. The origin is probably nautical, a *pole* being another name for (especially the upper part of) a mast, so that *up the* or *a pole* developed such meanings as 'in trouble' and 'in difficulty'. The only other citation is 1917.
woozy 1897	The origin is unclear, but it feels like a blend. The first part might be *woolly* (as in *woolly-headed*) or onomatopoeic (as in *whoa*); the second follows a familiar pattern, seen in *boozy, muzzy, dizzy, fuzzy, hazy*, and so on. However, the *English Dialect Dictionary* records an old use of *wooze* meaning 'ooze, distil', so perhaps the source lies there.
toxic † 1899	Advances in nineteenth-century medicine gave a new lease of life to the adjective *toxic* 'poisonous', and introduced new expressions, such as *toxic insanity*. The topers were listening, noted the overlap with *intoxicated*, and (in the solitary recorded example) joked about drunkenness being a 'toxic state where a man can't see the holes through a ladder'.

polluted 1900	An adaptation of the technical sense of *polluted* ('contaminated with poisonous substances'), originally US slang. As with *gassed* and *toxic*, it illustrates the way 'dark' sources prove especially attractive to drinkers, the exaggeration implicit in the semantic contrast effectively playing down the seriousness of a drunken condition.
pie-eyed 1904	The wide circles of eyes, dilated pupils, and distorted vision that accompanies drunkenness motivated *owl-eyed* in the seventeenth century and *pie-eyed* in the twentieth. The alcoholic context is less common today, as the word has also come to be used with reference to the effect of drugs.
spiflicated 1906	The verb *spiflicate* or *spifflicate* emerged in the mid-eighteenth century, perhaps on analogy with *suffocate*, with echoes of *stifle*, and became widely used in English dialects. The meaning is harsh ('crush, overcome, totally destroy') but the context is invariably humorous or light-hearted – hence its application to drinking, where the idea is that the drinker has been completely wiped out. Idiosyncratic coinages abound. Mr Pyke, in Charles Dickens's *Nicholas Nickleby* (1839, ch. 27) gets it wrong, threatening to *smifligate* someone. And around the same time we find *pifflicated* (1905), where the echo is of *piffle* ('talk nonsense, behave ineffectually').
on one's ear 1906	The first *OED* citation illustrates the context: drunks 'rollin' round on their ear' – their faces are on the floor. The expression originated in Australia, but eventually travelled and was further adapted. In *Behold, We Live* (1932), the London playwright John van Druten has a character say: 'I shall be on my little ear if I don't get some food soon.'
piped 1906	Several semantic strands could have motivated this US slang usage. The throat can be referred to as a *pipe* (as in *windpipe*). In some English dialects, a *pipe* was a cask containing beer or spirits. And there is the expression *as drunk as a piper*, recorded from the early eighteenth century (in Scotland, *as fou as a piper*). As with *loaded* and *pie-eyed*, the phrase was later applied to the effect of drugs, thereby losing some of its attraction in relation to drink.
jingled 1908	If something *jingles*, it produces a mingling of ringing sounds. *Jingled* and *jingling* were often used in English dialects to describe noisy mirth or a confused situation. The slang adaptation for a mildly drunken state is found in the USA in the first half of the twentieth century. The first recorded use talks of someone getting 'comfortably jingled'.

skimished 1908	*Skimis* is a strong drink in Shelta, the language of Irish travellers, and *skimisk* is 'drunk'. The English form is recorded just once, in William H. Davies's *Autobiography of a Super-Tramp* (1908, ch. 24), where the author meets a beggar who tells him how successful he has been in his trade: 'I seldom lie down at night but what I am half skimished' – helpfully glossing the phrase as 'half drunk'.
tin hat(s) 1909	Eric Partridge found *to be tin-hatted* or *to have on one's tin hat* in Royal Navy slang for being tipsy, presumably because the tin hat provided head protection when moving about below decks. *Tin hats* (usually in the plural) then became a synonym for 'drunk', and could be quantified, as in this extract from James Redding Ware's dictionary, *Passing English of the Victorian Era* (1909): 'Tin hat … drunk – two tin hats very drunk – three, incapable, and to be carried on board.'
pipped 1911	The origin is obscure. It may be another violent expression, as with *shot* (above), for *pipped* was military slang for being wounded. But John Masefield is the first *OED* citation, in his poem 'Everlasting mercy': 'Si's wife come in and sipped and sipped | (As women will) till she was pipped'. It could well be a euphemistic avoidance of *pissed*.
canned 1914	Many products were being canned by 1914, such as milk and beef (but not beer, which came some twenty years later). The idea seems to be, like *tanked* (above), that one has been completely filled with drink – an interpretation reinforced by *canned up*, military slang from the First World War.
lit 1914	The facial rosiness and animated expression that accompanies a bout of drinking was aptly reflected in this slang use of the verb *light*. We find people described as *lit*, *a bit lit*, and *well lit*, and more emphatically as *lit up* and *all lit up*. Later use extended to the effect of narcotics.
blotto 1917	The analogy is probably with blots and blotting paper, which soaks up ink as a person soaks up drink. It was a favourite piece of upper-class slang in the first half of the twentieth century. Here is Freddie, hungover, in the opening chapter of P. G. Wodehouse's *Jill the Reckless* (1920, ch. 1): 'I was possibly a little blotto. Not whiffled, perhaps, but indisputably blotto.'
zigzag 1918	A fairly literal extension of the basic meaning of the word, 'turning sharply at angles in alternate directions', to describe the walking pattern of a drunkard. It began as army slang, and spread around the English-speaking military world after the First World War, but lost its popularity by the Second.

stung 1919	Another slang expression of injury, as with *shot* (above), though less violent, chiefly known from Australia.
stunned 1919	To *stun* is to make someone dazed or unconscious through a blow, which makes it a rather appropriate word when applied to the effects of drink. It seems not to have travelled much beyond Australia and New Zealand.
potted 1922	A further slang development of *pot*, as a container for liquor, first used in North America and later elsewhere, especially South Africa. Confusion with the more widespread sense relating to drugs (someone who has taken *pot* [cannabis]) has now reduced its drink-related use.
poggled 1923	Military slang for 'wildly drunk'; also spelled *puggled*, and in Scotland *pagard* or *pagart*. The form seems to have travelled from India, where Hindi *pagal* came to be used by Anglo-Indians in the sense of 'madman' or 'idiot'. It must have been the associated crazy behaviour, often leading to a state of exhaustion, which motivated the 'drunk' sense, though the Scots forms have also been explained as a euphemistic variant of *buggered*.
cock-eyed 1926	The way drunkenness affects the eyes is a familiar source of new adjectives (as with *owl-eyed*, *pie-eyed* above). Since the early nineteenth century *cock-eyed* has been a popular colloquial way of describing someone who has a squint, so there was an obvious parallel with the way drink can make one's eyes turn towards each other as they lose focus. The usage began in the USA, with Ernest Hemingway the first *OED* citation in *The Sun Also Rises* (ch. 26): '"You're cock-eyed," I said. "On wine?" "Why not?"'
fried 1926	A further instance of the 'cooking' analogy. The first *OED* citation, from a dictionary of American slang, attributes the usage to a US university: 'Princeton has completed the idiom of the cuisine by adding *fried* to *boiled* and *stewed*, meaning intoxicated.'
bottled 1927	British society slang, from the way the noun is routinely used for a liquor container (*bottle of beer, gin*, etc.). The adjectival use was reinforced by related idioms, such as having a discussion *over a bottle* ('while drinking'), *going on the bottle* ('frequently drinking'), and *coming off the bottle* ('no longer drinking').
crocked 1927	American slang, of uncertain origin, but probably from *crock*, referring to someone or something broken-down or worn-out. Jack Kerouac liked it, as seen in the first part of his novel *On the Road* (1957): 'I had traveling money and got crocked in the bar.'

lubricated 1927	As with *oiled* (above), *lubricated* quickly attracted a *well*-modifier: in J. S. Neaman and C. G. Silver's *A Dictionary of Euphemisms* (1983), we read that 'the human machine functions better when it is well oiled or lubricated'.
liquefied 1928	The basic meaning of *liquefied* is 'transformed into a liquid state'. No more to say, really.
steamed 1929	In the nineteenth century, *steamed* was an adjective chiefly applied to food – potatoes, puddings, and suchlike. In the 1920s it developed the meaning of 'excited' or 'roused', especially to anger, usually in the phrase *steamed up*, and this is the expression most often encountered with reference to drunkenness. But there is another strand behind the usage, for from around the same time, in Australia and New Zealand, cheap fiery liquor was being called *steam*, and by the 1940s the term was being used for any kind of cheap wine.
overshot 1931	The use of *be overshot* meaning 'be mistaken', especially because one is befuddled with drink, dates from the sixteenth century, but as an adjective meaning simply 'drunk' it seems to have had a brief period of colloquial use in the mid-decades of the twentieth century.
swacked 1932	An originally onomatopoeic Scots noun for a heavy blow, *swack* developed the sense (in the late eighteenth century) of a deep draught of liquor. Somehow it crossed the Atlantic in the early twentieth century and became a feature of US slang, first recorded in the periodical *American Speech*.
looped 1934	The 'doubling-up' element in the meaning of *loop*, probably heavily reinforced by the aeronautic use of *loop the loop*, clearly appealed to slang coiners in the USA. A *loop* also helps things (and people) to stand up straight. A cluster of *OED* citations suggest its popularity in the mid-decades of the twentieth century.
stocious 1937	A puzzle. It seems to be Anglo-Irish in origin, which then travelled abroad, spelled also as *stotious*. A Gaelic source is likely, though no obvious source-word is detectable, other than some words in the semantic field of 'drink' which begin with the same sounds, such as *stab* 'stoup' and *stuagach* 'pitcher'. It could of course be an artificial word, coined by people with a real penchant for wordplay (remember James Joyce), and similar to *goluptious* ('delightful') or the neologisms of Lewis Carroll (*frumious*, *frabjous*).

whistled 1938	The analogy with the musical instrument seems to have motivated the slang use of *whistle* to mean the throat (as with *neck* and *pipe* above), and led to the phrase *wet one's whistle* ('take a drink'), known from the fifteenth century. *Whistled* ('drunk') seems to have begun in the services, especially the RAF. But other sources have been suggested, such as an adaptation of Scots *whiskied* or arising out of the weird effect observed when a drunk tries nonchalantly to whistle.
plonked 1943	Clearly from *plonk*, the facetious pronunciation of *blanc* (as in *vin blanc* 'white wine') which was widely used in Australia and New Zealand before travelling around the English-speaking world as a term for any kind of cheap wine. A drunkard addicted to plonk (a *plonko*) would be very definitely *plonked*, or *plonked up*.
stone 1945	A short-lived usage in the USA for 'drunk', which became obsolete after drug-users took it over as *stoned*.
juiced 1946	A slang usage which, judging by the *OED* citations, seems to have been especially popular among African Americans, often with a reinforcing *up*. We see it in the earliest citation, from Chester Himes's *Negro Story*: 'She was an old wino used to come there every night and get juiced up.' However, the history of the usage is much older, relating to a dialect and colloquial tradition of referring to any kind of culinary liquid (such as gravy or sauce) as *juice*. Benjamin Franklin includes *juicy* as a word for 'drunk' in his *Drinker's Dictionary* (1737) .
schnockered 1955	Probably, along with *snockered* (1961), a jocular adaptation of *snookered*, the analogy being based on the way snooker players find themselves unable to hit their target ball directly because other balls are in the way. The word had long been used figuratively to refer to people in a difficult or impossible position. The *sch-* variant might have been an echo of drunken speech, or even of Yiddish (as in *schnozzle* – see Chapter 2).
honkers 1957	Several strands of meaning lie behind this unusual word. Eric Partridge found *honking* used as Royal Navy slang for a drinking session during the Second World War. In the late 1940s, the word was used in Britain for a wild drinking party. And *honk* could also mean 'vomit', especially after a drinking bout. The *-ers* ending is public school, university, and sporting slang, as seen also in *champers* ('champagne'), *preggers* ('pregnant'), and *Johnners* (as in cricket commentator Brian Johnston).

bombed 1959	The most aggressive of all the slang expressions for 'drunk', suggestive of total incapacity. The word usually occurs after a verb: one *gets bombed* or *is bombed* – or, often, *bombed out*. We don't usually hear it used before a noun, as in *a bombed student*. It's now more commonly used in relation to drugs.
zonked 1959	*Zonk* arrived in the 1940s as an onomatopoeic word representing the sound of a heavy blow. The implication was always one of finality: a door would close (*zonk!*) or somebody would be knocked down (*zonk!*). So, when it began to be used adjectivally in the context of drink (at first in North America) the implication was always one of being overcome, to the point of being seriously incapable or even falling unconscious, the finality often reinforced by other words (*completely zonked out*). Later uses of the adjective, both in relation to drugs and as a slang term for exhausted, have made it ambiguous. We need to know the context before we can interpret someone who says 'I'm zonked'.
bevvied 1960	In the nineteenth century (from 1889), a *bevvy* was a drink, especially of beer – a slang abbreviation of *beverage*. It was also sometimes used for a tavern. It took a surprisingly long time for it to be used as a verb 'to drink' (1934, 'They...bevvy till all the money's gone') or as an adjective 'drunk' (1960, 'both of them bevvied').
plotzed 1962	A Yiddish expression, from the verb *plotz* 'crack, split', which led to several US slang uses, recorded since the 1920s, such as 'display strong emotion' ('she plotzed for joy') and 'sit down wearily' ('I plotzed into an easy chair'). Either or both of these nuances could have led to the association with drunkenness.
over the limit 1966	This phrase arrived when laws were introduced limiting the amount of alcohol that could be taken before driving a vehicle, or engaging in other potentially dangerous activities. The actual expression seems to have been earlier used in card games, where a maximum stake is agreed (as in poker) or the strength of a hand does not exceed a certain value (as in bridge). Because people can be 'over the limit' without necessarily feeling very drunk, the term sits uneasily in this listing, being more legalistic than descriptive.
the worse for wear 1966	An idiomatic euphemism which neatly captures the mental and physical deterioration which accompanies or follows a bout of drinking. The source is in clothing, where an earlier idiom was *the worse for the wearing*.

wasted 1968	A description, popular among teenagers (especially in the USA), which suggests that the mind and body of the drunkard is analogous to land which has been devastated or ruined. Today, the dominant use relates to the effect of drugs.
blasted 1972	The analogy is with the savage effects of a lightning strike, a gunshot, or some other violent force. It is nowadays used indiscriminately with reference to both drugs and alcohol, and one has to look to the context to see which is intended.
wired 1978	The notion of being connected by wires to a source of electrical power proved to be a fruitful metaphor, especially in the USA. It came to be used in several contexts with the common theme of 'being in a state of nervous excitement', and reinforced by the particle *up*, as in this 1990 *OED* citation: 'A weirdo wired up on speed and brandy'. As this quote suggests, both drugs and alcohol are implicated.
tired and emotional 1981	One of the most jocular euphemisms for 'drunk', with early citations showing its use in satirical and comedy settings. The first *OED* citation is from the British TV series *Yes Minister*: 'Hacker tired and emotional after embassy reception'.
ratted 1982	British slang for 'drunk'. But why a rat? A traditional expression (1553) is *drunk as a rat*, and there is a long-standing association between rats and water (as in somebody looking like *a drowned rat*). The word is chiefly used as part of a phrase – one *gets ratted* – and is often accompanied by an intensifying word, such as *mildly*, *totally*, or *absolutely*.
rat-arsed 1984	In US slang of the 1950s, if you *don't give a rat's ass*, you don't care anything at all – a rat's ass evidently being thought of as something of the least significance. Whether this relates to the British use (with *arse* for *ass*) isn't at all clear. It feels like a separate development. Eric Partridge found it mainly among teenagers.

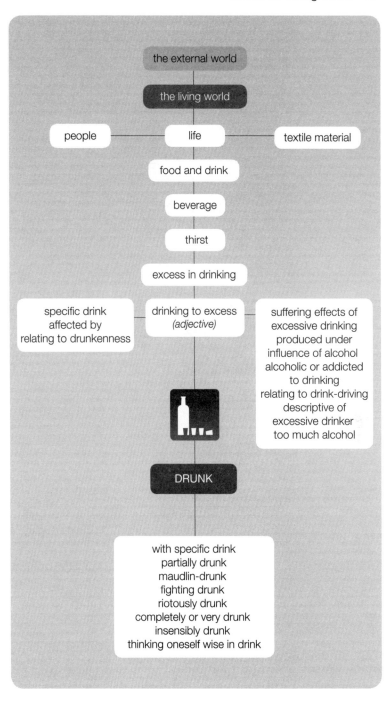

4

From *meatship* to *trough*, and *nuncheon* to *short-eat*

WORDS FOR A (LIGHT) MEAL

The ancient origins of *meal* lie in words to do with measuring, distantly related to *metre* and *moon*. In its earliest citations in Old English, it was a measure: one would talk about 'pouring three meals of wine', for example. And until the late Middle Ages people continued to form words in which the *meal* element meant 'a quantity at a time', as in Old English *drop-meal* ('drop by drop'), *foot-meal* ('step by step'), and *heap-meal* 'in large numbers', or Middle English *gobbetmeal* ('in gobbets'), *cupmeal* ('cup by cup'), and *littlemeal* ('little by little'). Coinages of this kind then died out, apart from isolated instances (such as *pagemeal* 'page by page' in 1827). Today we have only one word left to remind us of what was once a highly productive formation: *piecemeal* 'one piece at a time'.

In Old English *meal* was also being used to mean 'time' or 'occasion', especially when it referred to a specific moment a person had in mind. 'Time to go', says Beowulf at one point (*Beowulf*, line 316): *mæl is me to faran*. So it was a very short semantic step from here to the sense of a 'customary occasion for taking food or drink', which allows this word to open the listing below.

The other word that was very influential in this semantic field was *meat*, which in its oldest use simply meant 'food' – especially solid food, as opposed to drink (though some writers in the Middle Ages used it for everything). It later lost this sense in standard English, apart from in a few proverbial expressions, such as *one man's meat is another man's poison* and in the names of the foodstuffs *mincemeat* and *sweetmeat*, but in regional dialect it remains strong. The *English Dialect Dictionary* contains several expressions, such as *meat-board* ('dining table') and *meat-house* ('larder'), or *meatable* ('having a good appetite') and *fall from your meat* ('having a poor one'). It's still common in parts of Scotland, where we find such expressions as *he likes his meat* (said of someone looking especially well-fed) or *that's a good meat-house* (a place where there's good food to be had).

There are relatively few general words for 'meal' (18), and the list below shows a remarkable gap (between 1538 and 1804) where there seems to be no lexical development of this field at all. When words do start to emerge, in the nineteenth century, the contrast with the earlier period is striking. The first ten words in the list are all in general educated use – most, indeed, suggesting an 'upmarket' social setting (*meatship, mealtide, refection, repas, repast, recreation*). Then after 1800, we find very 'downmarket' words like *grub* and *nosh*, as well as departures from normal grammar (*cooking, eat*), and colloquialisms from abroad (*scoff, khana*).

Light meals

The paucity of items in the general category is because in everyday life it is individual meals and mealtimes that provide the talking-point, and the hierarchical organization of *HTOED* enables this kind of difference to be easily seen. The second list below illustrates a lower-level category, the words for a light meal. It contains three times as many items as in the general category, and this is certainly an underestimate, for the kind of usage we see in the final item (the South Asian *short-eat*) is likely to be repeated, with interesting variations, in other parts of the English-speaking world that have as yet received little or no lexical study.

As things stand, we see in the list a great deal of local dialect usage (such as *bagging, crib, morsel*) as well as international variants (*nuncheon, merenda, mug-up, smoke-ho*). The time of day at which snacks are taken is evidently an important regional factor (*undern, four-hours, fourses, elevens*). So is the time available to eat, as seen in the words for a hasty snack (*snatch, snap, bait*). Social variation can be observed in society's *dinnerette* and *tray*, schools' *bever* and *munchin*, and religion's *mixtum* and *collation*, as well as in the usage controversies that accompany the history of *luncheon* and *lunch*. There is a hint of weight-watchers' euphemism in *second breakfast* and *a little something*.

Timeline

I Meals in general	
meal eOE	King Alfred, in his translation of St Gregory's *Pastoral Care*, provides the earliest *OED* citation for the sense of a specific mealtime. In a chapter (44) on the merits of fasting, he points out that it's not very good fasting practice to keep your leftovers from one meal so that you can eat them at another meal; rather, you should give them to the poor.
meatship † lOE	The earliest term incorporating *meat* in its general sense of 'food'. The *-ship* suffix here means 'being in a state to do with', so *meatship* has the connotation of a special occasion, such as a feast or banquet. A similar example of the formation in modern English is *courtship*. The usage died out during the Middle Ages.
meal of meat c.1330	The earliest combination of the two basic terms, also found as *meal's meat*, widely used in dialects throughout the British Isles. 'Ah wadn't give'm a meal's meat if he was starvin', says a Cumberland speaker, recorded in the *English Dialect Dictionary*. *OED* citations from authors such as John Dryden and Charles Lamb show that the expression had some currency for a while in standard English.
refection c.1425	A communal meal, especially one taken in a religious house. The word has a somewhat self-conscious tone when used outside of such settings. In Christian tradition, it is recalled on the Fourth Sunday of Lent (*Refection Sunday*), when the first reading is the story from the Old Testament of Joseph feeding his brothers, and the Gospel for the day is the report of Jesus feeding the five thousand.
eating † 1483	An everyday word which, surprisingly, never achieved much dialect presence in the sense of 'meal'. That it had any popularity at all is probably due to Myles Coverdale, who used it in his Bible translation: 'Be not greedy in every eating' (Ecclesiasticus 37), though this usage failed to impress the King James translators, who used *meats*. Edward Bulwer-Lytton opts for it in his novel *Kenelm Chillingly* (1873): 'Epochs are signalised by their eatings.'
mealtide † 1485	Literally, 'mealtime', but then applied to the actual meal itself. The first *OED* citation refers to someone paying six shillings and eight pence for his 'mealtides from Sunday till Friday'.

repas *c.*1485	Directly from French *repas* ('meal'), the word had some popularity in the eighteenth century (though Samuel Johnson does not record it in his *Dictionary*). It has resurfaced as a 'new' French loan in modern writing that tries to capture an olde-world flavour, as in a *Mail on Sunday* (2004) citation in the *OED*: 'Horses bearing knights or maidens wound along the streets towards the evening's repas.'
breakfast 1526	Only the first meal of the day is now called a *breakfast*, but it was formerly also used in a wider sense of a 'meal' which could occur at any time of day, as long as the eaters are especially hungry – a usage still encountered in the notion of a *wedding-breakfast*.
repast 1530	Today, *repast* is used more figuratively than literally: nourishment for the mind rather than the body (as when in a 1992 *OED* citation a periodical is described as 'a satisfying intellectual repast'). When applied to food, it describes the quality or quantity of what is on offer rather than the occasion per se (as in 'a rich repast'). The associations are always positive (*rich, full, luxurious, plentiful* ...), so when used in the sense of 'meal' the implication is usually that one is being provided with something special.
recreation † 1538	The modern sense of 'pleasurable activity' is anticipated in the earliest meaning of this word in English, 'refreshment through eating', which was narrowed further when used to mean a particular meal. The first *OED* citation is actually from a bequest, in which the writer leaves to the Fellowship of Drapers the sum of five pounds 'for a recreation or a dinner'.
cooking † 1804	A quotation from the essayist William Taylor of Norwich ('swallowing two cookings a day') heralded a possible countable future for this noun, as had happened with *baking* ('a batch of bread baked at one time'), *drinking* ('an occasion of drinking'), *tasting* (as in 'a wine-tasting'), and some other alimentary nouns. But it remains the only citation in the *OED*.
eat 1844	One of the earliest and simplest attempts to find a colloquial way of referring to a meal: turning the verb into a countable noun. The earliest *OED* citation is of a plural, the writer talking of activities that might take place 'between the eats', but the singular was also routine, judging by the way a Tennessee innkeeper described his establishment as '25 cents a sleep, 25 cents an eat' (1904). The usage is still with us – indeed, it's evidently quite trendy. We find people organizing an *eat-in*. And a 2009 restaurant review in a lifestyle section of a magazine is headed 'Quite an eat'.

scoff 1846	A South African colloquialism, from Dutch *schoft*, which spread around English-speaking southern Africa, and eventually travelled abroad. Twentieth-century *OED* citations illustrate its slang use in Australia, Canada, and Britain, in various spellings (*schoff, skoff, scorf*). The word was common among tramps and in the criminal underworld, but has been given a class makeover, if this 1981 quotation from the *Guardian* is anything to go by: 'Ah! Scoff ahoy! I spy Florida Cocktail and Gammon Steak Hawaii!'
grub † 1857	*Grub* – slang for 'food' – was an uncountable noun when it arrived in the seventeenth century, and it stayed that way (as in *grub up!* and *lovely grub*). But there is a single *OED* citation from Thomas Hughes's novel *Tom Brown's School Days* which shows that it had (and perhaps still has) a countable potential: 'Twice as good a grub as we should have got in the hall.'
khana 1859	*Khana* is Hindi for 'food, dinner'. The word arrived in English in the middle of the British Empire period in India: an invitation to dinner was called a *burra khanah*. These days, the word is most often seen as part of the name of Indian Restaurants, *khana* having other meanings such as 'house, cook-room'. Research into this item produced one of the best puns encountered during the project – an aphrodisiac cookbook called *Khana Sutra*.
nosh 1964	*Nosh* was at first a Yiddish word which emerged in the USA towards the end of the nineteenth century for a nibbly snack, especially one eaten between meals. When the British took it over, it came to be used as slang for any meal – and in *nosh-up* for one that has been prepared informally but likely to be large and satisfying.
trough 1981	*Trough* has long been a feature of upper-class slang for a dining-table: P. G. Wodehouse has someone 'digging in at the trough' in *Very Good, Jeeves* (1930, ch. 4). Dylan Thomas has Mrs Pugh describe her husband's plate in the same way: 'What's that book by your trough?' (*Under Milk Wood*, 1954). The *OED* citation for a possible sense of 'meal' is from a Michael Innes novel – 'If he didn't stir his stumps he would be late for the trough' – but the context could also support the other senses.

2 Light meals	
nuncheon 1260	A *shench* ('cupful, drink of liquor') at *noon* ('the ninth hour of the day', according to the Roman method of calculating times from sunrise). The earliest *OED* citation actually spells it *noonschench*. A pronunciation with a 'shun' ending emerged, leading to such spellings as *nuncion* and *nuntion*, and eventually (because of the influence of such words as *truncheon*) as *nuncheon*. It remains a popular regional dialect word, often abbreviated as *nunch*, especially in the southern counties of England; but it also turns up in North America. It was a 'word of the day' in the Newfoundland *Telegram* (22 December 2010): 'snack taken between any two of the main meals, especially in the woods or while fishing or sealing'.
morsel *c.*1382	Today this is a small piece of food, or mouthful (from French *morceau*). But Wycliffe used it to mean a small meal (Job eats a *mossel*), and this usage spread (as in 'we were eating our morsel at home' by the socialite Lady Sydney Morgan in 1818). Today it is heard only in some regional dialects in England.
refection *c.*1439	Although used as a word for a meal (see above), *refection* also came to be used for a light meal, often in the phrase *a little refection*. If a man has such a mid-morning snack, says Thomas Elyot in *The Governour* (1531), he will have 'his invention quicker, his judgement perfecter, his tongue readier'.
mixtum † *c.*1490	A single quotation from William Caxton shows this Latin word used to mean a light monastic meal. He defines it specifically as the kind of meal eaten by the monk who reads aloud while others are eating.
bever † 1500	The word arrives in the mid-1400s meaning a drink (from Latin *bibere* 'to drink' via French), but soon broadened to mean a snack, usually taken between the midday and evening meals. It was widely used in British dialects, but Joseph Wright at the end of the nineteenth century thought it was becoming obsolete. In some public schools (such as Eton), it was slang for an afternoon drink.
banquet † 1509	Today a *banquet* can be only a sumptuous feast marking a special occasion. We therefore have to be careful when we see the word used in the sixteenth and seventeenth centuries, when people would talk of a 'running banquet' (as in Shakespeare and Fletcher's *Henry VIII*, 1613, 5.3.63) or of 'banquets between meals', where only the lightest of snacks is intended.

collation
1525

Another monastic word for a light snack taken at close of day, or replacing a main meal on a fasting day. Outside of the Church, it meant any light meal, especially one that needed little preparation (as in a 'cold collation'). Dr Johnson came to realize there was more to a collation than simply 'a repast' – the definition he gives in the first edition of his *Dictionary*. In the fourth edition he adds, albeit with some understatement: 'a treat less than a feast'.

bite
1562

One of the oldest and most widely used colloquialisms for a snack. In regional dialect it was often used in the expression *bite and sup* ('food and drink').

snatch
1570

The primary sense of the verb transfers to this usage: a light meal prepared or eaten quickly. One would 'take a snatch' before going to do something. 'A mouthful between meals', says a Suffolk dialect collection (1823).

beverage †
1577

A single quotation, from William Harrison's *Description of England* (ch. 7), talks about the way people used to have 'beverages or nuntions after dinner'. He is delighted that these 'odd repasts' have died out – but regrets that there are still 'here and there some young, hungry stomach that cannot fast till dinner-time'.

a little
something
1577

Another first recorded use from William Harrison (ch. 6), but popular in present-day writing, though often referring to an alcoholic drink rather than food. This is however not the sense used by Pooh (in A. A. Milne's *Winnie-the-Pooh*, 1926, ch. 6), who decides that it is 'time for a little something' – and takes the top off his jar of honey.

anders-meat †
1598

Two dictionary citations over a decade are the only illustrations of this curious expression in the *OED*. It is probably a development of Old English *undern-mete*, 'food eaten at the third hour of the day' – that is, at around nine o'clock (see *undern* below).

four-hours †
1637

A Scots expression: a light refreshment taken at around four o'clock in the afternoon, and also called a *four hours penny*. A 1651 historian explains: 'the name of the after-noon refreshment of ale (etc)'. A splendid quotation from Galloway, reported in the *English Dialect Dictionary*, illustrates: 'The Archangel Gawbriel (nae less) is waitin' to tak' his fower-'oors wi' him.' The *Chambers Concise Scots Dictionary* finds the expression obsolete by the early twentieth century.

watering † 1637	The word is normally used only with reference to liquid refreshment (as in the twentieth-century British use of *watering-hole* for a bar), but a single *OED* citation suggests it did once mean a light afternoon meal. In *The Elder Brother* (1637, a collaboration of dramatists Francis Beaumont, John Fletcher, and Philip Massinger) Andrew gives a description of his master's dietary day: 'he breaks his fast with *Aristotle*, dines with *Tully*, takes his watering with the *Muses*, sups with *Livy*' (1.2).
refreshment 1639	'Refreshments are available in …' This is the standard modern use, usually in the plural, and often preceded (somewhat tautologously) by *light*.
snap 1642	Like *snatch* (above), a hasty snack, widely used in dialects of England and Scotland, and the source of several other expressions, such as *snap-time*, *snap-tin*, and *snap-box*. One would take 'a snap and away' (i.e. a quick bite to eat and then leave). A woman who sold gingerbread cakes was, in some parts, called a *snap-wife*. Miners and railwaymen would take a *snap* to work. In standard English, the notion is reflected in *brandy-snap*.
luncheon *c.*1652	The word still has echoes of its original colloquial meaning: a light repast taken between two of the main meals, usually between breakfast and midday. For those for whom *dinner* was the word for the main meal of the day, eaten in the evening, then *luncheon* would describe the meal taken in the middle of the day – a less substantial and less ceremonious occasion. It has been replaced by *lunch* in everyday discourse (see below), other than in very formal contexts, such as menus for special occasions.
crib *c.*1652	A dialect word that travelled from Britain to Australia and New Zealand, showing a similar development to *snap* (above). Workers would take their crib in a *crib-bag* or *crib-tin*, and would eat it at *crib-time*.
munchin † 1657	*Munch* is onomatopoeic, but probably influenced by French *manger* 'to eat'. The only *OED* citation for *munchin* is a slang schoolboy use (as with *bever* above), probably on analogy with *nuncheon* and *luncheon*. There is also an isolated example (1611) of *muncheon* as a verb. A related dialect use from Yorkshire, *munching and eating*, refers to a habit of eating at any time of the day.

bait † c.1661	*Bait*, 'attractive food for fish', broadened its meaning in the sixteenth century: it came to be used for a light meal taken by travellers on a journey, and during the following century for any hasty snack taken between meals. Like *crib* and *snap* (above), it became widely used in regional dialect, along with associated words such as *bait-time*, *bait-bag*, and *bait-poke*.
whet † 1688	The core sense of the verb ('sharpen') had by the sixteenth century developed an association with meals (to *whet the appetite*), and a noun use of *whet* to mean 'appetizer' was a natural next step. At first a small draught of liquor, it soon included small portions of food – what would later (from around the 1740s) be called *hors d'oeuvres*. A household book from 1769 contains instructions about how 'to make a nice whet before dinner'.
undern 1691	A light meal, usually taken in the afternoon, but sometimes mid-morning. It is widely represented in Scottish and English dialects, in a huge variety of spellings, such as *andren* (see *anders-meat* above), *ontron*, *horndoon*, and *yender*.
merenda 1740	Travelling in Europe brought English speakers into contact with foreign eating-habits. The *merenda* was encountered in Italy – a light meal usually taken in the afternoon.
bagging 1746	A word widely used in the northern counties of England for food taken between regular meals – usually mid-afternoon, but sometimes mid-morning. Related words include *bagging-time* and *bagging-can*. In Lancashire, if you missed your afternoon tea, you were said to be *baggingless*.
snack 1757	Originally in English, a *snack* was a snap or bite, especially from a dog. Later (seventeenth century), it was used for a small quantity of drink: one would take 'a snack of brandy', for example. The modern sense emerged in the eighteenth century, and has remained popular, developing quite a family of associated expressions, such as *snack food*, *snack bar*, and *snack-sized*.
coffee 1774	The word for the drink arrived at the very end of the sixteenth century, and was occasionally used to mean a light meal at which coffee is taken. This sense has disappeared now, but echoes of it can still be heard. If you go to a *coffee-morning*, you would expect to be offered something to eat as well as coffee. And in twentieth-century US slang, a *coffee-and* unambiguously points to a combination of coffee and – doughnut, roll, or similar.

second breakfast 1775	A snack taken late in the morning, or even into the early afternoon. The word is achieving a new lease of life. According to a news report in *Time* magazine (29 February 2012), 'more Americans are consuming breakfast in stages thanks to on-the-go lifestyles and the belief that multiple, smaller meals are healthier than three large ones'. The headline: *More Americans Are Treating Themselves to 'Second Breakfast'*.
stay-stomach † 1800	A snack which keeps hunger-pangs at bay. William Cobbett, in his *Rural Rides* (1825) kept some bits of bread and meat in his pocket 'as stay-stomachs'. A similar later usage (1833) was a *stay-bit*.
damper † 1804	A small amount of food or drink that 'damps down' feelings of hunger between meals. Charles Lamb, in the persona of Edax, wrote a letter to the editor of *The Reflector* periodical in 1811 complaining about being afflicted with a 'most inordinate appetite', requiring him to 'make up by a damper' before he goes out to dinner, to stop him eating too much. His companions nicknamed him 'Doublemeal'.
noonshine † 1808	An adaptation of *nuncheon* (see above), used by Jane Austen in her letters: 'The tide is just right for our going immediately after noonshine'. She may have made up the word herself, as a facetious coinage, but *noonchine* is recorded from Hampshire in the *English Dialect Dictionary*.
by-bit † 1819	In parts of Scotland, a light snack between main meals. Walter Scott is the sole *OED* citation, from *The Bride of Lammermoor* (ch. 5): Lord Turntippet hopes to receive some money from the local privy council 'for a bye-bit between meals for mysell'.
fourses 1823	A word in the tradition earlier established by *four-hours* (see above) for a light meal taken by workers in the afternoon. It is always found in the plural, and parallel to *elevenses* for the corresponding refreshment taken in the morning. Dialect variants include *fours* in Hertfordshire and *a four o'clock* in the Midlands.
lunch 1829	*Lunch* has had a chequered history. When it emerged in the early nineteenth century as an abbreviation of *luncheon*, some socialites considered it the latest thing in fashion and adopted it, while others thought it a vulgarism and avoided it. According to the earliest recorded use of the word, it was given a social boost when accepted by the London social club, Almack's, the writer commenting that '*luncheon* is avoided as unsuitable to the polished society there

exhibited'. In some dialects, it developed a more general sense, related to the original (sixteenth century) use of *lunch* to mean a thick piece (or *lump*) of meat: a light meal taken at *any* time of the day. *OED* citations show people preparing a lunch in the evening or even at midnight. The daytime use is also found in *HTOED* in the subcategory 'midday meal or lunch'.

picnic meal 1839	Picnics were fashionable social events, with each guest contributing a share of the food, before they became informal out-of-door excursions. Today a *picnic meal* (or the later *picnic luncheon* (1855), *picnic lunch* (1865), and *picnic tea* (1869)) is usually far less elaborate than one taken at home, reflecting the relaxed nature of the occasions.
elevens 1849	Eleven o'clock in the morning, like four in the afternoon (see above), was the time for a refreshment break. Dialect words in England and Scotland include several variants: *elevens*, an *elevener*, and an *eleven o'clock*. A typical example, from Suffolk: 'I commonly has a drop [of ale] for my elevens'. The word later travelled up the social scale, emerging as *elevenses* (1887) among the middle classes.
dinnerette 1872	A society coinage, illustrated by a single *OED* citation from Mortimer Collins's novel *The Princess Clarice*. The word is still with us: a US online cooking class in 2013 includes a recipe for 'A full circle meal with a sit down dinnerette after with all the guests'.
smoke-ho 1874	An expression for a rest period that emerged in Australia and New Zealand, but also known among sailors worldwide. The 'smoking' part is one of the options, as a 1953 *OED* citation illustrates: 'a billy of tea and a slice of brownie…a smoko tea'.
soldier's supper 1893	A jocular usage, reflecting the fact that, after tea, the final meal of a soldier's day, the only option was a smoke and a drink of water. From a food point of view, a soldier's supper = nothing at all.
mug-up 1909	A chiefly Canadian word for a snack and hot drink, mainly used by trappers and traders in the far north of the country. The snack could be substantial, as in this 1972 verb use: 'We…mugged up on boiled eggs, toast, jam, and coffee.'
tray 1914	A typically high-society usage: a tray of food brought to someone who is unable or unwilling to eat at a dining table. Because of the small size of a tray, it would need to be a light meal, often contrasted with a full meal. In Edward Frederic Benson's *Trouble for Lucia* (1939), Lucia suggests that her proposed visit to Sheffield Castle at an inconvenient time would cause the hostess no problems: 'My maid would bring me a tray instead of dinner'.

café complet 1933	The 'complet' part lies in the accompanying food. As Pamela Price puts it in her *France: A Food and Wine Guide* (1966), the expression means 'coffee with milk and lumps of sugar accompanied by bread or rolls and butter; sometimes jam is included'. It is not a good substitute for breakfast, according to M. V. Hughes in *A London Home in the 1890s* (1937): 'Our breakfast consisted of *café complet*. I made it as "complet" as I could, but was ravenous by midday.'
nosh *c.*1941	Before *nosh* became British and hearty (see above), it was a North American between-meals snack. A Baltimore paper refers to 'a light and tasty premeal nosh' (1997).
snax 1947	A respelling of *snacks*, used chiefly in brand-names and advertising, and widely seen in shop names, such as *Snax Cafe*, *Snax in the City*, and *Snax 2 Go*. The first recorded usage is in *Say the Word* by journalist and language pundit Ivor Brown, who doesn't like it at all: 'Why does such shop-window spelling, Sox and Snax, irritate me so?' I have no idea.
ploughman's lunch 1956	A traditional British cold meal, based on bread, cheese, and salad, served in public houses at lunchtime; informally shortened to *ploughman's*. An 1837 *OED* citation refers to a *ploughman's luncheon*, but there is no further example of this, and indeed we do not see the notion again until the 1950s. Views vary. Barry Maitland has a character in his novel *The Marx Sisters* (1995) grumble that 'No ploughman ever survived on these scraps.' On the other hand, I have sometimes been served up with one of these lunches that would have needed two ploughmen to eat.
munchie 1959	Another word in the tradition of *munchin* (see above), heard among British schoolchildren, and also recorded in Australia and North America. In the USA, the word was adopted by drug-users for the snack that alleviates hunger after taking marijuana.
playlunch 1960	In Australia and New Zealand, a snack taken by children to school to eat during the morning break.
short-eat 1962	A word from Sri Lanka and India, referring to a variety of small, easy-to-eat items, such as egg or vegetable rolls, buyable from *short-eat shops*. 'Order your short-eats, cakes and pastries' says a catering advertisement. There will doubtless be equivalents in other parts of the English-speaking world that have still to be recorded.

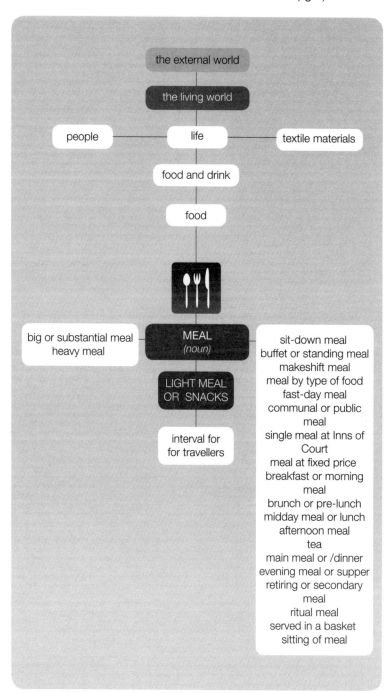

the external world

the living world

people — life — textile materials

food and drink

food

big or substantial meal
heavy meal

MEAL
(noun)

LIGHT MEAL
OR SNACKS

interval for
for travellers

sit-down meal
buffet or standing meal
makeshift meal
meal by type of food
fast-day meal
communal or public
meal
single meal at Inns of
Court
meal at fixed price
breakfast or morning
meal
brunch or pre-lunch
midday meal or lunch
afternoon meal
tea
main meal or /dinner
evening meal or supper
retiring or secondary
meal
ritual meal
served in a basket
sitting of meal

5

From *gong* to *shitter*, and *closet* to *the House of Lords*

WORDS FOR A PRIVY

In the beginning, judging by the words in Old English, it was all about 'going'. A *gong* (also spelled *gang* and *geng*), the root of many derived forms, was a passage, drain, or privy. The Anglo-Saxons had a surprising number of synonyms for privy, but none of them show the imaginative coinages of the kind we so often encounter in Old English literature, where the sea is a 'whale-road' and the sun is a 'sky-candle'. Rather, what we find is a repeated use of *gang*: a *gangpytt* ('going-pit'), *gangeen* ('going place'), *gangsetl* ('going-seat'), and *gangtun* ('going-yard'), or an *utgang* ('outgoing'), *forthgang*, and *earsgang* ('arse-going'). *Nidhus* ('necessary house') is a welcome departure from the pattern.

We see the same predictability throughout the history of this semantic field, which is basically the story of the contrast between 'telling it like it is' and 'telling it like it isn't'. At one extreme we have a group of words which remain as close as possible to the bodily processes of urination and defecation (*crapper, shitter, shithouse*) or the actual objects involved (*siege, stool, can*) or the disposal of the contents (*draught, bench-hole, dike*). At the other extreme, we have a group of words that are bland (*place*) or comforting (*convenience*), and which take us as far away from lavatorial reality as it is possible to get (*lavabo, House of Lords*), sometimes into a very alien-sounding world (*kocay, cloaca*).

In between these extremes, we find the words which have achieved a long-term presence in the language, usually because they acquired status as terms of choice when officials needed to write about such matters: *privy* and *latrine* are the oldest examples, with *lavatory* and *toilet* their nineteenth- and twentieth-century successors. At a colloquial level, the equivalents are *jakes* and *bog*, for the older period, and *john* and *loo*, for recent times.

The search for a fashionable euphemism is the story of 'variations on a theme'. *Closet, water-closet, closet of ease. Office, house of office, gingerbread-office.* The 'room' series in modern times: *washroom, restroom, small room, throne-room, bathroom, cloakroom.* And the remarkable use of *house*, which first appears in the thirteenth century and turns up in some shape or form in every century thereafter: *room-house, house of office, privy house, house of easement, common house, necessary house, long-house, passage-house, shithouse, little house, outhouse, shouse* – and the cheeky *House of Lords*.

The problem of categories

In a taxonomy, we normally expect the range of the semantic categories to reduce as we go further down the hierarchy. Beginning with X, we expect the next level down (X1) to be aspects of X, and the next level down again (X2) to be aspects of X1, and so on. The diagrams at the end of each chapter in this book illustrate this process in action. But sometimes there is overlap between higher and lower categories, and this is the case with the topic of the present chapter.

The basic idea behind the classification of words for 'privy' is that the subcategories deal with special cases. Thus within the general category of 'privy/latrine' we see such special settings as 'in a ship', 'in a convent', and 'used by a king', or special pieces of equipment such as 'urinals', 'chamber-pots', and 'bed-pans'. The subcategory I selected for illustration is headed 'water-closet/lavatory' – focusing on the room in which the lavatorial facility is situated, rather than the facility itself. Sometimes this distinction is clear-cut. There is no ambiguity with such words as *restroom* or *bathroom*. One always 'goes to' these places, and never 'sits on' them. But not all the words are like these.

For example, the *OED* definition of *water-closet* begins 'a closet or small room fitted up to serve as a privy'. This seems clear enough until we read the usage note: 'sometimes applied to the pan and the connected apparatus for flushing and discharge; also, loosely, to any kind of privy'. For semanticists and taxonomists, the devil always lies in such details – here, in those words 'sometimes' and 'loosely'. The multiple applications of words like *water-closet*, made more complex always by the vagaries of language change and uncertainties over usage, both socially and regionally, means that there are bound to be arbitrary decisions over which category to assign a word to (as with *little house*, which has been put in the first group of words below, and *smallest room*, which has been put in the second). If the taxonomist feels that the 'bowl + pedestal' (or equivalent) is the dominant element, the word will be assigned to the first category; if 'the room in which this is situated' is felt to be the dominant element, it will be assigned to the second. In several instances, everything depends on the context, and even on the choice of grammatical construction, as we see below with *lavatory*, *toilet*, *loo*, and *john*, which allow both 'going to' and 'sitting on'.

Timeline

1 Privy/latrine	
gong † OE	A primeval form for this semantic field, derived from the verb 'to go'. It forms the base of a cluster of Old English words, such as *gong-hole*, *gong-house*, and *gong-pit*, and also the surprising (to modern eyes) *gong-farmer*, from a verb *farm* 'cleanse, empty' – a different etymology from *farmer* in its present-day sense.
privy *c.*1225	The French had a word for it: it arrives in English in the early thirteenth century from *privée*, 'private place'. We see it first in the phrase *privy thirl* ('hole'). It became very frequent, used in many figurative as well as literal ways, such as the proverbial expression recorded in 1659: 'A true friend should be like a Privie, open in time of necessity.' In later centuries, the term became increasingly used for a facility situated outside a house or without plumbing.
room-house † *c.*1275	A word that occurs only in a single poem, *The Owl and the Nightingale*, at a point where the owl lays into the nightingale, accusing it of singing only in dirty places, such as behind the seat in a 'rum huse' (line 592). The *rum* element has been much discussed. It could be a word related to *rime* ('to make empty') or *rune* ('secret', much as happened with *privy*), or simply a jocular usage (like *little room* today).

chamber foreign † 1297	This is *foreign* in the sense of 'out of doors'. Within a few years of its first recorded usage, we see it abbreviated to *foreign* (1303). Chaucer, in *The Legend of Good Women* (c.1385), describes a tower that 'was joining in the wall to a foreign' (line 1962, in the story of Ariadne).
wardrobe † 1382	A *wardrobe* was originally a room in which clothes were kept; only in the eighteenth century did it develop the sense of a moveable closed cupboard. As a new word in the fourteenth century, its meaning was evidently flexible, and several writers of the time (including Wycliffe and Chaucer) use it to mean a privy.
siege c.1400	This is *siege* in the sense of 'seat', not of 'army action', used especially in the phrase *go to siege*, and in *siege-house* and *siege-hole* (both first recorded in 1440). The application to privies died out in the seventeenth century, but the sedentary meaning is still encountered in historical writing. The vacant seat at King Arthur's Round Table was called the *Siege Perilous*.
house of office c.1405	In its earliest use, it's unclear whether a usage referred specifically to a privy or to any of the other outhouses belonging to a property. But it's perfectly clear in later *OED* citations, such as actor David Garrick's comment, in a letter written in 1764, that he has regaled himself 'with a good house of Office', adding that 'the holes in Germany are . . . too round, chiefly owing to the broader bottoms of the Germans'. It has become a modern euphemism.
stool † 1410	A *stool* was originally any kind of seat, including even royal or episcopal thrones, as well as being used for the simple wooden structure familiar today. The seat enclosing a chamber utensil is therefore often found with a qualifying word to make its meaning clear, as in *close stool* (1410), *privy stool* (1528), and *stool of ease* (1561).
kocay † c.1440	An unusual word, known from a translation of Latin *cloaca* in a bilingual Latin–English glossary, *Promptorium parvulorum* ('storehouse for children'). The author is thought to be Geoffrey the Grammarian, of Norfolk, and this is significant for the word's etymology, as *cockey* is known in East Anglian dialects as a word for a drain or sewer.
privy house 1463	A small building or room used as a *privy* (see above). The term continues to be used, especially in historical descriptions and novels.

withdraught † 1493	The verb *withdraw* led to two nouns: *withdraw* and *withdraught* (modern *withdrawal* was much later, 1824). Any place of retirement, or private chamber, could be called a *withdraught*, so inevitably the word came to be used for one of the most private places of all.
house of easement † 1508	The *OED* definition of *easement* runs: 'the process or means of giving or obtaining ease or relief from pain, discomfort, or anything annoying or burdensome'. First recorded in 1405, it was quickly applied to the evacuation of excrement, and thus to the associated location. The earliest recorded usage of *house of easement* is not until a century later, and *stool of easement* still later (1580), but it's likely both phrases were around in the fifteenth century.
draught † 1530	This could be an abbreviation of *withdraught* (above), but it might have been a separate development, from the use of *draught* in senses related to water. Either way, we find people described as 'sitting at the draught' or in a *draught-house* (1597). The word has maintained its presence by being used in both of these ways in the King James Bible: 'whatsoever entereth in at the mouth goeth into the belly, and is cast out into the draught' (Matthew 15: 17) and those who destroyed the house of Baal 'made it a draught house' (1 Kings 10: 27). In other contexts, there are no *OED* citations after the seventeenth century.
jakes 1530s	This popular colloquialism, still often heard in regional dialects (such as in Ireland), along with *jakes-house* (1577), has a totally obscure etymology. Might it be from the proper name *Jaques*, as has sometimes been suggested? Certainly, the association with the name, pronounced identically, was frequent in the sixteenth century. Sir John Harrington opens his book introducing his flushing toilet (*The Metamorphosis of Ajax*, 1596 – the name is a humorous spelling of *a jakes*) with an anecdote of a courtier's maid who was so confused by the arrival of a visitor named Jaques Wingfield that she introduced him to the assembly as M. Privie Wingfield.
shield † 1535	The sense of 'protective covering or shelter' led to this word being used in the sixteenth century for the seat of a privy, and then to the privy as a whole. It was especially known in Scotland, where a *shiel* was also a dialect word for a 'small house' or 'hovel'.

boggard † 1552	One of the commonest colloquial words for a privy is *bog*, probably with a link to the general sense of the word (from Gaelic *bogach*) for a type of wet spongy ground. This usage isn't attested before 1665 (in the form *bog-house*) and 1789 (both as *bog* and *bogs*), though this is perhaps not surprising given the nature of the subject-matter and the slang character of the word. The form in *-ard* is recorded first – a construction quite common in Middle English to form nouns meaning 'one who does something excessively or discreditably' (as in *drunkard* and *sluggard*), and it was doubtless the pejorative connotation which led to its use here, also as *boggards*. The anti-Catholic clergyman Nathaniel Ward illustrates the latter, in *The Simple Cobler of Aggawam in America* (1647), when he recounts the story that when Satan showed Jesus all the kingdoms of the earth, he did not show him Ireland, as he wanted it kept 'for a Boggards for his unclean spirits'.
bench-hole † 1555	'We'll beat 'em into bench-holes', says Scarus to Antony, in the middle of a battle (Shakespeare's *Antony and Cleopatra*, c.1607, 4.7.9). There are no *OED* citations later than the seventeenth century.
purging place † 1577	*Purge* always suggests 'removal' – of sins, of people from a political party, or of unwanted bodily contents. *Purging place* came to be used for both the first of these (i.e. purgatory) and the last.
issue † 1588	This is *issue* in the sense of 'outlet', as when we talk of a river issuing into a sea. It seems to have had a short-lived usage in the sense of 'privy' around the year 1600.
common house † 1596	Sir John Harrington (see *jakes* above) uses this expression for a privy when he writes disapprovingly of people 'placing the common houses over rivers'. The same idea appears in the 1640s in the word *commons*.
private † 1600	A single *OED* citation appears for this word, used as a noun for a privy. It was one of the many neologisms of the period that never caught on.
necessary house 1612	*Necessary* has been in English since the fourteenth century, so I find it surprising to see over 200 years pass before it comes to be used in a lavatorial context, chiefly as a *necessary house*, but also with *house* replaced by *vault*, *stool*, and *place*. It then became widespread in dialects in England as a euphemism, usually in abbreviated form as *a necessary* (recorded from 1633).

vault † 1617	A sixteenth-century development was the use of *vault* for a drain or sewer, and thus, eventually, for a privy. The poet John Taylor is the first recorded user, reporting in one of his travels that a hangman 'hath the emptying of all the vaults or draughts in the city'.
long-house † 1622	An early but short-lived euphemism. The translator James Mabbe points to its euphemistic status when he writes (1622) of 'those that go to the Long-house (you know what I meane)'.
gingerbread-office † c.1643	Slang uses of *gingerbread* were common. It was used for money (see Chapter 12), and anything showy or tawdry (such as clothing) might be described figuratively as gingerbread. There is just one *OED* citation for *gingerbread-office*, from playwright William Cartwright's *The Lady-Errant*, so it may not have had much use outside of its literary setting.
passage-house † 1646	The verb *pass* and noun *passage* are often used with reference to excretion, but *OED* citations do not begin until the 1680s. This locational expression antedates them, though probably that is fortuitous. It seems not to have lasted much beyond the turn of the century.
latrine c.1650	A term that developed an occupationally restricted use, as the *OED* definition indicates: 'a privy, in a camp, barracks, hospital, or similar place'. The fact that, especially in an army context, the latrines were often rough-and-ready, led to the word being used as the term of choice whenever a critical comparison was made. In a 1673 *OED* citation, the River Tweed is described as 'the latrons [a Scots spelling] and receptacle of the universe'. The services also introduced the expressions *latrine rumour* (in the First World War) and *latrine wireless* (in the Second) for the gossip that originates there. The slang abbreviation *lats* dates from the 1920s.
retreat † 1653	Another short-lived euphemism, which seems to have been ambiguous, as the two *OED* citations both make the context explicit: 'the jakes and retreats of a house' and 'a jakes retreat'.
shithouse 1659	One of the most popular colloquialisms for an outhouse privy, but today avoided in polite conversation and formal writing, though the omission of letters in the written form (as *s--t* or *s**t*), commonplace since the eighteenth century, is now rarely seen. The word is more often used these days in a figurative application to any wretched place or despicable person, and in its adjectival use, describing virtually anything thought to be bad or disgusting (*a shithouse job/philosophy/linguist...*).

closet of ease † 1662	A continuation of the theme of 'easing' (see *house of easement* above). This phrase competed with others between the seventeenth and nineteenth centuries, as people searched for the most polite way of avoiding direct mention. *House of ease* is recorded in 1734; *easing-chair* in 1771; *seat of ease* in 1850.
backside 1704	*Backside* has long been used in regional dialects for the rear premises of a house or building. A privy was often one of these, especially in rural areas, so it provided a useful euphemism. Jonathan Swift uses it as a polite way of describing what happened to Jack, when he was 'suddenly taken short' and unable to find 'an authentic phrase for demanding the way to the *backside*' (*A Tale of a Tub*, 1704, Section 11).
office 1727	A somewhat archaic euphemism, but still heard, especially in the phrase *the usual offices*. The word was generally used as a collective noun for all the parts of a house devoted to household work and storage, including any outhouses. The euphemism appears either in the singular (as in Ngaio Marsh, *Opening Night*, 1951, ch. 9: 'I went to the usual office at the end of the passage') or the plural (as in John Braine, *Room at the Top*, 1957, ch. 1: 'The bathroom's to the right and the usual offices next to it').
little house 1750	A rather self-conscious euphemism that became very popular, especially in Australia and New Zealand. Mid-twentieth-century genteel usage changed the noun and added a gender distinction: *little girls' room* (1949) and *little boys' room* (1957).
outhouse 1819	Any outside building might be called an outhouse, especially in northern dialects in England and Scotland, and this usage travelled abroad, especially to the USA, where it became one of the colloquialisms for a privy. The first recorded use is from diarist William Sewall, who goes on board a paddle-steamer in Connecticut (14 June 1830) and discovers, near the giant wheels, 'two outhouses, which is a very great convenience'. *Backhouse* (1847) made a similar journey to North America.
cloaca † 1840	A single literary citation in the *OED*, from novelist Frederick Marryat, records the use in English of this Latin word for 'privy'. It never caught on.
petty † 1848	The word (French *petit*) has been widely used as an adjective since the fourteenth century. As a noun for 'privy', it was common in northern and eastern England dialects, as well as in Ireland, and had some society use as a euphemism, as seen in the *OED*'s first citation, from one of the letters in Nancy Mitford's *The Ladies of Alderley*: 'if these houses had been built by his Lordship every one would have had his *petty*'. In the form *petty-house*, it parallels *little house* (above).

crapper 1932	The verb *crap* in its sense of 'defecate' provided several low slang expressions, such as this one, as well as *crapping case*, *crapping ken*, and even *crapping castle*.
shouse 1941	Australian and New Zealand slang, a shortened form of *shithouse* (above), avoiding the perceived unpleasantness of the full word. In Les Ryan's novel *The Shearers* (1975), the abbreviated character of the word is underlined by the use of an apostrophe: 'all alone like a country s'house'.
shitter 1967	A chiefly American colloquial usage, avoided (like *shithouse* above) in polite conversation. It has a similar figurative range of use, in such expressions as *be in the shitter* or *go down the shitter*, all descriptive of various really bad situations.

2 Water-closet/lavatory

closet † 1662	A euphemism of a euphemism: an abbreviation of *closet of ease* (see above), popular in the Victorian era. Modern slang has taken the word in other directions, as in *closet case* or *to come out of the closet*.
water-closet 1755	Defined by the *OED* as 'a closet or small room fitted up to serve as a privy'. Although still common in estate-agents' house descriptions, only the acronym *W.C.* (first recorded in 1815) is in everyday use. And that, in turn, is sometimes euphemistically shortened to the simple *W*, as heard when one of the gossiping neighbours in Dylan Thomas's *Under Milk Wood* (1954) criticizes Mr Waldo for 'singing in the W'.
washroom 1806	A euphemism that can at times be ambiguous: does it or does it not contain the required facility? W. H. Auden in *New Year Letter* (1941) refers to 'Pullman washrooms', where it definitely does. Stephen Spender in *Learning Laughter* talks about 'the indoor separate lavatory and washroom with shower', where it's unclear. And an online sales ad in 2013 tells us that a house has '…a fitted kitchen, washroom, separate lavatory…', with the picture showing that it definitely doesn't.
convenience 1841	A euphemism most often used for an outdoor toilet facility, or a room in a hotel, museum, or other place frequented by the public, and often in the fuller form of *public convenience* (1938). It can be either a singular ('There's a public convenience in…') or a plural ('There are public conveniences in…').

lavatory 1845	The meaning has see-sawed between the room and the facility within the room. An 1864 newspaper *OED* citation illustrates the former: 'There are separate lavatories for the men and for the women.' A 1967 citation from *The Listener* illustrates the latter: 'flush conscience down the lavatory'. The twentieth-century meaning has largely been in this second direction, though people who use this word do still talk of 'going to' the lavatory – or, more colloquially, *lav* (1913) or *lavvy* (1961).
restroom *c.*1856	The American equivalent of a *washroom* (above). Originally, the word was used on both sides of the Atlantic for a room in a public building or workplace set aside for rest and relaxation, but in the twentieth century it has increasingly come to refer to a room containing toilet facilities. Its frequent use in films and on television has given it some currency in other parts of the English-speaking world.
small room 1858	This euphemism received a royal sanction. Its first recorded use is in one of Queen Victoria's letters: 'Has the railway carriage got a small room to it?' It follows in the tradition of *little house* (see above), but was taken a step further in the 1930s with the colloquialism *the smallest room*.
throne-room 1864	A grandiose euphemism, often used in a jocular way (as with *crapping castle* above), especially when referring to the needs of royalty. The usage led to the use of *throne* for the actual lavatory bowl and pedestal, first recorded in James Joyce's *Ulysses* (1922, ch. 1), when Arius is described as dying in a Greek watercloset 'stalled upon his throne'.
can 1900	North American slang, at the opposite end of the semantic scale from genteel euphemisms. J. D. Salinger captures the contrast in *The Catcher in the Rye* (1951, ch. 10), when he describes Marty as someone who 'kept saying those very corny, boring things, like calling the can the "little girls' room"'.
place 1901	The many meanings of *place* militate against frequent use for this slang euphemism – at least, not without further specification (as in *the place where you cough*, 1951). The *OED* citations show the importance of having more explicit words nearby to avoid ambiguity. When, in *Lie Down in Darkness* (1951), one of novelist William Styron's characters says 'I guess I'll take the opportunity to go to the place', another provides a gloss: 'She means the little girls room.'

toilet 1917	A similar ambivalence to *washroom* (above) is found with this word – a development from *toilet* meaning the process of dressing, washing, and grooming, and even earlier, meaning a cloth (French *toile*) used during the process. One *OED* citation (1955) is 'she...poured the perfume into the toilet'. Another (1959) is: 'he met you coming out of the toilet'. Both senses continue side-by-side, with context invariably indicating whether the user means 'room' or 'bowl'. There was a long-running battle in the mid-twentieth century between the relative social standing of *toilet* and the older *lavatory*: it was asserted that the latter was 'U' (upper-class) while the former was 'non-U' (used by everyone else). The debate seems dated now, especially as other words, such as *john* and *loo* (below), have achieved a widespread use.
dike 1923	This is a development of the 'watercourse' sense of this word, also spelled *dyke*, used chiefly in Australia and New Zealand for an outside community facility. As with several other words in this semantic field, it's used both for the room ('the outside lavatory, known locally as the dyke', 1965) and the object within the room ('the dyke's in the bathroom', 1960).
lavabo 1930	From Latin *lavabo* 'I will wash', an expression used during a ritual washing ceremony in the Roman Catholic celebration of Mass. The basin employed in the washing came to be called a *lavabo*, and this acted as a precedent for its use in other ways. The erudite origin seems to have given it a chiefly literary use.
john 1932	Chiefly US slang, with wider use through familiarity via films and television. *John* is one of the commonest first names in English, and has often been used in generalized contexts (*John-a-dreams, John Citizen, John Doe*...), as has the colloquial diminutive *Johnny* (*Johnny-come-lately, Johnny-on-the-spot*), so an application in this semantic field is unsurprising. There could well be a connection with the first name of the inventor of the flushing toilet, Sir John Harrington (see *jakes* above), as there are anecdotes suggesting his invention was referred to as 'John' in the nickname-conscious Elizabethan court.
bathroom 1934	A twentieth-century euphemism, analogous to earlier *washroom* and *restroom*, but with a wider reach around the English-speaking world, especially in the expression *go to* (*visit*, etc.) *the bathroom*, which makes it clear what sense is intended. Outside of this, there can be uncertainty, as illustrated by a *Times* (1960) citation in the *OED*, where someone from Britain remarks, following a visit to the USA: 'I did find it odd...when told that a small day school...had a bathroom on every floor.'

loo 1940	'Etymology obscure', says the *OED* – but there is no shortage of theories. Paul Beale, in an appendix to the eighth edition of Eric Partridge's *Dictionary of Slang* (1984), lists five. From *Waterloo* [station], because of the association with water and French *l'eau* (*le water* being a colloquialism for 'water-closet'). From the medieval warning call *gardy-loo* (as a chamber-pot was emptied onto the street below). From *bordalou*, a portable privy, hidden in a muff, used by fashionable ladies in the eighteenth century as they travelled. Related to *leeward* on a boat, as this is the side one would use. An Anglicization of French *lieu* 'place', already used in English (see above). Whatever the origin, it remains the noun of polite colloquial choice among the British middle-class.
cloak-room 1953	An alternative to the other *-room* euphemisms, listed in P. C. Berg's *Dictionary of New Words* in 1953. It has not displaced them.
karzy 1961	Alternative spellings, *carsey* and *carsy*, suggest more clearly the origin of this word in Italian *casa* 'house'. It is Cockney slang, which has replaced earlier senses of the word (such as a brothel, pub, or grafters' hangout). It achieved national recognition in Britain when used by Johnny Speight's East-End character Alf Garnett in the British television sitcom of the 1960s and 70s, *Till Death Us Do Part*.
House of Lords 1961	A usage which follows the grandiose tradition (see *throne-room* above) of referring to the 'lowest' part of the house by the name of the highest – an example of British cheeky humour at its best. It is described as 'Business Man Jocular' in a *Listener* article in 1967. *House of Commons* also had some use in the same way, but never became as popular – presumably because Lords, rather then MPs, provided a more imaginative contrast.

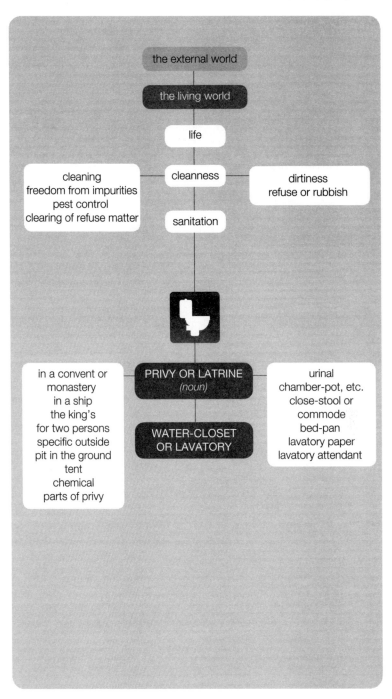

the external world

the living world

life

cleaning
freedom from impurities
pest control
clearing of refuse matter

cleanness

dirtiness
refuse or rubbish

sanitation

PRIVY OR LATRINE
(noun)

in a convent or
monastery
in a ship
the king's
for two persons
specific outside
pit in the ground
tent
chemical
parts of privy

urinal
chamber-pot, etc.
close-stool or
commode
bed-pan
lavatory paper
lavatory attendant

WATER-CLOSET
OR LAVATORY

6

From *dizzy* to *numpty*

WORDS FOR A FOOL

Chapter 5 illustrates the kind of 'vertical' problem taxonomists have to deal with when relating words between superordinate and subordinate categories. This chapter illustrates the corresponding overlap and inter-dependence that occurs 'horizontally': relating words in categories operating at the *same* level in a taxonomy. Within the broad domain of 'mental capacity' there is a cluster of subcategories headed 'stupid/foolish/inadequate person'. How are the words to be assigned to these three closely related areas?

Clearly a potential distinction can be drawn between the two extremes of 'blockhead' (someone with their senses intact who is acting stupidly) and 'simpleton' (someone with a weak intellect). 'Fool' hovers somewhat uncertainly in between. And when we examine actual contexts of use for the various words, it is often difficult to say which of these three emphases is dominant in an individual citation. As a result, some sideways cross-referencing between the categories is inevitable.

This can be seen in the selection of words for this chapter. If I restricted myself to only the words in the 'fool' list, there would be several cases where the etymological story would be only partly told. For example, look up *nigion* (1570) in the *OED*. The entry states '= NIDGET *n*.', and the cross-reference shows that this is indeed a relevant part of the explanation of the word. But *nidget* is not in the 'fool' listing: it is in one of the divisions of the 'simpleton' category. Similarly, the etymology of *silly ass* (1901) needs a reference back to both *silly* and *ass*: *silly* is in the 'fool' list, but the etymological reference to 'ass *n*. 2' (1578) takes us to the 'block-head' category. *Goof* (see also *goff*), *niddipol* (see *noddypoll*), and *gump* (see also *numps*) are further examples of the need to go sideways through the thesaurus to complete a lexical history.

The moral is plain: when dealing with a semantic field where the categories are closely related, we need to look in both taxonomic directions if we are to provide a complete account of where a word comes from. In addition to the 'horizontal' examples just illustrated, there are several cases in the present chapter analogous to those discussed in Chapter 5. *Gobdaw* (1966) obviously needs to be linked to *daw* (c.1500), but that is in a subcategory of 'fool'. And similarly in this subcategory we will find *goose* (needed to complete the story of *saddle-goose* and *goosey*), *noodle* (needed for *doodle*), *noddy* (needed for *nodcock*), *hoddypeak* (needed for *noddypeak*), and *ninny* (needed for *nincompoop*).

The scale of the problem needs to be appreciated. There are over 100 items in the list below, but these need to be seen alongside the additional 40 in the 'weak intellect' category (*sucker, dope, softy . . .*), the over 200 in the 'blockhead' category (*nitwit, moron, thicko . . .*), and the 70 in the further subcategory of 'fool'. In all we are dealing with the classification of over 400 words of an extremely colloquial kind. There are hardly any formal words in the list below (*insipient, foolane,* and *liripipe* are exceptions). People are not usually being formal when they refer to each other as fools. But the more colloquial the words in a semantic field, the more difficult it is to categorize them uniquely.

Important themes

Sound symbolism is a powerful explanatory principle in this semantic field. Almost half the words in the list below have an unclear or unknown etymology – a remarkable proportion. And one of the reasons will be that the words have been, quite simply, made up on the basis of how they sound. *Gump, tonk, zob,* and *yuck* are individual examples. And only the onomatopoeic potential of what we might call the 'N' group explains their extraordinary diversity: in alphabetical order, *niddipol, nidget, nigion, nigmenog, nig-nog, nincom, nincompoop, ning-nong, ninny, ninnyhammer; nod, nodcock, noddy, noddypeak, nokes, noodle;* and not forgetting *nana, numpty, nup,* and *nupson.* Further examples will be found in the related categories.

Similarly, we can see other groupings based on phonetic similarity. There is something about the *oo* sound which makes it recur (*doodle, fool, goof, noodle, poon, poop*). The initial *f* of *fool* carries through several words (*folt, fon, fond, fondling, foolane, fop*) as does initial *g* (*goff, goof, gowk, gubbins, gorm*). A final *-p* seems to be important too (*ape, fop, joppe, mop,* *mope, nup, poop, sap, sop*), especially when ending the *-ump* consonant cluster (*gump, numps, wump*).

But phonetic impact does not explain everything. We see the focus on the appearance or movement of the head (as in the *nod* series, and in *fool's head, dosser-head,* and *hulver-head*). And there is a regular search for apt analogies from the animal kingdom, starting with *ape* in the fourteenth century, and continuing with *goose, daw, ass, cuckoo, stirk, glow-worm, buffle, prawn, suck-egg,* and *possum.*

Words in time... One of the most striking features of this semantic field, apart from the number and ingenuity of the words for 'fool', is the way they are spread evenly (with one exception) across time. Early references are understandably sparse, as the predominantly formal documentation that survives from the Old and early Middle English periods provides relatively few opportunities to use colloquial terms of abuse. We see them coming into their own as the literature becomes more demotic, with Chaucer, Shakespeare, and others (especially playwrights and novelists) reflecting all social classes in their work. The most creative period for 'fool'-words was the sixteenth and seventeenth centuries, which introduced almost half the words in this chapter's list. The least (this is the exception) was the 'polite' eighteenth century, which provides only two examples – a dip that can't be entirely explained by limited lexicographical coverage of that period. Things pick up again in the nineteenth century, with novelists reflecting everyday usage and journalists reporting it, and this continues in the twentieth century, where the specialized dictionaries – notably Joseph Wright's *English Dialect Dictionary* and Eric Partridge's *Dictionary of Slang* – bring to light many examples.

Words in place... This is a field where home-grown words rule. Almost all the words in the list are Germanic or French. This was a pattern which began in Old English, where the words for 'fool' include *gedysigend* ('one who acts dizzily, foolishly'), *open sott* ('manifest fool'), *sotman* ('fool man'), and *wanhoga* '(lacking in understanding'). Borrowings from elsewhere are few – the occasional Irishism (*omagdhaun, gobdaw*) and Yiddishism (*schmoll*), and Spanish *tonto*. It is the regional British dialect forms that dominate the list, especially from northern England and Scotland, and there is a good representation from outside Britain around the English-speaking globe, especially from the USA and Australia.

Timeline

dizzy † OE	It's the adjectival use that we know today: if we're *dizzy* we feel a whirling sensation in the head, or feel metaphorically giddy ('my head is dizzy with thinking of the argument', wrote Benjamin Jowett in 1871). But when the word arrived in Old English it meant 'foolish, stupid', and the associated noun is the earliest example we have of a word for 'fool' that was still being used after 1066. In *Lambeth Homily* 33 we read: 'Hwet seið þe dusie' ('what says the fool').
cang † c.1225	A word that appears (in various spellings) only in the West Midlands text *Ancrene Riwle*, a monastic guide for anchoresses, as both adjective and noun. The etymology isn't known, but the variants in the different surviving manuscripts make it clear what the meaning is: *old cang* in one appears as *ald fol* in the other. There could be a dialect connection with *cank* 'chatterer, prater', known from Midlands dialects, given the proverbial biblical association between foolishness and idle talk.
fool c.1275	The defining word for this semantic field, used consistently since the thirteenth century, but with a stronger sense of insult developing as time goes by. In Shakespeare, for example, we see it used as a term of endearment or pity, as when Hermione says to her maids in *The Winter's Tale* (c.1610, 2.1.118): 'Do not weep, good fools.' And it is a source of sympathetic humour when we see it used as a name for a professional jester or clown (such as Feste or Touchstone). But there is no such empathy when Hamlet angrily tells Ophelia to 'marry a fool' (*Hamlet*, c.1600, 3.1.138), and it is this sense of a stupid person or simpleton that is the dominant meaning today.
fon † c.1300	The etymology is uncertain, but the meaning is not, as the antonyms in a 1450 *OED* citation make clear: 'God some tyme chastys [chastises] a fonn And he is made mare wyse.' The word probably relates to *fond*, which meant 'foolish' in its earliest use (see below), and *fun* may be a later development. A 'little fool' would later (1591) be called a *fonkin*.
folt † 1303	A French loan (*folet*, from *fol* 'foolish'), which survived into the sixteenth century. It seems to have been quite forceful, judging by this 1566 example: 'The foolish frantycke foultes'.

God's ape † c.1330	The earliest animal allusion. Chaucer's fraudulent pardoner (prologue to *The Canterbury Tales*, c.1405, line 706) 'with feigned flattery and japes | ... made the person and the people his apes'. And in 1553 we see the use of *God's apes* for a natural born fool.
mop † c.1330	The word must have had a slightly different nuance from *fool*, judging by a 1390 example, where someone talks about 'chidying of fool oþer [or] of moppe'. The sense may be more of 'simpleton' or perhaps 'innocent', given the related use of the word to mean a sweet baby or toddler (as in modern *moppet* – see Chapter 6).
saddle-goose † c.1346	'Only a fool would try to do such a thing' is probably the reasoning behind this curious expression. An example from John Skelton's play *Magnyfycence* (c.1530) suggests it became a proverbial name, along with *daw* (see below): 'Sym sadylgose was my syer [sire] and dawcocke my dame'.
mope c.1390	Probably a regional variant of *mop*, one of several derived forms around the dialects of the British Isles, including *mope* in Ireland, and *mopus* and *mopy* for a dull-witted person in northern England. The word remains strong in the USA, as seen in this 1995 *OED* citation: 'he's just the kind of mope everyone picks on'.
buffard † c.1430	The word is known from a single *OED* citation from a poem by John Lydgate ('The prohemy [introduction] of a marriage betwix an old man and a young wife'): a young woman is advised not to couple with 'a fresh man of innesse [youthfulness]' but rather with 'a buffard rich of great vilesse [old age]', in the hope that the latter will shortly die and she can then go for a youngster. It seems to mean 'foolish fellow', with the *-ard* suffix used in the same way as in *boggard* (see Chapter 5), but it is one of several words of this kind ultimately onomatopoeic in character. *Buffer* is widely reported in English and Scottish dialects as a word for a fool, and was used by Wycliffe in his translation of *Isaiah* 32 to mean 'stammerer'.
fondling † c.1440	This is nothing to do with the verb *fondle*: it is *fond* (see below) + *-ling*. The suffix here simply means 'a person that has the quality denoted by the adjective'. The word was used in this sense of 'foolish person' until the eighteenth century, when a different sense ('one who is fondly loved') took over. Dr Johnson has only this latter sense in his *Dictionary* (1755). But the earlier sense remained in some dialects, such as Yorkshire, where the word is often written down as *fonlin*.

fop †
c.1440

The etymology is unclear, though some sort of link with Latin *fatuus* ('fool') has been proposed. The *OED* citations suggest that the word was quite forceful: in the Coventry Mystery Play cycle (295), Caiphas harangues Jesus to speak: 'Speak man, speak! speak, thou fop!' The word didn't develop its modern sense of 'a dandy' until the seventeenth century. In the interim, there is a single recorded instance of *fopper* (1598) in the same sense.

joppe †
c.1440

The word is found only in a bilingual Latin–English glossary, *Promptorium parvulorum* ('storehouse for children'), where it translates medieval Latin *joppus*. Its origin is obscure. There may be a link with *jape*, but the origin of that word is obscure too.

daw †
c.1500

An abbreviation of *jackdaw*, applied contemptuously to people who were lazy, untidy – or foolish. The jackdaw's chattering sound is presumably the link, as in this Lincolnshire quotation in the *English Dialect Dictionary*: 'What's good o' listenin' to a daw like that'.

hoddypeak †
c.1500

A *hoddy-dod* is an old word for a shell-snail, whose horns provided an apt way of describing a fool, especially one who didn't know his wife was being unfaithful. *Hoddypeak* seems to have taken this nuance a stage further. It's certainly present in *The Anatomy of Absurdity* (1589), where Thomas Nashe describes the behaviour of a wife becoming someone's paramour 'under her husbands, that hoddy-pekes nose'. The *peak* element was also used as a separate noun, meaning 'fool'.

insipient †
c.1513

A scholarly word which arrived as part of the obsession with Latinisms in the 1500s. It seems to have survived for little more than a century.

fond †
1519

The adjective, meaning 'foolish', is known from the fourteenth century, and had earlier led to the noun *fondling* (see above), but as a noun in its own right it isn't recorded until the sixteenth century. 'The fond will read . . . but cares for nought' writes the soldier Thomas Churchyard in 1595. There are no later *OED* citations.

noddy
1534

Several words use the verb *nod* as their source for nouns for a fool, such as *noddypoll* (1529), *noddypoop* (1598), the mock title *noddyship* (1589), and the plain *noddy*. Mrs Squeers, in Charles Dickens's *Nicholas Nickleby* (ch. 7) exclaims: 'To think I should be such a noddy!' The word received a new lease of life in the twentieth century after Enid Blyton's creation of the innocent elf Noddy.

bobolyne † c.1540	It is known from just one *OED* citation, in a rhyming diatribe against monks by poet John Skelton, who needed a rhyme for *gobolynes* ('devils'). It is probably a literary coinage, therefore, though it has similarities with several onomatopoeic words, both in English (*bob*) and other languages (Spanish *bobo* 'fool').
dizzard † 1546	This is *dizzy* resurfacing after several hundred years, with the demeaning *-ard* suffix attached (see *dizzy, buffard* above). It was still being used in the nineteenth century, both in formal writing (as in Isaac Disraeli's *Curiosities of Literature*, 1871) and in regional dialect (especially Yorkshire, according to the *English Dialect Dictionary*).
goose 1547	The goose in folklore is proverbial for its stupidity, seen also in such expressions as *saddle-goose* (above), *goose-cap* ('fool'), *goose-gabble* ('chattering like a fool'), and *goosedom* ('foolishness'). A typical use is in Rosa Carey's novel *Uncle Max* (1847): 'What a goose I was to leave my muff behind me.'
Witham † 1548	The name of certain villages in the south-east of England, pronounced 'wittam', prompted a pun: Little Witham = 'little wit'. Writer Thomas Nashe, in *The Anatomy of Absurdity* (1589), talks about one who would 'prove a wittome whiles he fisheth for finer witte'. It became proverbial to say of a fool that 'he was born at Little Witham'.
nod † c.1563	Judging by the *OED* citations, this abbreviation of *noddy* (above) was valued by poets for its ease of use. Its monosyllabic character made it a useful metrical alternative to *noddy*, as we see in this line from John Collop's *Poesis Rediviva* (1656), 'No dialect of nodds, thee Noddy speaks'.
nigion † 1570	The only example of this word in the *OED* is in Peter Levens's *Manipulus vocabulorum* ('handful of words'), the first rhyming dictionary. It appears between *niggon* ('a niggard') and *onyon* ('a onion'), and is glossed as 'a fool'. Despite its earlier date, it is probably a variant of *nidget*.
goff 1570	A widely used dialect word in northern England and Scotland, also spelled *guff*, and heard also in such forms as *guffin* and *gowfin*. The word seems to have come from French *goffe* 'awkward, stupid'.
fool's-head † 1577	A short-lived expression (latest recorded use, 1650), though given some presence through its use by Shakespeare. In *The Merry Wives of Windsor* (1597, 1.3.123), Dr Caius is called one (behind his back) by Mistress Quickly.

nodcock † 1577	A further development of *noddy* and *nod*, this time with a pet-name suffix (seen also in such dialect words as *meacock*, and in surnames such as *Hancock* and *Adcock*). The dialects show several related forms, such as *nodgecock* (1566) and *niddicock* (1587) – the latter perhaps a blend of *nodcock* and *nidiot* (1533, itself an adaptation of *an idiot*).
ass 1578	One of several beasts of burden that were proverbial for their supposed stupidity, hence the many expressions such as *to make an ass of someone* or *as dull as an ass*. In the nineteenth century, *donkey* came to be used in the same way.
nidget † 1579	A variant of *a nidiot*, with the spelling reflecting the new pronunciation. A jingle from a 1675 ballad illustrates the use: 'Ridiculous Niget, │ To scoff at St Bridget'. In the nineteenth century, there was a similar development in *eejit*, used in Irish English. I recall being regularly labelled one by my Christian Brothers teachers in secondary school.
cuckoo 1581	The slang use of *cuckoo farm* for a mental hospital, and the popularity of the 1975 film *One Flew Over the Cuckoo's Nest*, has caused a division between the slang adjectival use of this word ('crazy, out of one's wits', 1918) and the noun sense (where since the sixteenth century it usually means 'silly person'). The origins of the usage seem to lie either in the lack of variation in the bird's call or its habit of laying its eggs in other birds' nests.
niddipol † 1582	As with *niddicock* (see *nodcock* above), this could be a blend of *noddy* and *nidiot*, but this time suffixed by *poll*, the old word for 'head' (as reflected today in the notion of a poll or 'head-count'). Later dialect words for 'fool' such as *nidderling*, *niddle-noddle*, *niddlety-nod*, and *niddy-noddy* suggest it could have been more commonly used than its single *OED* citation suggests.
stirk c.1590	A *stirk* is a young bullock or heifer (*steer* is a related word). It became a popular word for a fool in Scotland.
ninnyhammer 1592	Originally quite a strong word, judging by some early quotations: 'whoreson Ninihammer' (1592), 'Clod-pated, Numskulled Ninny-hammer' (1712). The *hammer* element suggests 'blockhead'. It is much milder in later usage, as illustrated by the quotation from J. R. R. Tolkien's *Two Towers* (1954, Book 4.1) when Sam Gangee calls himself 'nowt but a ninnyhammer'.

ninny 1593	A widely used word that has become more colloquial and dialectal over the centuries. It is another case where the etymology is unclear, but there's a plausible suggestion that it is from *innocent* (in its sense of 'half-witted'): *an innocent* became *a ninnocent* (like *a nidiot* – see *nodcock* above) and then shortened to *ninny*. It probably predates *ninnyhammer* (above), though an earlier *OED* citation hasn't yet been found.
Gibraltar † 1593	The Gibraltar monkeys were known in Britain long before it became a British possession in 1704, and the animal allusion probably lies behind the short-lived use of the name to mean a fool in the decades around 1600. The spellings *gibaltar* and *giberaltar* suggest colloquial pronunciations.
plume of feathers † 1598	*A feather in a cap* was the badge of a fool (not, as in the modern idiom, a mark of achievement), so expressions such as a *plume of feathers* or *Jack with the feather* (c.1633) came to be used for the person. 'What plume of feathers is he that indited this letter?' asks the Princess in Shakespeare's *Love's Labour's Lost* (c.1595, 4.1.95).
noddypeak † 1598	Probably a development of *hoddypeak* (see above), showing the same kind of change as seen in *a nidiot* from *an idiot*. But it could just as easily have been a further adaptation of *noddy*.
numps 1599	The name *Humphry* was often shortened to a pet-name, as *nump* or *numps*. Presumably a particular Humphry lies behind its use for a 'stupid person', but who this might be is lost to history. The word is used either as a singular or plural, but in the singular both with the *-s* ('The man's no better than a numps', 1919) and without it ('That nump!', 1955).
gowk c.1605	In Scotland and northern dialects of England, a cuckoo was called a *gowk* (originally pronounced 'gohk'). So, as with *cuckoo* (above), it soon adapted to human folly. April Fools were called *April Gouks*. If you *hunted the gowk*, you made an April fool of someone, or sent a person on a fool's errand. People would shout 'hunt a gowk' in much the same way as today we call 'April fool!' The nineteenth-century *gawk* (in its sense of 'fool') has a different origin, from the verb *gawk* 'gape stupidly'.
nup † 1607	*Nup* and *nupson* are both first recorded in the *OED* in the same year, found in the same text, playwright Thomas Tomkis's comedy *Lingua*. The two later citations of *nupson* are both taken from plays by Ben Jonson. The words could therefore be literary coinages, but a listing of *nupson* in Francis Grose's *Classical Dictionary of the Vulgar Tongue* (1785) plus a similar word from the *English Dialect Dictionary* (*nuppit* 'simpleton' from Yorkshire) suggest a wider use.

fooliaminy †
1608

Playwright Thomas Middleton (in *A Trick to Catch the Old One*) seems to have coined this word to mean both a company of fools ('the Fooli-aminy...of the Country') and an individual fool ('Now good-man fooleaminy, what say you to me now'). Playwrights Dekker and Massinger also used it in *The Virgin Martir* (1622), but there are no other recorded instances. Middleton may have got the idea from French *brouillamini* ('confusion'), first recorded in 1566.

dosser-head †
1612

A *dosser* was a basket carried on the back (from French *dos*, 'back'). In its human application, it evidently meant something like 'basket-head'.

glow-worm †
1624

Why the glow-worm should have been singled out to mean a fool is not at all clear, but it was used in that way during the seventeenth century. The *English Dialect Dictionary*, though, does record a nineteenth-century use of *glow-basin* in Somerset to mean both a glow-worm and a 'bold, impudent fellow', so the earlier writers were clearly not alone in seeing an animal-human connection. Perhaps it was the blindness of the worm that fostered the analogy. As John Dryden later wrote, in *The Conquest of Granada* (1672, 2.3.99) 'For, Glow-worm-like, you shine, and do not see'.

liripipe †
c.1625

The etymology is unknown, beyond it being a medieval Latin import. The word, also spelled *liripoop*, originally described the long tail of a graduate's hood, but became more widespread in a figurative sense of 'lesson' or 'part' (one would *know one's liripoop* or *play one's liripoop*). In its *-poop* form, the word is found in eighteenth-century Devonshire dialect to mean a foolish person. Joseph Wright, in the *English Dialect Dictionary*, quotes the view that it was the jingling sound of the word that gave it dialect appeal (as with *whippersnapper*).

doodle †
1629

The word may have come in from German, where *dudeltopf* is a simpleton. The modern use of *doodle* ('aimless scrawl') seems to have completely replaced the earlier meaning.

sop †
1637

When something like a piece of bread is thoroughly soaked in a liquid, it is called a *sop*. The word had long been used (since the fourteenth century) with reference to people in the form *milksop* for a timid or ineffectual (especially male) person. The seventeenth-century use to mean a 'foolish fellow' seems to be a development of this, but there are only two *OED* citations, and the only sign of it in the *English Dialect Dictionary* is in the form *sope*. The sense of foolishness is however still present in *soppy* ('foolishly affectionate').

spalt † 1639	Another word of obscure origin. The two *OED* citations, from the same writer in a translation from French, suggest its unfamiliarity, for each instance is given a French gloss. The nearest we get to it elsewhere is much later, in the *English Dialect Dictionary*, where an adjectival use of *spalt* was recorded in Kent in the sense of 'awkward, clumsy'.
simple † 1643	The adjective is known from the thirteenth century, with its meaning of 'foolish' probably best known in the nursery rhyme 'Simple Simon'. As a noun, meaning 'ignorant or foolish person', it is seventeenth century, with only sporadic signs of (chiefly dialectal) later use. *Simpleton*, first recorded a few years later (1650), seems to have been a playful development of *simple*. *Idleton* 'idle fellow' illustrates the same process, but whereas this word remained dialectal, *simpleton* became the term of choice in relatively formal settings.
buffle 1655	An animal choice, from *buffalo* (French *buffle*), but recorded in only two *OED* citations. The derived *bufflehead* (1659) was still being used at the end of the nineteenth century.
nincompoop 1673	The second element in this curious word is very likely the same as in *noddypoop* and *liripoop* (above), the word *poop* having developed the meaning of 'to fool, deceive' in the late sixteenth century. The question is: what does the first element refer to? *Nin-* could be from *ninny* (above), and there are many spellings supporting this; but there are also spellings without the *n*. Indeed, the first recorded usage lacks it, from poet laureate Thomas Shadwell: 'you Nicompoop'. The spelling *Nickumpoop* (1685) suggests a name, as happened with *Nicodemite* (from Nicodemus) and *Old Nick* (for the devil), but who the 'Nick' might be is lost to us.
nokes 1679	Another uncertain etymology. It may have a person origin, as *Nokes* or *Noakes* has long been a common surname (someone who lived by 'an oak'), and *John-a-nokes* is known in the legal world (as a fictitious name for one of the parties in an action). After some seventeenth-century usage, it resurfaces in Canada in the twentieth: *noax* in Newfoundland (1937), glossed as 'a simple minded fellow'.
foolane † c.1681	One of a group of humorous adaptations of *fool*, popular in the eighteenth century, with Latin-derived endings. The jocular Latinity is even more apparent in *foolarum* and *foolatum*.

hulver-head †
1699

Hulver is an old name for holly. The origins of the dialect use of *hulver-head* for 'a silly foolish fellow' are suggested by this 1825 explanation in an East Anglian lexicon: 'stupid; muddled; confused; as if the head were enveloped in a hulver bush'. Quite so.

Jack Adams †
1699

Low slang for a fool, recorded into the nineteenth century, and according to lexicographer Eric Partridge popular among seamen. Whether Jack Adams was a real person or an imaginative coinage isn't known.

nigmenog †
1699

Probably another adaptation, along with *nimenog*, of the lexical strand seen above in *ninny*, *niddicock*, and *nidget*. It led in turn to further adaptations, notably *ning-nong* (1832), *nong* (1944), and *nig-nog* (1953 – though Eric Partridge claims it was army slang of the late nineteenth century). In the second half of the twentieth century the use of *nig-nog* was affected by a folk-etymology confusion with *nigger*, which led to it becoming a racist insult.

single ten †
1699

The expression is defined as 'a very foolish, silly fellow' in a canting dictionary. The source may be cards, in which case Eric Partridge's explanation of 'an age-old juxtaposition of fools and knaves' (the adjacent card in a suit) is plausible. But it could also be a popular adaptation of *simpleton* (above).

mud †
1703

A word for a fool during the eighteenth and nineteenth centuries, reflecting the various connotations of mud (thickness, slow-moving, dregs). It is remembered today in the idiom *one's name is mud* (1823, often spelled with a capital initial), and also in the form *mudhead* (1882).

noodle
1720

A colloquialism used widely throughout the English-speaking world. Its etymology isn't clear: it could be a playful variant of *noddle* 'head'. Today, both words tend to be used only in light-hearted ways. The rhyme with *doodle* (above) has often brought the two words together, as in one of politician Richard Cobden's speeches (1845): 'the Noodles and Doodles of the aristocracy'.

nincom
1800

An abbreviation of *nincompoop* (above), also spelled *nincum*, popular throughout the nineteenth century. Folk etymology today has given the word a new lease of life, as in this blog post (2006): 'is a nincompoop something a nincom has left behind in a field?'

sap 1815	A widely used colloquialism, often recorded in British dialects, with quotations from such diverse sources as Sir Walter Scott, P. G. Wodehouse, the Philadelphia *Saturday Evening Post*, and the Toronto *Globe and Mail*. It is a shortened form of *sapskull* (1735), used along with *sap-head* during the eighteenth and nineteenth centuries to mean a fool. There is indeed a relation to the sap of plants: the notion is that one's head is so full of fluid that it reduces mental capacity.
omadhaun 1818	A word found in over twenty spellings, due to its unfamiliar Celtic etymology – in Gaelic (Irish and Scots, *amadan*) and Manx (*ommidan*). James Joyce in *Dubliners* (1914) talks about 'these thundering big country fellows, omadhauns'. *Oonchook* (1825) has a similar background (Gaelic *oinseach*) for a (usually female) fool. The words are still used in Newfoundland, thanks to Irish immigration. Irish settlers accounted for half the island's population by the mid-nineteenth century.
gump 1825	There's clearly a strong element of sound symbolism in *gump* – heard in several other words, such as *numps* (above), *wump* (below), *chump, frump, lump, thump*. Derived forms include *gumph, gomph*, and *gumphead*, but the basic form remains the most widely used, reinforced today by its media presence (as in the film *Forrest Gump*, 1994).
silly billy 1834	The rhyming reduplication made this a popular name for a type of fairground or street entertainer in the early nineteenth century – the 'stupid' partner of another clown. Anyone called William thus attracted the nickname – most famously King William IV. An alternative form, *silly Willy*, is found in some dialects.
prawn 1845	A foolish-looking person, likened to a prawn in appearance. The point is captured by Charles Dickens in one of his letters (27 January 1845) when he describes a man with 'his eyes protruded infinitely beyond the tip [of his nose]. You never saw such a human Prawn as he looked.' The analogy has been widely taken up, especially in Australia, where the colloquial idiom *the raw prawn* ('an act of deception') is common in both speech and writing, as in this quotation from the Melbourne *Sunday Herald Sun* (2005), where someone is given advice to 'check that he isn't coming the raw prawn over you' – that is, treating you as a fool.

suck-egg 1851	A dialect word for a *cuckoo*, a bird-name already in use for a fool (see above). It's often heard colloquially in the US South, especially as an adjective meaning 'worthless' or 'stupid': 'I'll be a suck-egg son of a bitch' (1958).
goosey † 1852	A colloquial diminutive of *goose* (above). In Harriet Beecher Stowe's *Uncle Tom's Cabin* (1852, ch. 1), Mrs Shelby dismisses what she thinks are the silly fears of her maid Eliza, calling her 'you goosie'.
silly 1858	A colloquial noun development from the adjective, first recorded as a plural ('great sillies'). These days the word is everywhere, from pop music (The Sillies, a Detroit punk rock group) to film (*A Tale of Two Sillies*, 2013) to computer apps ('Escape of the Sillies', 2012 – from Silly Monsters).
damfool 1881	A euphemistic or jocular spelling of *damned fool*, reflecting a colloquial pronunciation, and used more commonly as an adjective. Mark Twain, in an 1881 letter, makes the spelling even more opaque: *damphool*.
poop 1893	Finally, after a long history of use as an element of other words (see *noddy, liripipe, nincompoop* above), *poop* appears on its own as a colloquial noun for a fool. 'They . . . think us such poops for dressing in the evening', says Mrs Dalloway (in Virginia Woolf's *The Voyage Out*, 1915, ch. 3). It then gave birth to slang forms of its own: *poop-stick* (1930) and *poop-head* (1955).
silly ass 1901	A twentieth-century application of *ass* (above), 'an amiable upper-class idiot', as the *OED* circumspectly puts it.
wump 1908	Another example of the *-ump* sound effect (see *gump* above), used sporadically for 'foolish person' in the first half of the twentieth century.
zob 1911	US slang, probably an invented word coined for its sound. But two of the four *OED* citations show 'poor zob', suggesting it could be a euphemistic alteration of *sod* (short for *sodomite*), used as a rude colloquialism for 'fellow' throughout the twentieth century, often in the commiserating phrase 'poor sod'.
goof 1916	Although apparently originating in British dialect *goff* (above), the earliest *OED* citations are American. The usage spread rapidly, perhaps influenced by the similarity with *goose*, and reaching a global public through the Walt Disney cartoon character of Goofy. *Goofer* ('one who goofs') followed soon after (1925), as did *goof-ball* (1938), the latter reinforced by the use of this expression for a marijuana or barbiturate tablet.

gubbins 1916	The word is a variant of *gobbon*, a word from French meaning 'portion, gobbet', and usually referring to bits and pieces of little value, with uses known from the sixteenth century. In the sense of 'fool', there's nothing recorded before the twentieth century, though *gobbin* is found earlier with this meaning in several dialects of northern England.
B.F. 1925	A euphemism for *bloody fool*. It seems to have emerged as forces' slang in the First World War.
berk 1929	A shortened form of Cockney rhyming slang for *Berkeley Hunt* or *Berkshire Hunt*, well-known English fox-hunting locations, also spelled *birk* and *burk*. Although the origin is to avoid the explicit use of *cunt*, the most powerful of English rude words, *berk* developed a much gentler and often comedic force, becoming especially popular after its frequent use in television sitcoms of the 1960s and 70s, such as *Steptoe and Son*. It's occasionally used facetiously in a fuller form, as in 'You always was a berkeley' (1940).
loogan 1929	US slang, etymology unknown. Various suggestions have been made: there could be a relationship with *hooligan*, or with *loon* ('rogue') or even *loony* (from *lunatic*). Writer Damon Runyan is the first recorded user, in an article for *Hearst's Magazine*: 'The poor loogan she is marrying will never have enough dough to buy her such a rock.'
nelly 1931	A derogatory colloquialism, at first used with reference to effeminate men, but later for anyone considered to be fussy or silly. A *Sunday Times* citation in the *OED* from 1962 refers to getting 'on the same wavelength as the nellies who write in'.
gorm 1936	A noun development related to *gormless* 'lacking sense', which in turn is from an Old Norse word meaning 'heed, attention'. It's widespread in dialects (also as *gaum* or *gawm*) of Scotland and the north of England. Novelist Nicholas Blake (aka C. Day Lewis) uses it in *Thou Shell of Death* (1936, ch. 2): 'There's a gorm of a girl comes up from the village every morning.'
slappy 1937	A US slang reduction of *slap-happy* (in its 'punch-drunk' sense), shown in a single *OED* citation from Ernest Hemingway's *To Have and Have Not* (ch. 22), when someone in a fight is told 'Shut up, slappy'.
poon 1940	Australian slang for 'a simple or foolish person', possibly related to *poind*, recorded by the *English Dialect Dictionary* in northern England and Scotland for 'a silly, useless, inactive person; one easily imposed upon'.

tonk 1941	Used in Australia and New Zealand as a general slang term of abuse, alongside a range of other uses to do with effeminacy and foppery. Eric Partridge thought it might be an adaptation of *tony* (used in the sense of 'simpleton' in the seventeenth century), but it could just as easily be a made-up word valued for its punchy phonetic quality.
clot 1942	A middle-class colloquialism for 'fool', but also found widely in dialects of northern England and Scotland in such forms as *clothead* and *cloit*, as well as in earlier 'blockhead' expressions such as *clotpoll* (1609). It is often no more than a mild or friendly term of abuse, frequently with a nuance of clumsiness, as in the expression 'clumsy clot!'
yuck 1943	A US slang name for 'fool', the first *OED* citation – in a rare show of lexicological certainty – asserting a definite origin: 'a word introduced into the language by [radio show host] Fred Allen [for] a dope who makes a practice of going around appearing on quiz programmes'. It would seem obvious to derive this from the exclamation of disgust, usually also spelled *yuck* (though with many variants, such as *yuk, yech, yecch* . . .), but the first recorded use of the interjection is not until some 30 years later.
possum 1945	Australian slang for 'fool', but recorded only in a single dictionary source.
nana 1965	A shortened form of *banana* – a fruit that had become slang before (during the 1950s) in the phrase *be/go/drive bananas* 'go crazy'. The meaning is usually reinforced by an intensifier (a *right nana, complete nana*).
gobdaw c.1966	An Anglo-Irish coinage, a blend of *gob* ('mouth') and *daw* (see above). Radio broadcaster Terry Wogan's memoir, *Day Job* (1981) comments: 'It is the mark of any eejit [see *nidget* above] and gobjaw to enter any Irish drinking establishment and order, say, a "Vodka and lemonade".'
schmoll 1967	A term for 'fool' found in novelist John Wainwright's writing, thought to be from Yiddish *shmol* 'narrow'. It's unusual to find a British writer taking words from Yiddish. This source is much more commonly encountered in US English, as with *schmuk* (1892), *schmo* (1948), and *schlump* (1948).
dork 1972	US slang, perhaps a variant of *dirk*, given an earlier slang sense of 'penis', and maybe influenced by *dick*, which has a similar history. *Dork* seems not (yet) to have generated further 'fool'-words (unlike *dick*, which has given rise to *dick-ass* and *dickhead*).

tonto 1973	The only borrowing from Spanish (*tonto* 'fool') in this listing, mainly used in US slang as an adjective in such phrases as *going tonto* ('going crazy').
plonker 1981	The origin seems to be the verb *plonk* in its sense of 'put something down clumsily', but in the 1940s *plonker* came to be used (chiefly in Britain and Australia) for a penis, and – as with several other slang terms – a sense of 'foolish person' followed soon after. Its use was boosted in Britain by its frequent use in the television sitcom *Only Fools and Horses* (1981).
wally 1983	Originally a slang term for an unfashionable person, but by the 1980s in general use in Britain as a mild term of abuse for anyone considered to have done something stupid. It is often intensified, especially by *right*, as in this quotation from a *Daily Telegraph* article (1984): 'They looked a right load of wallies.'
numpty 1988	The word probably goes back to *numps* (above) or it might be an abbreviation of *numbskull* (1699), with an attractive analogy for the ending being *Humpty-Dumpty*. Its modern use seems to have started in Scotland, but by the turn of the century was a widely used colloquialism, as in this *OED* citation from the *Guardian* (2001): 'What a bunch of numpties'.

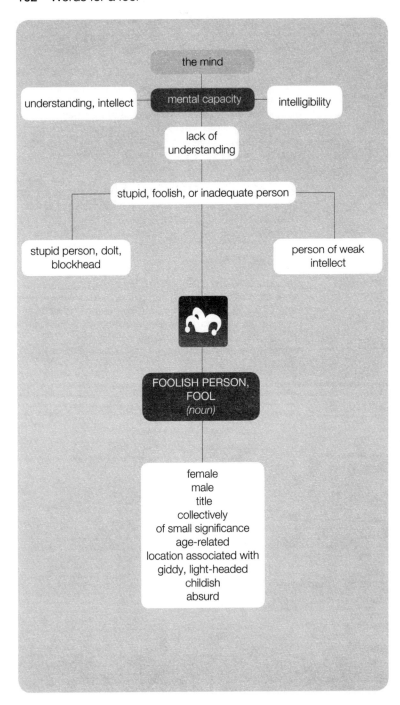

the mind

mental capacity

understanding, intellect — intelligibility

lack of
understanding

stupid, foolish, or inadequate person

stupid person, dolt,
blockhead

person of weak
intellect

FOOLISH PERSON,
FOOL
(noun)

female
male
title
collectively
of small significance
age-related
location associated with
giddy, light-headed
childish
absurd

7

From *darling* to *lamb-chop*

TERMS OF ENDEARMENT

The number of ways we have of addressing each other in an endearing way is probably quite limited. After all, what options are there once we have exhausted the three lexical stalwarts of this semantic field – *darling, dear,* and *love*? If the object of our affection is to be pleased with the term of address we use, there has to be a shared sense of the pleasurable; and judging by the items in the list below, very few areas of the lexicon qualify.

This explains one of the most important features of this field: the same basic item is frequently adapted. There are 98 items in this category of the thesaurus, but the field is not actually so diverse, as several words cluster into groups, so that we find only 73 entries below. *Sweet*, for example, motivates *sweetheart, sweetkin, sweetikins, sweetling,* and *sweetie. Honey* gives us *honeycomb, honey-sop, honey-bunch,* and more. *Love* leads to such forms as *lovey, sweetlove, lover,* and *luvvie.*

Taste seems to be the dominant motif. We see it also in the eatables that are adapted to terms of address: *cinnamon, powsowdie, sucket, bag-pudding, cabbage, pumpkin, sugar,* and *lamb-chop*. These are the attested instances. Probably far more foodstuffs have an idiosyncratic or nonce usage than are recorded in *OED* pages. Some seem to be influenced by fashion: types of *fish*, for example, were once attractive names, it would seem, judging by *whiting, sparling,* and *prawn*. This seems unlikely today, though evidence of *my little codfish* or suchlike would prove me wrong.

There is little sign of truly innovative expression in the list below (unlike in some of the other fields covered in this book). Several of the items are predictable, such as *beautiful* and *pretty*, the kinship term *coz*, or the literary choice of *soul, joy, dainty,* and *treasure*. Indeed, the only field that generates a significant number of items is the animal kingdom. The farmyard and the field seem to be the favourites (*chuck, cocky, bawcock, duck, duckling; suckler, bulkin, lamb, bun, bunny*), but flying things figure as well (*culver, dove, butting, sparrow, ladybird, flitter-mouse*), and a few household animals seem to be permanent fixtures as endearments (*mouse, pussy, pet*).

What is surprising is the absence of lexical fields we might expect to see, such as flowers (apart from *daisy*). Doubtless nonce-usages of *daffodil, tulip*, and the like occur, but evidently not with sufficient frequency to be caught within the lexicographer's net. Appearance is likewise missing, apart from colour in *golpol*, a reference to the eyes in *nye* and *nykin*, and some examples relating to size (*pug, fub, pinkany*). Behaviour is conspicuous by its absence, apart from *wanton*.

A few borrowings enliven the list below (Irish *acushla, alanna, machree*; Welsh *bach*; French *belamy*; Italian *frisco*), and there are some interesting cases where the etymology is unknown. The use of babytalk could be a fruitful field of enquiry, too, given that *pussums* and *snookums* are already recorded, but obtaining a relevant corpus of such informal and revealing intimacies would require more than the usual amount of lexicographical ingenuity.

Timeline

darling OE	A word that has stood the test of time, deriving from the adjective *dear* (see below) with the suffix *-ling* – here meaning simply 'a person showing the quality of [dearness]'. It first appears in King Alfred's translation of Boethius, where the author discusses the afflictions borne by virtuous men, adding 'Se godcunda anweald gefriþode his diorlingas' ('the divine power saved his darlings'). It is recorded as a term of address from the fourteenth century, and was probably used in this way a lot earlier.
belamy † c.1225	A direct translation of French *bel ami* ('fair friend'). In 'The Offering of the Magi' (line 343), one of the fifteenth-century Towneley Mystery Plays, one of the three wise men, Jaspar, greets a messenger with 'Welcome be thou, belamy.'
culver † c.1225	The earliest of the bird names used to express tender affection, usually found in religious contexts with reference to God. *Culver* was used for both doves and pigeons, and later became a widely used dialect word for a wood-pigeon.

dear
*c.*1230

The word is found throughout the Germanic family of languages, and was frequent in Old English as an adjective. It developed noun-like functions during the Middle Ages in the sense of 'dear one'. Subsequent use brought the use of the superlative (*dearest*, 1616) and several associated expressions, such as *my dear*, *darling dear*, *deary*, and *old dear*.

sweetheart
*c.*1290

This combination of *sweet* ('lovely, charming, delightful') and *heart* (as the seat of the emotions) was originally written as two words, a practice that continued into the seventeenth century. It is traditionally used both for someone with whom one is in love and more generally for anyone with whom one has an affectionate relationship; but since the nineteenth century it has developed ironic or contemptuous slang uses, as seen in Frank Parrish's novel, *Fire in the Barley* (1977): 'Try harder, sweetheart, or I'll plug you in the guts.'

heart
*c.*1305

The two elements in *sweetheart* had lives of their own as terms of endearment – *sweet* recorded a little later (*c.*1330) and its diminutive form *sweeting* (*c.*1375). Either could be used alone, but most *OED* citations record *heart* along with *dear* or *dearest* and *sweet* preceded by *my*. Tennyson uses both forms of *sweet* in *Maud and Other Poems* (1855): 'my own, my sweet' (21.11) and 'take me, sweet' (24.12).

honey
*c.*1375

A hugely popular extension of the 'sweet' motif. Any honey-related word could in principle appear. Attested examples are *honeycomb* (*c.*1405), *honey-sop* (1568), and *honeysuckle* (1598), none of which seems to have outlasted the seventeenth century. The twentieth century saw a resurgence of interest, with *honey-bunch* (1904), the abbreviated *hon* (1906), *honey-bun* (1911), the southern US *honey chile* (1926), and *honey-baby* (1948). I haven't seen any endearment reference to *honey-bee* or *honey-cup*, but I expect they're out there somewhere. People might draw the line at *honey-fungus*, though.

dove
*c.*1386

The replacement of *culver* (above) as the bird of choice for expressing tender affection. The turtle dove, in particular, was proverbial for the affection it shows for its mate. As a result we find *turtle dove* also used as a term of endearment (1535), sometimes simply as *turtle* (1548). *Dove* (typically in the form *my dove*) was usually used by men to women, but sometimes by women to men – as when Ophelia reflects on her dead father (Shakespeare, *Hamlet*, *c.*1600, 4.1.168), 'Fare you well, my dove'. It retained its popularity: *dovey*

(1769) was used into the nineteenth century, and the reduplicated rhyme *lovey-dovey* (1781) is still with us, though associations of excessive sentimentality ('none of the usual lovey-dovey stuff', 1969) have reduced its use as a term of address.

cinnamon †
*c.*1405

The only *OED* citation is from Chaucer's *Miller's Tale*, when Absolon calls Alison 'my sweet cynamome' (line 3699).

love
*c.*1405

The archetypal form of address to one's beloved, usually with a possessive *my*, and in the twentieth century often spelled colloquially as *luv*. In regional dialect, it's long been widely used colloquially in addressing any close acquaintance, or even people one does not know (such as a shopkeeper to a male or female customer). *Lovey*, first recorded in 1684, became an equally popular form, especially in Britain.

mulling
*c.*1475

A word of uncertain etymology, used as a term of endearment during the fifteenth century. *Mully* (1548) seems to be a later derivation, used in a piece of verse to rhyme with *bully* (see below). The *English Dialect Dictionary* records two similar terms: *mullach* in Scotland (Scottish Gaelic *muileach* 'dear') and *mulley* in Suffolk (a child's pet-name for its mother).

daisy
*c.*1485

A rare flower appellation, a general term of admiration to a woman, not recorded after the early seventeenth century. The Scots poet Alexander Montgomerie (1605, *Miscelleneous Poems*, 39) begins an address to his mistress with the words 'Adieu, O daisy of delight'.

powsowdie †
*c.*1513

The word is recorded only in a William Dunbar poem ('In secreit place this hyndir nycht') in the phrase 'My sweit possodie', one of a long string of fantastic endearments. It could be from the sweetly flavoured hot milk drink, the *posset*.

suckler †
*c.*1513

Another Dunbarism, a few lines later: 'My sowklar' – from *suckle*, used in relation to lambs and calves.

mouse
*c.*1520

A very popular term of endearment, especially to a woman. Hamlet tells his mother not to let Claudius 'call you his mouse' (Shakespeare, *Hamlet*, *c.*1600, 3.4.167). It has retained its popularity into modern times.

butting †
*c.*1529

An endearment found in a single *OED* citation from a John Skelton poem, 'Against Garnesche', where he imagines his target in Fenchurch Street, London, addressing a prostitute

	with the words 'Bas me, buttyng' ('Kiss me'). The etymology is unknown. Eric Partridge thought there might be an association with the bird, the *bunting* – a name recorded as a term of address in the seventeenth century, as well as in the nursery rhyme, 'Bye baby bunting'.
whiting † *c.*1529	Comparing one's darling to a fish is no longer fashionable, but perhaps it never was a totally complimentary term, for the only *OED* citation is in a savage character assassination by John Skelton, 'The Tunning [putting into an ale-barrel] of Elynour Rummyng'. Eleanor says of her husband 'He calleth me his whiting,	His mulling [see above] and his miting [little creature, as in *mite*]'. The use was probably influenced by its value as a rhyme.
fool † *c.*1530	An endearment recorded in the sixteenth and early seventeenth centuries, usually accompanied by a supporting adjective, such as *poor, young, heavenly*, and *sweet*. The other, much more dominant sense of *fool* (see Chapter 5) probably crushed its tenderness potential.
beautiful 1535	As a term of address, first recorded in Myles Coverdale's translation of the biblical Song of Solomon (2: 10): 'My love, my dove, my beautiful'. In twentieth century usage, it became colloquial, used in talking to babies, in casual compliment, and in set expressions such as 'Hey Beautiful' – the name of various beauty salons and the title of a 2007 pop song by The Solids.
soul *c.*1538	A chiefly literary endearment, always used with *my*, as when Lysander calls Helena 'My love, my life, my soul' (Shakespeare, *A Midsummer Night's Dream*, *c.*1595, 3.2.247). Even more literary is *soul of my soul* (1654).
bully † 1548	At first either men or women could be addressed as *bully*, meaning 'sweetheart', but by Shakespeare's time it was men only. The innkeeper in *The Merry Wives of Windsor* (1597) calls all the men *bully*, both with an accompanying noun ('bully Sir John', 'bully doctor') and as a single vocative ('Mockwater, in our English tongue, is valour, bully').
lamb *c.*1556	By the end of the Old English period, *lamb* was being used metaphorically for anyone meek and gentle, so it was a short step to its use as a literary term of endearment. It is usually accompanied by an adjective, such as *sweet* or *dear*.

pussy c.1557	This use of a cat's call-name as an endearment is found in a ballad as early as the sixteenth century ('Adieu, my pretty pussy...'), but there is a significant gap before *OED* citations resume in the nineteenth century. The reason is probably to do with the way *puss* developed negative associations in the interim (such as spitefulness and slyness). When Samuel Pepys writes in his diary (6 August 1663), 'His wife, an ugly puss...', this is a long way from endearment. But when Doctor Jeddler calls his daughter *puss* (in Charles Dickens's novella *The Battle of Life*, 1846, ch. 1), we see a very different usage. The change seems to have taken place during the eighteenth century, and heralded later adaptations of the *pussy* motif (see *pussums* below).
sweet-love † c.1560	A compound found only in a literary translation of Virgil, motivated by the metre of the line: 'O husband sweet-love most desired'.
coz † 1563	A much-used term of familiar address in Shakespeare, and still in use in the nineteenth century. Although an abbreviation of *cousin*, it was used to other relatives as well as to people who were not kin at all. For example, in *Hamlet* (c.1600, 3.2.102), Claudius calls Hamlet his cousin, though the latter is his stepson; in *Henry IV Part 1* (c.1597, 3.1.49) Mortimer calls Hotspur cousin, though the latter is his brother-in-law; and in *The Two Noble Kinsmen* (c.1613, 1.1.222), Theseus calls Pirithous cousin, though they are no more than comrades-in-arms.
ding-ding † 1564	A playful adaptation, probably of *darling* (above), with *OED* citations into the early seventeenth century. *Ding-dong* and *ding-a-dings* took it a stage further.
golpol † 1568	Probably a colloquial variant of *gold-poll* 'golden head'. *Goldilocks* ('golden hair') is first recorded during the same decade.
sparling † 1570	Another fish-term of endearment, this time for the smelt. As with *whiting* (above), it has just a single *OED* citation from *The Play of Wit and Science*, and seems to have been motivated by the need for a good rhyme: 'I will be bold with mine own darling, | Come now, a bas [kiss], mine own proper sparling.'
lover 1573	In several British dialects, especially in the Midlands and West Country, a familiar address that has no romantic or sexual connotations at all. The earliest use of the word (thirteenth century) meant simply 'friend'. Since the seventeenth century, the context of an extra-marital

	relationship has become the dominant sense, and is the only one known in the USA. This explains the look on the faces of American tourists travelling around Warwickshire when a pub-owner calls one 'me lover'.
pug † 1580	Most of the meanings of *pug* are to do with 'small size' – a dwarf animal, an imp, a nose, a doll – so presumably this endearment was used for people of small stature. *OED* citations are found throughout the seventeenth century. There was usually an accompanying adjective: the alliterative *pretty pug* was popular.
bulkin † 1582	This is *bull* with a diminutive suffix, as in *lambkin* – a bull-calf. It is recorded only once, in a literary translation: 'My sweete choise bulcking'. One imagines the implied size of the recipient would have made it a not entirely welcome term of endearment, but it does resurface in seventeenth-century cant in the forms *bulch* and *bulchin*, especially for a chubby young lad.
mopsy 1582	The word is probably an amelioration of *mop* in its sense of 'fool' (see Chapter 5). It was often used when talking to a child, especially a young girl, along with *mops* (1584) and *moppet* (1601), and moved from there to any woman, especially one of small stature. The name in this sense remained popular in northern and eastern dialects of England, and continues to turn up from time to time in present-day literature, though today it's more likely to reflect a pejorative use ('a dowdy, dirty, or untidy woman') that developed in the seventeenth century. A witch in Harry-Potter-world has the name of *Mopsy*.
bun 1587	A popular pet-name for both squirrels and rabbits, with the cuddly nature of the latter the primary motivation for its use as a term of endearment. *Bunny* (1606) became even more popular, reinforced in literary use by its rhyme with *honey*. Today the term has a mixed pattern of use, due to its having developed negative associations during the twentieth century: a poor player at a game might be called a *bunny*, and *dumb bunny* has been US slang since the 1960s for a stupid girl, perhaps influenced by the night-club hostesses called (from their imitative costumes) *bunny girls*.
wanton 1589	A name for anyone – child or adult – displaying playful or roguish behaviour. The use never became widespread, because during the same period *wanton* was being used to mean 'lascivious person', and it is this sense which eventually dominated.

ladybird † 1597	The Nurse in Shakespeare's *Romeo and Juliet* (*c.*1595, 1.3.3) is the first recorded user of this endearment, when she calls out to Juliet: 'What, lamb? What, ladybird?' During the seventeenth century, it came to be applied to mistresses and prostitutes, so its use as an 'innocent' term of address faded.
chuck 1598	*Chuck* has long (at least since the seventeenth century) been a dialect word for *chick* or *chicken*, so it's not surprising to see it appearing as a familiar term of address, along with later *chucking* (1609) and *chucky* (1728). It had a very wide range of use: husbands could use it to wives and vice versa; parents to children; and close companions to each other.
muss † 1598	The origin is unclear. It could be a dialect form of *mouse* (above) or *mouth* (as in *muzzle*). The latter is known especially in northern dialects of England, mainly used in talking to children ('wipe your muss'), and probably originating in baby-talk. Ben Jonson evidently liked it, as it appears several times in his play *Every Man in his Humour* (1601).
pinkany † 1599	Essentially, 'pink eye', but without any connection with colour. *Nye* is occasionally recorded as a popular adaptation of *eye* (*an eye > a nye*). And if eyes are *pink-eyed*, or *pinkie-eyed*, they are small and narrow or half-shut (there is a connection with *blink*) – the small size also seen in modern English use of *pinkie* ('little finger'). So this endearment probably started out when addressing a girl whose eyes were the main attraction. Writer Thomas d'Urfy later (1696) adapted it as *pinkaninny*.
sweetkin 1599	A natural combination of *sweet* with a diminutive suffix. Judging by the *OED* citations, it was an idiosyncratic usage – just one for *sweetkin* and one for the by-form *sweetikin* (1596) – both from playwright Thomas Nashe. However *sweetikin* (along with *sweetikins*) turns up again in the 1970s, so it evidently meets a need.
duck 1600	'O dainty duck', Pyramus calls Thisbe, in Shakespeare's *A Midsummer Night's Dream* (*c.*1595, 5.1.276). It remains popular in general familiar address, both as *duck* and *ducks*. In the nineteenth century it appears also as *ducky* and *duckie* (1819), often used today as a mock-endearment between people who aren't on good terms with each other.
joy 1600	A term of address for 'someone who causes delight'. It is usually found with an adjective or possessive – *my joy*, *gentle joy*, *pretty joy*, *sweet joy*, and so on.

sparrow *c.*1600	A single *OED* citation suggests that this was never a common endearment outside of some dialect use. It did however become popular among Cockneys, as part of a phrase reflecting their chirpy, quick-witted character: *me old cock sparrow*. Used mainly between male friends or comrades, it eventually shortened to *cock* and *cocker* (1888).
bawcock *c.*1601	This is a man-to-man endearment, 'fine fellow, my good man', from French (*beau coq* 'fine cock'). It was often used sarcastically, as when Sir Toby Belch teases Malvolio, calling him 'my bawcock' (Shakespeare, *Twelfth Night*, *c.*1602, 3.4.112).
sucket † 1605	An ingenious variation of the *sweet* theme (above): a *succade* (fifteenth century), with the stress on the second syllable, is a fruit preserved in sugar. It seems to have altered its stress pattern and developed the variant form *succate*, with the spelling *sucket* one of the consequences. It is recorded just once as a term of endearment.
nutting † 1606	The modern use of *nut* ('crazy person') makes it difficult to appreciate the way this word was earlier (seventeenth century) used to mean 'source of delight', especially in the phrase *for nuts* ('for fun'). A single *OED* citation from the play *Wily Beguiled* shows the unusual (to modern eyes) association: Will Cricket addresses 'sweet Pegge' with an extravagance of endearments: 'my nutting, my sweeting, my love, my dove, my honey, my bonny, my duck, my dear, and my darling'.
tickling † 1607	Another single *OED* citation, this time from Ben Jonson's play *Volpone* (3.7.69), when Volpone addresses his 'parasite' Mosca as 'my joy, my tickling, my delight'. The meaning is 'one that gives a thrill of pleasure' (as in twentieth century *to be tickled pink*).
bagpudding † 1608	The word does indeed mean 'a pudding boiled in bag', and might seem out of place in this list. But the context of its single recorded use, in playwright John Day's *Humour out of Breath*, suggests a jocular sense of 'clown' or 'buffoon'.
dainty † 1611	Another instance of a single *OED* citation from a playwright – Ben Jonson again, in *Catiline* (2.1.232), when Curius calls Fulvia 'daintie'.
flitter-mouse † 1612	And yet another from Ben Jonson. In *The Alchemist* (5.4), Subtle calls Dol Common 'my fine flitter-mouse, | My bird o' the night' – a bat.

fub † 1614	An onomatopoeic word, spelled both as *fub* and *fubb*, and usually used as if a plural, *fubs*. Echoing *full* and *chub*, it was used when addressing pretty little children or women, especially if they were chubby.
pretty 1616	Both people and animals could be addressed with this word, often with a preceding possessive: *my pretty* or – if addressing more than one – *my pretties*. 'Back to back, my pretties', says Mrs Hardcastle, as she measures Tony Lumpkin and Miss Neville against each other (Oliver Goldsmith, *She Stoops to Conquer*, 1773, 2.42).
old thing c.1625	An expression that has ameliorated with age. It was originally an expression of contempt or reproach aimed at anyone who was literally old, often found with demeaning adjectives (such as 'ugly old thing', 1717). But in the nineteenth century we see it used with warmhearted adjectives (especially as 'dear old thing', 1852), and eventually on its own as an affectionate form of address to a person of any age.
duckling † 1630	This diminutive use of *duck* (above) as a term of address is recorded again in 1716, but not thereafter. It may have been overtaken by the collocation 'ugly duckling' (1844, from one of Hans Andersen's tales).
sweetling † 1648	A continuation of the *sweet* motif (above), with examples of use into the early twentieth century. The *-ling* suffix had solely a diminutive force (as in *duckling*), lacking the dismissive nuance that is found in such words as *princeling*.
frisco † c.1652	The word seems to be a sixteenth-century pseudo-Italian formation, based on *frisk*, referring originally to a brisk dancing movement. As a term of address, it is recorded in a single *OED* citation from playwright Richard Brome's *The New Academy* (1.1.3) 'Where's my Boykin? my Frisco? my Delight?'
machree † 1689	This is Gaelic, as in Irish *mo chroí* 'my beloved', and little encountered outside of Irish settings. When the word became known from the 1910 sentimental song, 'Mother Machree', and the 1928 silent film of the same name about a poor Irish immigrant in America, it was interpreted as a proper name.
cocky 1693	A further development of the *cock* motif (above), also spelled *cockie*, but with no *OED* citations after the eighteenth century. Dialect use was mainly in Scotland and the south of England. Eric Partridge also found it in Canada.

nykin † 1693	Another use of *nye* ('eye'), as in *pinkany* (above), with the diminutive suffix expressing affection. In William Congreve's play *The Old Bachelor* (1693, 4.4), Fondlewife and Laetitia repeatedly call each other *nykin* – and also *cocky* (above).
nug † 1699	A canting dictionary provides the only citation in the *OED*: it defines *nug* as 'a Word of Love, as, my Dear Nug'. It may be a playful adaptation of *pug* (above).
pet 1767	The word originally (sixteenth century) referred to a lamb or other domestic animal reared by hand (from Scots Gaelic *peata* 'tame animal'), and by the eighteenth century had developed its modern meaning. Any sweet, obedient, or obliging person then came to be called *pet*, as a familiar form of address, as did anyone specially cherished.
sweetie 1778	The direction *sweet* took colloquially in the USA as a term of endearing address, but now widely used around the English-speaking world, along with the more elaborate *sweetie-pie*. The direction of use is more towards someone considered as a lovable person rather than as a lover.
toy † 1822	A single use in a literary translation of Aristophanes, evidently prompted by the rhyme: 'Why, Xanthias, my toy, | Why, what ails the poor boy!' The meaning of 'plaything' makes an endearing use almost inconceivable today.
acushla 1825	An Irishism (from *a chuisle*, 'heartbeat'), used to mean 'darling, dear' – the *a* being a particle that shows the noun is being used to address someone. In Virginia Brodine's novel, *Seed of the Fire* (1996, ch. 13), about Irish immigrants in America, we read 'Bridget, acushla, how is it with you?' The early nineteenth century also saw *macushla* (from *mo chisle*, 'my heartbeat') used in the same way.
alanna 1825	Another Irishism (from *a leamnbh*, 'child'), used as a familiar form of address usually to someone younger than the speaker: 'my child'. We hear it in George Bernard Shaw's play, *John Bull's Other Island* (1907, Act 3), when Aunt Judy addresses Nora Reilly: 'Come on, alanna, an make the paste for the pie'.
cabbage 1840	One of relatively few vegetables that have become endearments, often in the form *my (little) cabbage*. The usage shows the influence of the equivalent expression in French, *mon (petit) chou*.

bach 1889	One of the few Welsh words to have achieved widespread recognition in English. It literally means 'little', but as a term of endearment it would be best translated as 'dear' or 'mate'. It is often used along with a proper name (as in *Dai bach*), always coming after the noun, this being normal Welsh word order.
prawn 1895	The dominant human application of *prawn* was unflattering (see Chapter 5), but there is a single *OED* citation suggesting that, for some people at least, the noun could be an endearment. 'I expect you're a saucy young prawn, Emma', says a character in William Pett Ridge's *Minor Dialogues* (1895).
so-and-so 1897	A euphemistic term of abuse, with the two *so*'s replacing words of more explicit intent; also, with softened force, a term of affectionate address. Depending on the intonation, an expression like *you so-and-so* could be cajoling or angry. An accompanying adjective can make all the difference: *you old so-and-so* vs *you ignorant so-and-so*.
pumpkin 1900	A food which has accumulated both negative and positive associations, so that it is sometimes used contemptuously and sometimes endearingly. As a term of friendly familiar address, it has a similar range of application to *sweetheart* (above).
pussums 1912	The source is ultimately baby-talk, where *diddums* (*did 'em* = 'did they') as an expression of commiseration is known from the late nineteenth century. The *-ums* ending then had a limited productivity in jocular pet-name vocabulary between playful adults. *Pussums* came to be used in talking to both people and cats; *snookums* (1919) for people and lap-dogs. Most recently, we find people and dogs addressed as *pookums* (probably from *pooch*), though sociolinguistic lexicography has yet to establish who is responsible.
treasure 1920	Friends, children, and other people held in special esteem have long been referred to as *treasures*, but the use of the word as a form of intimate address is twentieth century, often accompanied by modifiers, such as *my (little) treasure*. Anything considered to be precious could of course be used in the same way, in a wide range of idiosyncratic usages (*my jewel, my precious, my pearl* ...).

sugar 1930	Given that *sugar* is recorded in English from the thirteenth century, and often used figuratively and proverbially since then, it's surprising that the fashion to use the word as a term of address seems to be not much older than the 1930s. Among the more popular compound words since then are *sugar-babe* and *sugar-pie,* but a wide range of possibilities exists. A 2001 song by Woody Guthrie begins: 'Tippy tap toe, my little sugar plum'.
lamb-chop 1962	A woman in Ellis Lucia's memoir, *Klondike Kate* (1962, ch. 2) is described as 'quite a lamb chop'. It strains my imagination to think of lamb chops being used for direct intimate address, but that's one of the risks you take when you engage in thesaural lexicography.

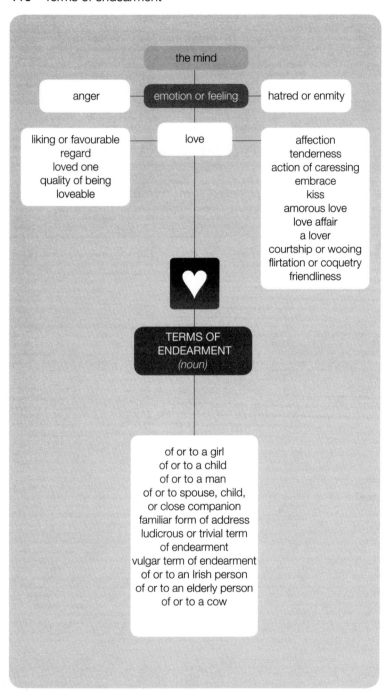

the mind

anger — emotion or feeling — hatred or enmity

liking or favourable
regard
loved one
quality of being
loveable

love

affection
tenderness
action of caressing
embrace
kiss
amorous love
love affair
a lover
courtship or wooing
flirtation or coquetry
friendliness

TERMS OF
ENDEARMENT
(noun)

of or to a girl
of or to a child
of or to a man
of or to spouse, child,
or close companion
familiar form of address
ludicrous or trivial term
of endearment
vulgar term of endearment
of or to an Irish person
of or to an elderly person
of or to a cow

8

From *Io* to *knickers*, and *aplight* to *sapristi*

OATHS AND EXCLAMATIONS

In Act 2 Scene 2 of Shakespeare's *Romeo and Juliet*, Romeo tries to swear his undying love to Juliet: 'by yonder blessed moon I vow...'. Juliet cuts him off: 'O swear not by the moon, th'inconstant moon...'. Romeo, totally taken aback, asks her: 'What shall I swear by?' To which Juliet replies: 'Do not swear at all. | Or if thou wilt, swear by thy gracious self...'

If Romeo had had the *HTOED* available, he would have had little trouble finding an original and apt expression, for this section of the work contains over 300 options (see Wordmap 8 below). Assuming he would have avoided the categories of 'Obscene oaths' and 'Euphemisms for stronger oaths', and probably not wanting to use any of the explicitly 'Religious oaths' to a young Catholic girl, he would doubtless have found the present category useful: 'Oaths other than religious or obscene', for there are a dozen '*by*-expressions' to choose from in the first part of the listing below and in the first, second, and third subcategories ('Word or honour', 'With reference to life', 'With reference to parts of the body').

He would not have used the items listed in subcategories 4 ('Imprecations'), 5 ('Damn'), 6 ('Mild oaths'), and 7 ('Implying rejection'); and the words in subcategory 8 ('Foreign words') had not yet arrived in the language as exclamations. At least, he would not have used them to Juliet. But they would have done him good service in his encounter with Tybalt.

Motifs

The recorded examples start relatively late, in the thirteenth century. People must have sworn as much in the first millennium as they do today – Beowulf would surely have let out something rather more Anglo-Saxon in his various fights than the expressively elegant locutions we know from the poem – but the words would never have been written down. As with many other categories in *HTOED*, the lists show an increasingly colloquial character as time goes by, and writers more accurately incorporate the language of everyday into their work.

There are relatively few cases in the present semantic field where the etymology is unclear or unknown (*goodyear, I snore, hokey, horn spoon, Sam, pize, cargo*). In most cases, it is perfectly clear what is going on. We see several examples of a progressive weakening of oath-force over time, as with *rot* leading to *rat, rats, rabbit, drabbit,* and *drat,* or the adaptations that stem from *damn.* And there is a certain logic underlying most of the expressions.

Swearing by the two fundamentals, 'life' and 'death', provides the basic motivation. We see both these terms in the list, as well as the factors that are most implicated – disease (*pestilence, murrain, plague, pox, rot, cancro, pest*) and punishment, both in this life (*hang, vengeance*) and the next. The threat of eternal destruction is an especially powerful motif in the early centuries (*confound, wild-fire, confusion, perdition, consume,* and most of the *damn* set). Echoes of a religious mindset remain in several secular expressions (*Lord Harry, yea and nay, pody-cody, splutterdenails, goodness sake, George, Christmas*). These echoes are not always Christian (*Jove, waniand, wanion*).

A level down from death is affliction and bad luck, central to the use of *mischance, woe, dahet, sorrow, evil theedom, maugre, deuce, foul fall,* and *cess.* The affliction can be wished on body or mind – either on particular parts of the body (*ten bones, vitals, eyes, windpipe*) or on what one most believes in (*truly, aplight, troth, honour, word*). People also swear by the things they need in order to live healthily (*bread and salt*) or to protect themselves, such as clothing (*hood, knickers*) or weapons (*sheath, hilts*).

Compared with oaths that are religious or obscene in character, several of the examples in the present section are much less predictable. This is especially so when people wish to exclaim in a weak way. One does not really expect to see people swearing by tiny animals (*mouse-foot, Jiminy Cricket*), a vegetable (*peasecod*), a card game (*capot*), or an Irishman (*Mike*), but they do. And there comes a point, in exclamations, when meaning is left behind. There is probably little semantic content motivating *jingo* and *yerra*, and the way people home in on foreign expressions and use them, often without any clear sense of their original meaning (*sapristi*, *merde*, and the others in section 8 below) is an interesting feature of this semantic field.

The chapter also illustrates the classification of a field into several subcategories. As with most other subclassifications, there is no balance of coverage between the different domains. There is just a single item in section 3 below, for example, and only two entries in sections 2 and 7. It is a typical taxonomic scenario in linguistics. A lexicon does not evolve symmetrically over time.

Timeline

lo † OE	*Lo* is attested in Old English, but this was hardly an oath – more like a modern *oh!* It has long lost its exclamatory function, being used today as an attention-directing particle chiefly in historical and biblical narratives. Outside these contexts, it's sometimes heard in breezy, jocular story-telling: *lo and behold . . .*
spi † *c.*1225	This too is hardly oath-like – more an exclamation of disgust, used in the same way as later *fie!*
how mischance † *c.*1330	*Mischance* is 'bad luck, ill fortune'. Chaucer uses it both as a single word and in construction with *how* and *with*. It must have been a fairly genteel oath, as Criseyde uses it when thinking of her future in the Greek camp: 'Or how, meschaunce, sholde I dwelle there' (*Troilus and Criseyde*, *c.*1385, Book 4.1362). On the other hand, the Host – never one to avoid a meaty oath – uses it in the prologue to *The Manciple's Tale* (*c.*1390, line 11): 'Is that a cook of Londoun, with meschaunce?' where he means 'ill luck to him!' (because the cook had fallen asleep). *How meschaunce* would probably equate today with 'how the devil . . .'
by my hood † *c.*1374	Hoods were worn by monks as a sign of their calling, so using a hood as an oath would originally have meant more than referring just to a piece of clothing – more like 'by my faith'. But as time went by, and men and women started to wear different styles of hood, the oath lost a lot of its force. It is almost jocular when Gratiano, amazed at Jessica's actions, comments: 'Now by my hood, a gentile and no Jew!' (Shakespeare, *The Merchant of Venice*, *c.*1597, 2.6.51).

by my sheath † 1532	A *sheath* was the covering into which a blade was placed when not in use. The associations with weapons and manhood gave it some force. There are no *OED* citations after the sixteenth century.
by the mouse-foot † 1550	The expression contrasts with the various religious oaths of the time, where *by God's foot* was one of many that used parts of Christ's body as a serious oath. A mouse's foot goes to the opposite extreme, and suggests an oath that doesn't mean very much. 'I'll come and visit you, by the mouse-foot I will,' says the parasite Weathercock to Sir Lancelot (in *The London Prodigall*, author unknown, 1605, 2.2).
what a/the goodyear † *c.*1555	In Shakespeare's *Much Ado about Nothing* (*c.*1599, 1.3.1), Conrade addresses Don John: 'What the goodyear, my lord, why are you thus out of measure sad?' The origins of the expression are obscure. There is a parallel in Dutch, where the source seems to lie in the optimistic exclamation 'as I hope for a good year'. But any literal meaning had gone by Shakespeare's time, so that a modern equivalent is more like 'what on earth' or 'what the dickens'.
bread and salt † 1575	Two of the necessaries of life, so a fairly weighty oath for anyone in a domestic setting. Dame Chat and Gammer Gurton both use it, in *Gammer Gurton's Needle* (1575, unknown author, 2.2, 5.2).
by Jove 1575	*Jove* was a poetical name for Jupiter, the highest deity of the Ancient Romans. An important religious oath at the time, it lost its force as belief systems changed, and today is one of the mildest exclamations in this category.
by my truly † 1580	*Truly* on its own is simply an emphatic assertion of fact, with a formal tone (as in *yours truly* at the end of a letter). It's unusual to see an *-ly* adverb used in a noun-like way, but this one developed several forms, such as *upon my truly*, *in truly*, and *in good truly* (1672), all affirming the truth of what the speaker is saying. The first recorded usage is from one of Gabriel Harvey's letters: 'By my truly, I was never so scared in my life.'
by these hilts † 1598	Another example of the 'weapons' motif, and thus a strong oath. We still use the expression *up to the hilt*, but the oath seems not to have outlasted the seventeenth century, other than in literary historical allusions.

by yea and nay/no † 1598	The expression is biblical in origin, for Jesus tells people that they do not need to swear but need say only 'yea, yea; nay, nay' (Matthew 5: 37). *Yes* and *no* also cover the scale of affirmation to denial, so that an oath which uses them is all-inclusive – as well as ambiguous. It has a euphemistic character, avoiding any really serious words, hence its force is rather weak. Simple-minded people, however, would treat it as a very serious oath, so playwrights saw its comedic potential. Master Shallow swears by it in Shakespeare's *The Merry Wives of Windsor* (1597, 1.1.80): 'Sir, I thank you; by yea and no I do.'
by the Lord Harry 1693	Who *Harry* was isn't clear. The most likely candidate is the Devil, who was often referred to as *Old Harry*. A 1708 *OED* citation also has 'in the Lord Harry's name', which echoes the commonly used expression, 'in the devil's name'. It feels archaic and literary today.
by the pody cody † 1693	A mock-religious oath, a euphemistic mispronunciation of *body of God*. It is known from a single *OED* citation in a translation of Rabelais.
by jingo 1694	*Jingo* seems to have been first used as a nonsense word by conjurors (like *abracadabra*), but people would have been aware of the association between the initial *J* and the name of *Jesus* (as with *bejabers, jeepers,* and so on). The first *OED* citation for *by jingo* is actually a translation of French *par dieu* ('by God') in Rabelais. The later (1766) *by the living jingo* also suggests a religious parallel. *By jingo* remains in modern usage around the English-speaking world, sometimes appearing as *by jing* (first recorded in 1786) or *by jings*.
splutter-denails † 1707	Both *splutter* (1731) and *splutterdenails* are oaths usually attributed to the Welsh. The *p* and *t* sounds are typical ways of showing Welsh pronunciation, here replacing their voiced equivalents in the source religious expressions *blood* (short for 'God's blood') and *blood and nails*.
I snore 1790	A curious US expression, used in some regional dialects (mainly New England) as a mild expletive, roughly equivalent to the more widely used *I declare* (1811). *The Montreal Gazette* instanced it in an article on snoring (7 October 1981), the author adding 'it's so old that even the oldest New Englanders don't remember it'.

by hokey 1825	Probably another nonsense expression, though with echoes of *hocus-pocus*, used as a magical formula in conjuring. It has been widely used in British and Irish dialects in a variety of forms, such as *by the hokey, by the hokeys, by the hokey fiddle* (1922), and *by the hokey farmer*.
shiver my timbers 1834	Have sailors ever genuinely used this oath? The first recorded use is in Frederick Marryat's *Jacob Faithful* (ch. 9), where Tom's father tells him: 'I won't thrash you, Tom. Shiver my timbers if I do.' It seems to have inhabited pirate literature ever since.
by the (great) horn spoon 1842	A US expression, of obscure origin, but with some tantalizing links to Scotland, where *horn and spoon* was a dialect expression for 'food and drink', so there may have been a parallel development to *bread and salt* (above). The *horn* was also a local name for the Little Bear (Ursa Minor), so there may be a link with navigation. The expression had virtually died out until Sid Fleischman used it for the title of his children's adventure novel (1963) about the California Gold Rush.
upon my Sam 1879	The etymology is unknown, but this jocular expression seems to have started out in Devon and Somerset, where it is sometimes recorded as *zam*. The general assumption is that *Sam* is a shortening of *Samuel*, which is why it is usually written with a capital initial, but it could be a euphemistic alteration of *upon my soul*. The phrase is often expanded with an adjective, such as *sacred* or *solemn*.
for goodness' sake 1885	The use of a religious name or word in this expression can be traced back to the fourteenth century: *for God's/ Christ's/heaven's sake. Goodness* is a nineteenth-century euphemistic substitution for *God*.
yerra 1892	An Anglo-Irish exclamation, common since the end of the nineteenth century, and typically spoken in a jocular or enthusiastic way. Brendan Behan makes the point explicitly in *Borstal Boy* (1958, ch. 3): '"Yerra, 'tis nothing," said I, jovial and Irish.'
for the love of Mike 1901	*Mike* (and also *Mick*) became nineteenth-century slang for an Irishman (first recorded use, 1859). Around the turn of the century we see it used in a euphemistic exclamation of exasperation, with the pet-name substituted for *God*, as in John Brophy's novel *Waterfront* (1934, ch. 1): 'For the love of mike... shut those blasted windows.' Used on its own, and often preceded by *well*, it expresses dramatic surprise: 'Well, for the love of Mike!'

knickers 1971	The name of the undergarment (in British English), used as a 'rude word' by little children, transmuted to the adult world in the 1970s as an exclamation expressing exasperation, annoyance, and other such emotions. I suppose it just about qualifies as an oath.

1 Word or honour

aplight † 1297	Old English *pliht* had several meanings, such as 'promise' and 'pledge'. Today we know it chiefly from the marriage ceremony: one 'plights one's troth' (see *troth* below). As an exclamation or expletive, in Middle English, it carried the sense of 'in faith' or 'in truth', as in this quotation from *The Sowdone of Babylon* (*c.*1400): 'Fifteen thousand left in the field aplight'.
by my troth *c.*1374	*Troth*, a variant of truth meaning 'good faith' or 'loyalty', went out of use in the early seventeenth century, other than in some North Country dialects in England and in special settings (such as 'wedded troth'). It was one of the most widely used oaths during the Middle Ages, and appeared so often in later historical literature that it remains in popular consciousness as a jocular use, along with *upon my troth*.
on one's honour *c.*1460	An expression of strong assurance of truthfulness (slightly stronger in the form *upon my honour*), as it is one's personal credit and sincerity that is being affirmed. In the Middle Ages, nothing could be more obligating than this expression, and it retains a powerful force to this day.
upon my word 1591	The expression parallels *on one's honour* (above), but with less force, so that its meaning approximates more to 'assuredly' or 'certainly'. It eventually weakened into an exclamation of surprise, occasionally as *on my word*, and colloquially reduced in writing to *'pon my word*. A 2003 cricket commentary illustrates its present-day use: 'The batsman . . . sends it to the outfield where, oh, upon my word, a Georgian lady . . . scoops her hand down and catches in her hand a ball which never existed.' The expression feels somewhat dated today.
honour bright 1819	A protestation of sincerity – or a check on someone else's sincerity – which remains colloquial and often jocular. American essayist Ralph Waldo Emerson wanted nothing to do with it: 'The phrase of the lowest of the people is "honor-bright".'

2 With reference to life

by my life
*c.*1225

The preposition varies a great deal: we see *by/for/of/on my life*. In the twentieth century, it can be prepositionless, as in British novelist Frank Norman's *The Guntz* (1962): 'My life (I thought) what chance am I going to have.'

lifelikins †
*c.*1644

The *life* element is from *God's life*; the -*kins* a suffix found in a few old swearwords (such as *bodikins* and *lakins*). The puzzle is where the medial *li* comes from. It's probably an intensifying element, seen occasionally in other words (such as *bodlikins*); or it may be related to the -*ly* adverb ending (often spelled -*li* in early texts). It's recorded only in the seventeenth and eighteenth centuries.

3 With reference to parts of the body

by these ten bones †
*c.*1485

The fingers. The expression appears in late medieval times, used in oaths chiefly by unsophisticated people, such as apprentices, servants, and messengers. It's most often encountered today in productions of Shakespeare's *Henry VI Part 2* (*c.*1591, 1.3.193), when the armourer's man, Peter, swears that he is telling the truth in reporting his master's words: 'By these ten bones, my lords, he did speak them to me.'

4 Imprecations

woe
971

This expression of lament is one of the oldest in English, appearing in various forms throughout Indo-European languages. It is recorded early on as a curse, usually in the form *woe be to* – a wish that affliction or grief will fall on the recipient. With self-reference, the curse is made conditional, as in this 1583 example: 'Woe were us, if we were at the rule and government of creatures.' The use today is archaic ('woe is me'), but kept alive through historical films and television sitcoms. A car advertisement in 2013 was headed 'Woe, woe and thrice woe' – the reference being to the catchphrase used by Senna the Soothsayer, a character in the 1969 UK TV series *Up Pompeii!*

woe worth †
*c.*1275

This is *worth* used as a verb, meaning 'happen' or 'take place'. It was an important verb in Old English, but it fell out of use in the sixteenth century, apart from in a few set phrases, such as *woe worth*, used as a curse. Walter Scott uses it in *The Lady of the Lake* (1810, Canto 1.9), where the hunter exclaims over his dying horse: 'Woe worth the chase, woe worth the day, | That costs thy life, my gallant gray!' If you wanted to wish *good* fortune on someone, then *well worth* was also available.

dahet † c.1290	A borrowing from Old French, where it meant 'misfortune, evil', used only in imprecations. It is found variously spelled in fourteenth-century texts in such cursing constructions as 'dahet [someone/something]', 'dahet have [someone/something]', or 'dahet that [something should happen]'. *Maldehait* is also recorded (c.1400) as a stronger form.
confound c.1330	This verb entered English in the fourteenth century with a truly ferocious sense: 'defeat utterly, bring to ruin, totally destroy'. When in Shakespeare's *Henry VI Part 1* (c.1592, 4.1.123) the Duke of Gloucester shouts at two quarrellers, 'Confounded be your strife', he is absolutely furious with them. But the force gradually weakened, and this is seen in the associated oath, which since the eighteenth century has really been quite mild, expressing annoyance rather than anger. When, in Oliver Goldsmith's *She Stoops to Conquer* (1773, 4.79), Tony Lumpkin finds he cannot read some handwriting, he expostulates with 'confound me, I cannot tell'.
sorrow on † c.1330	The expression is most often seen with a following pronoun. In Shakespeare's *The Taming of the Shrew* (c.1593, 4.3.33) Katharina, starving for lack of food, harangues Grumio and the other servants for fooling her with 'Sorrow on thee, and all the pack of you' – that is, 'may affliction trouble you'. It had a chiefly dialectal use, especially in Ireland, Scotland, and northern England.
in the waniand † c.1352	This unusual word comes from *wane*, said of the moon. The idea behind it is that the time of the waning moon is unlucky, so that to curse someone in this way was to ask for bad luck to come to them. If you wanted to send *really* bad luck, you would intensify it as (c.1430) *in the wild waniand* or (c.1485) *in the wild waning world*. The expression isn't recorded after the sixteenth century, but with *wanion* replacing *waniand* it survives into the 1800s. In Walter Scott's *Peveril of the Peak* (1823, ch. 5), Sir Geoffrey Peveril curses a parson with one of his favourite phrases: 'with a wannion to him'.
woe betide you 1362	One of the *woe* expressions (see above) that has remained to the present day, but in a very weakened sense. It usually means little more now than 'you'll get into trouble if . . .'
wild-fire † c.1375	A *wild-fire* was a really destructive fire, and also a name for serious inflammatory diseases, so to wish such a thing on someone was quite a strong thing to say. 'Wildfire and brimstone eat thee', says a furious Earl Edoll to King Aurelius at the end of Act 3 of William Rowley's *Birth of Merlin* (c.1626).

evil theedom † c.1386	To *thee* (with the *th* as in *thin*) was an Old English verb meaning 'to thrive, prosper'. It was archaic by the sixteenth century, but continued to be used as an imprecation in folklore and ballads into the eighteenth century, especially in Scotland, in such expressions as 'may he never thee'. A noun based on the verb appears in Middle English: 'Evil theedom come to thy snout' appears in one of the Coventry Mystery Plays (c.1450).
a pestilence (up)on † c.1390	The first of the 'plague' curses, still used in the nineteenth century. 'A pestilence on him for a mad rogue', says one of the gravediggers about Yorick in Shakespeare's *Hamlet* (c.1600, 5.1.74).
hang c.1400	A curse originating in the days when hanging was a routine method of execution, so that it became quite a strong expression of anger or vexation. People would be addressed directly ('Hang thee!', 'Speak and be hanged!') or it could be self-addressed ('Hang me if . . .'). In the eighteenth century, it weakened when it began to be used with *it*, where the reference was often completely non-specific. In the nineteenth century, *hanged* came to be used as an adjectival intensifier of annoyance ('A confounded bad dinner and hanged bad wine', 1887), and this continues today, where *Hang it* and *Hang it all* have little more than emphatic force.
murrain c.1400	A *murrain* was originally the flesh of animals that have died of disease, and it transferred from here to any death caused by disease and to the disease itself. To invoke a murrain on someone was thus to call down a plague on them. But the word was also used with exclamatory force in such expressions as *what the murrain* and *how a murrain* (compare present-day *what the hell*): 'Who am I?' asks Luce in Act 4 of Thomas Dekker and John Webster's *Westward Ho* (1607), and Tenterhook replies: 'What the murrain care I who you are.' Despite its old-fashioned character, the word continues to be sporadically used. US versifier Ogden Nash (1961) was a fan: 'A murrain on every bridesmaid and every usher! | I hope they all get spattered with oil from a gusher!'
vengeance c.1500	An act of revenge would inflict hurt or harm on another, so simply wishing for this provided the basis for a strong curse. The word is almost always found with a preceding article: 'a vengeance on him!', 'what the vengeance!'

plague *c.*1566	Nothing was more feared in the Middle Ages than the arrival of the highly infectious diseases usually called simply *the plague*. To wish a plague on someone was therefore one of the strongest curses or exclamations. We see it in a wide range of expressions, such as 'a plague take Damon' (*c.*1566), 'what a plague mean ye' (1598), 'how the plague dost thou' (1600), and – probably the most famous plague-curse of all, from the dying Mercutio in Shakespeare's *Romeo and Juliet* (*c.*1595, 3.1.91): 'a plague on both your houses'. This last usage survives as an adaptable quotation today: a 1991 press report about the quality of television programmes comments: 'a plague on all their houses'.
maugre † 1590	This Old French loan came into English with the sense of 'ill will' or 'shame', and also developed a prepositional use meaning 'in spite of'. We might thus have expected it to have become popular as a curse, but the only example so far recorded is from Edmund Spenser, who in Book 2 (Canto 5) of *The Faerie Queene* curses Fortune with 'maugre her spite'.
pox *c.*1592	After the plague (above), the other feared group of diseases of the Middle Ages included smallpox and syphilis. As with the plague, a wide range of strong expressions developed, such as 'a pox of that jest' (1598), 'a pox on him' (*c.*1604), 'O pox!' (1695), and 'a pox take the House of Commons' (1702). *Pax* (1604) was a common alternative. The frequency with which the word was used (such as in Shakespeare) has kept it alive, so that we find it, for example, in the *New York Times* (5 April 1994): 'A pox on those services that suggest otherwise in their advertisements.'
rot 1594	'To suffer from a wasting disease while alive' or 'to decompose when dead': either way, it isn't a very nice thing to wish on somebody. So when we find it first used as an imprecation, along with *rot on* (1595), it is usually in an intense emotional setting, as with captured Aaron's summary curse in Shakespeare's *Titus Andronicus* (*c.*1591, 5.1.158): 'I'll speak no more but "Vengeance rot you all".' By the eighteenth century it had weakened into a fashionable expression of irritation: 'Rot you, Sir', says Richard Steele in an elegant exchange in *The Tatler* (1709).
cancro † 1597	An early word for 'cancer', used as a strong exclamation. Only two instances from the Jacobethan period have so far been recorded.

perdition c.1603	Wycliffe introduced this word in his translation of the Bible (1382), capturing the sense of 'damnation' and 'hell'. Shakespeare is the first recorded user of it as an exclamation, when Othello says of Desdemona: 'Perdition catch my soul | But I do love thee' (*Othello*, c.1604, 3.3.91). It later came to be used in a variety of ways to express irritation or impatience, such as 'perdition seize you', 'perdition take you', and 'why in perdition…?'
death c.1603	Another doom-laden word, used in its general sense, as with *confusion* (above), but with overtones of an earlier oath, *God's death*, often abbreviated euphemistically as *'sdeath*. It was a fashionable vehement expression by the time Oliver Goldsmith used it in *The Vicar of Wakefield* (1766, ch. 2). The narrator is horrified to be found playing 'hunt the slipper' on the floor by two unexpected lady visitors, and exclaims: 'Death! To be seen by ladies of such high breeding in such vulgar attitudes!'
pize 1605	One of the few imprecations where the etymology isn't known: it could be a euphemistic adaptation of *pox* or *pest*, or some other 'dangerous' word, such as *poison*. It came to be widely used in regional dialects of England and Scotland (in a variety of spellings) in such expressions as 'pies take him' (c.1643), 'out a pize' (1676), 'a pize on 'em' (1715), and 'what a pize' (1754), and is still heard.
vild † 1605	Seen in a single *OED* citation from *The London Prodigall* (author unknown). Sir Lancelot Spurcock, looking for his missing daughter, thinks Flowerdale has murdered her and curses him with 'A vild upon thee'. It is probably an adaptation of *vile*, which had a range of meanings to do with abhorrence and depravity, as his Uncle in the next line says: 'He is my kinsman, although his life be vilde.'
peasecod † 1606	A 'pea pod' – an unlikely source of a curse, but evidently used by some seventeenth-century playwrights as a mock imprecation. In John Day's *The Isle of Gulls* (1606, 5.1), Mopsa curses the absent Dorus with 'A peasecod on him'.
cargo 1607	Another unclear etymology, with an isolated *Cargo!* used just twice in seventeenth-century plays. It is probably a dismissive use of Spanish *cargo* 'burden, load'. The *English Dialect Dictionary* has examples from Nottinghamshire with a pejorative tone, such as 'a cargo of rubbish'.

confusion 1608	A use of this word as an exclamation. In Shakespeare's *King Lear* (*c.*1608, 2.4.90), the king, angry that Cornwall will not speak to him, produces a string of maledictions: 'Vengeance, death, plague, confusion'.
pest 1632	The French loanword *peste* 'plague' (1479) shows a similar development to other 'plague-words' used as curses, occurring as (*a*) *pest on* or *upon* someone or (*a*) *pest take* someone. The usage is still occasionally encountered: 'A pest upon people who would derail my dreams' appeared in a 1991 Australian newspaper article.
light upon 1642	The force of this expression depends entirely on the accompanying words. Both good and ill fortune could *light upon* someone. In the 1642 *OED* citation, it is a plague: 'The plague of Egypt light upon you all'.
deuce 1651	An imprecation or exclamation originally meaning 'bad luck', as in 'a deuce on him' (1651) or 'a deuce of his cane' (1709), and more common later in such phrases as *what the deuce, deuce take it, deuce knows,* and *go to the deuce,* where the usage is increasingly a euphemism for 'devil'. This is not *deuce* from French *deux* 'two', as encountered in dice, cards, and tennis, but *deuce* related to German *daus,* formerly used in the same exclamatory way (*der daus!*) – though there's probably a link between the two. If gamblers throwing a two (a low value) at dice were to exclaim in vexation 'the deuce', this could easily have turned into the expletive.
rat 1691	A euphemistic alteration of *rot* (above), usually used to express exasperation or disbelief in such phrases as *rat it!* or *rat me!* In John Vanbrugh's play *The Relapse* (1697, 1.3), the newly created Lord Foppington complains to his tailor about the height of a pocket. The hapless tailor protests that if it had been lower 'it would not have held your Lordship's pocket-handkerchief'. 'Rat my packet-handkerchief', replies his Lordship, 'Have not I a page to carry it?'
stap my vitals † 1697	Another exclamation from Lord Foppington, who is affecting a pronunciation that he thinks to be fashionable (as with *packet* in the entry on *rat* above). The expression was already in vogue: a 1699 canting dictionary glosses *stop my vitals* as 'a silly curse in use among the beaux'. The *stap* version was then picked up and used by other writers, and sometimes shortened to *stap me*. Always an older person's usage, it seems to have died out by the early 1900s.

strike me blind 1697	A more discriminating application of the 'health' motif, seen in *vitals* (above), and usually encountered in jocular contexts. One can chiefly ask to be struck *blind* or *dumb*, if what the speaker affirms is not true, but Charles Dickens (1830s) has *strike me bountiful* and *strike me vulgar*, and later examples include *lucky* and *ugly*. The expression *strike me pink* (1902) is chiefly used as an exclamation of astonishment. Adaptations go in two directions: more fanciful (as *strike me down with a feather*) and elliptical (*Strike me!*) – the latter common in Australia and New Zealand as simply *Strike!*
split my windpipe † 1700	The 'health' theme continuing, with the windpipe the focus this time. It was commonly shortened to *split me!* 'Split me if I ever sell it for less,' says a writer in an 1811 sporting magazine.
rabbit 1701	A euphemistic or jocular adaptation of *rat* (above), widely used in dialects of England south from Yorkshire and Lancashire in such ways as 'Rabbit the fellow!' (1742) and 'Rabbit me!' (1768). The *English Dialect Dictionary* records other local expressions, such as *drabbit!* and *What the rabbits!*
consume † 1756	This is *consume* in the old sense of 'waste away, rot'. It was a local dialect equivalent to *damn* (below): 'consume you' (1756), 'consume it' (1823), recorded in the English Midlands and East Anglia.
capot me † 1760	An unusual source for an imprecation: a card game (piquet). A *capot* was the winning of all tricks by one player, so if you *capotted* someone you had a real victory. A single *OED* citation from Samuel Foote's comedy *The Minor*, by Mr Loader, shows its use as an exclamation: 'Capot me, but those lads abroad are pretty fellows.' The implication is: 'if I'm wrong, you definitely win'. It seems to be an idiosyncratic usage, as Loader loves to swear in this way, peppering his speech with such oaths as 'Nick me', 'Slam me', and 'Strip me'.
foul fall † c.1775	'May evil fall' on someone or something. (The opposite was *fair fall*.) It is first recorded in this sense in a Scots ballad: 'Foul fa the breast first treason bred in!'
weary 1788	Another chiefly Scottish usage, found in such expressions as *weary fall* (or *fa'*), *weary set*, and *weary on*. The intent is to wish wretchedness on the receiver. 'O weary fa' thae evil days!' and 'O weary on him' says the grand-dame in Walter Scott's *The Black Dwarf* (1816, ch. 3).

drat 1815	A shortened form of *God rot!* (see *rot* above), in widespread dialect use as an expression of angry vexation, with the variant *drot* also used in the USA.
rats 1816	A further euphemistic development of the 'rat' motif, used on its own with appropriate tone of voice as an exclamatory sentence. It has a wide range of usage: on the one hand, it can express frustration or annoyance ('Rats! I've dropped it'); on the other, it can express incredulity or disagreement ('Rats! That's nonsense').
bad cess to 1859	An originally Anglo-Irish expression, possibly a shortened form of *success*, or – more indirectly – from a tax levied to help pay for the needs of the lord deputy of Ireland, known locally as a *cess* (from *assessment*). It has a wider colloquial presence today.
curse 1885	An unusual euphemistic avoidance of 'real' swear-words to express irritation or frustration by using the metalinguistic term. People don't usually say such things as 'swear' or 'imprecation' when they wish to let off steam, but *curses* has established itself in some literary writing. As a histrionic aside on stage, it has become a catchphrase for pantomime villains: 'Curses! Foiled again!'

5 Damn

damn 1589	The earliest of several expressions which, in their original and most forceful meanings, consign a person to eternal punishment (or an object to total destruction) in hell. As time passed, it weakened into an outburst of irritation or impatience, with all theological meaning lost in such expressions as *damn it, be damned*, and *damn your eyes*. When Shakespeare's Macbeth curses a messenger with 'The devil damn thee black' (*Macbeth*, 1606, 5.3.11), the word has its original strength. When, in William Thackeray's *Pendennis* (1850, ch. 66), Amory says to his daughter, 'D – n it, I love you', it hasn't. (The euphemistic dashes were common in the eighteenth and nineteenth centuries.)
damnation c.1603	While *damn* weakened (see above), *damnation* retained its strength. It's usually found in literary contexts where the character is in a real rage.

damme † 1645	The pronunciation is 'dammee', and it is often written in that way, or as *dammy*. It is a colloquial shortening of *damn me* that became a genteel male profanity. In the seventeenth century, a man who used this oath repeatedly was called a *damme-boy*. Lord Byron (in *Don Juan*, 1823, Canto 11) considered the British *damme* 'rather Attic', going on to say: 'But "Damme"'s quite ethereal, though too daring – | Platonic blasphemy, the soul of swearing'.
darn 1781	The first of the *damn*-euphemisms, with widespread dialect use in England and Scotland in such expressions as *I'll be darned* (1808) and *darn my soul* (1825), and now all over the USA most often as *darn it* and *darn it all*, or simply *darn!* It is found in all the contexts where *damn* could also be used, such as *by darn* (1840) or *I don't give/care a darn* (1850).
dash 1800	Another euphemism, even milder than *darn*, especially used in fashionable British slang. In Charles Dickens's *Bleak House* (1853), the London lawyer Mr Guppy likes to use it: 'I'm dashed…if I don't think I must have had a dream of that picture', 'Dash these notes!', 'Dash it!'
hot damn 1929	As *damn* weakened, alternatives were found to beef it up. This slang expression has been popular since the 1920s, especially in the USA.
dammit 1956	This is the modern colloquial shortening of *damme* (above), these days used most in the comparative expression *as – as dammit*. It has so lost its profane force that it can nowadays be seen even in the most elegant columns of Sunday newspaper magazines. What could be more genteel than a restaurant review in the *Sunday Telegraph* (25 January 1998)? 'An aubergine purée…was repeated, as near as dammit, as the topping of a pancake which came with a red mullet.'

6 Mild oaths

before George *c.*1592	The name of the patron saint of England, St George, often appears in a familiar form, with slang uses referring to objects as various as a coin and a loaf of bread. The image forms part of the insignia of the Order of the Garter, and this is something Shakespeare's King Richard is ready to swear by: 'Now by my George, my Garter, and my crown' (*Richard III*, *c.*1593, 4.4.366). During the seventeenth century it came to be increasingly used as a mild oath, as *for* or (1680) *before George*, then (1694) *by George*, and eventually, simply, as *George!* (1888).

Gemini † 1664	A euphemistic echo of the first syllable of *Jesus*, but without any content relating it to the standard meanings of *gemini* ('twins' or the star constellation). It seems to have stayed fashionable until the mid-nineteenth century, usually as a single exclamatory word or preceded by *Oh*.
dash my wig † 1797	It might seem difficult to make an imprecation milder than *dash* (above), but the eighteenth century managed it with *dash my wig* or *wigs*. Not to be outdone, the nineteenth century shortened this to simply *My wig(s)!* (1871) and added other articles of clothing: *Dash my buttons!* (1846).
Jiminy 1803	*Gemini* (above) gradually transmuted into *Jiminy*, and the sonic punch of the repeated *i*-sounds soon led to phonetically associated words, such as *crimini jimini* and the mock-name *Jiminy Cricket*, with further variations as *Jiminity Crickets*, *Jiminy Cripes*, and *Jiminy Christmas*. It was *Jiminy Cricket(s)* that achieved lasting fame, being used in quick succession by Judy Garland (as Dorothy in *The Wizard of Oz*, 1939) and then as the name of the puppet's cricket conscience in the Walt Disney animation *Pinocchio* (1940).
Christmas 1897	A euphemistic alternative to *Christ*, which – unlike most of the above – retains an element of identity with its point of origin.

7 Implying rejection

farewell **fieldfare** c.1413	The *fieldfare* is the name of a large migratory thrush, whose departure at the end of winter evidently gave rise to a proverbial expression meaning something like 'it's too late for action now'. As an exclamation, it was more like 'good riddance!' or, as an explanation in *Notes & Queries* (1869) put it, 'go, and never mind what becomes of you'. It is still encountered in folklore and historical allusions.
twenty-three **skidoo** 1926	North American slang, chiefly Canadian, of uncertain origin, though the second element probably relates to *skedaddle* 'go away, leave', with an onomatopoeic nuance added (as in *shoo!*). Eric Partridge surmises that the first element (usually written as a numeral) may be a remnant of telegraphers' slang, where code numbers were sometimes used to replace words, in much the same way that we hear items from the 'ten-code' system used today (as in *10-4* 'acknowledgement'). The expression means 'leave at once', 'scram!'

8 Foreign words

parbleu 1696	The earliest of the foreign exclamatory loanwords, chiefly used when representing the speech of a French person talking in English. It is in origin a euphemism of *par Dieu* 'by God'.
sapperment † 1815	If the speaker was German, nineteenth-century writers used *sapperment* – a euphemistic adaptation of *sakrament* 'sacrament'.
caramba 1835	This Spanish exclamation of surprise or dismay achieved some popularity in English due to its use in literature. In Herman Melville's *Moby Dick* (1851, ch. 43), the sailor Cabaco doesn't believe that his shipmate Archy has just heard strange noises, and reacts with: 'Caramba! have done, shipmate, will ye?' Richard Ford's tourist guide to Spain, published in 1845, seems to assume that travellers will know the word: 'More becoming will it be to the English gentleman to swear not at all; a reasonable indulgence in *Caramba* is all that can be permitted'. The word achieved a new lease of life at the end of the twentieth century thanks to its use by Bart Simpson in *The Simpsons*. *Ay caramba* were apparently his first words as a baby.
merde 1920	An exclamation of annoyance or surprise, borrowed from French, which came to be used mainly by those for whom the English equivalent (*shit!*) was felt to be too risqué. Its fashionable status was confirmed when it developed a use as a theatrical superstition, said to a performer before a performance (in a similar way to 'break a leg!') to wish them good luck.
sapristi 1932	Another euphemistic adaptation, from French *sacristi* ('sacristy'), used as an exclamation of astonishment or exasperation. It will be remembered by an older British generation as being one of the nonsense oaths used by Count Jim Moriarty in the BBC radio series *The Goon Show* in the 1940s and 50s. A younger generation is more likely to have encountered it from the mouth of the French comic hero Tintin, who uses it as his favourite exclamation of surprise (freely rendered as 'Great snakes!' in English translations). When Steven Spielberg's film *The Adventures of Tintin* was released in 2011, several reviews began with *Sapristi!* (without gloss).

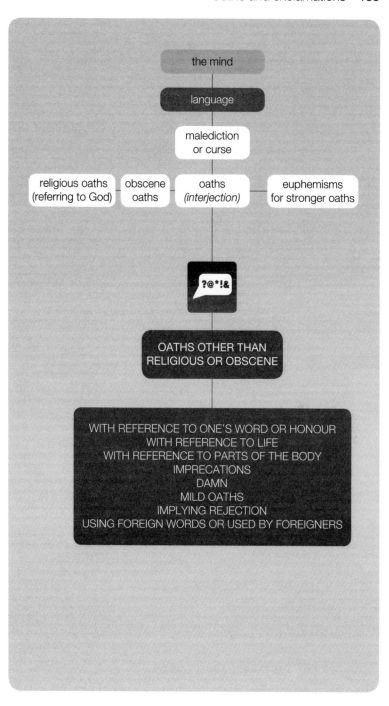

9

From *guest house* to *B & B*, and *hotel* to *floatel*

WORDS FOR INNS AND HOTELS

There were few 'foreign-looking' words in Chapter 8. Quite the opposite impression comes from the present chapter. The turning point in the first category below is around 1600. Before then, there were relatively few words for a traveller's lodging, and they form a close-knit etymological community. Apart from the two 'default' terms of *guest-house* and *inn*, they are all *host-* or *harbour-*related: *hostry, host, hostel, hostelry, hostelar, host-house*; *harbergery, harbergage*. (The initial *h-* was often omitted in the spelling, indicating the *h-*dropping character of contemporary pronunciation.)

Why 1600? The later decades of the sixteenth century saw a great increase in travel from England to the continent of Europe, during periods of relative peace. Some of it was motivated by the need to avoid religious persecution in England. Some was for cultural reasons. Travelling theatre companies brought their plays abroad, and the wealthy made cultural visits, especially to France and Italy – forerunners of the 'Grand Tour' which would become a major part of the European social scene during and after the late seventeenth century. Famous journeys include those made by Thomas Coryat in 1608 and Thomas Howard (the Earl of Arundel) in 1613–14, and their experiences are reported in letters and publications.

Linguistic consequences

The linguistic impact of these social trends on this semantic field is evident in the arrival of loanwords from the languages spoken in Europe. It's always difficult to know exactly when a foreign word enters a language, and how long it takes to 'settle down' as a naturalized item, so dates of first recorded usage need to be viewed with caution. But trends are readily apparent. In the sixteenth century we find examples from Italian (*fondego*, *albergo*), French (*auberge*), and Spanish (*rancho, posada*). The nineteenth century brings a second wave, in the form of Spanish (*meson, parador*), German (*gasthaus, gasthof*), Portuguese (*estalagem*), and Italian (*locanda*). Sometimes the European language has a relay function, as with *fonda* (from Arabic via Spanish) and *tambo* (from Quechua via Spanish). The pattern continues into the twentieth century, with travel becoming so much easier, and we see words also coming from further afield, as English becomes established as a global language (Portuguese *pousada*, Japanese *ryokan*, Hindi *sala*).

These loanwords dominate the 'inn' semantic field after 1599. It's notable that little subsequent use is made of the 'basic' terms *inn* and *house*. We see only the idiosyncratic *inn-house*, the Australian *bush inn,* and the uncommon *temperance inn*. *House* fairs slightly better, with *host-house, public house, roadhouse*, and the marginal *sporting house*. And we have *livery tavern* and *B&B*. But that is it. The lower end of the lodging-house market does not seem to have been lexically creative in modern times. Indeed, it sometimes demonstrates a lack of imagination, such as when a place calls itself *Hotel Meson La Posada* (a real example), which is basically the 'Hotel Inn Inn'. It often isn't clear whether the owners see the name as expressing a word in the source language (which would therefore not be included in the *OED*) or whether it is a real loanword.

By contrast, the upper end has done quite well by way of 'home-grown' lexical diversity. There are only 2.5 unfamiliar loanwords in the 'hotel' list: *gasthof, parador*, and *hotel garni*. *Hotel* itself appears in a range of functions (*palace hotel, temperance hotel, railway hotel, residential hotel, welfare hotel*), and in recent times has motivated a series of blends (*motel, botel, floatel*). Social and economic factors are important too (*lodge, trust house*), as is the drive towards increased luxury (*metropole, Ritz*). It is in the actual names of hotels that we see this creativity at its best, as well as presenting a difficulty of making a clear-cut distinction between the terms in these two categories. I would forgive any lexicologist who decided to throw in the towel after trying to work out where to place *The Silver Tarpon Lodge Motel Boatel* in any taxonomy.

Timeline

1 Inn	
guest house OE	*Guest* is a truly ancient word, widespread in the Germanic languages, and – as a result of a phonetic change in the initial consonant – related to *host* and *hospitable*. In the form *giest-hus* in Old English, it meant both an inn (a place that people pay to use as a temporary residence) and a house for invited visitors (without having to pay anything). The distinction continues today, though usage has changed. Visitors who stay overnight at my house are *guests*, as are the people who stay down the road at a local B&B. But only the latter place can now be called a *guest house*.
hostry † 1377	A great deal of uncertainty seems to have accompanied the earliest words for a 'public lodging house'. In a single decade (see below) we find *hostry, harbergery, host, hostel,* and *hostelry,* all from French. Sometimes the words seem to be no more than variants of each other. In the Hengwrt manuscript of Chaucer's *Canterbury Tales* we see the travellers staying at a *hostelrye*; in the Petworth manuscript, they are at a *hostrye*. *Hostry,* and its alternative spelling *hostery,* seem not to have lasted beyond the nineteenth century.
harbergery † 1382	The sources behind *harbergery* (or *herbergery*) all have something to do with 'place of shelter' (*harbour* is related). In its sense of 'inn', it is first found in John Wycliffe's translation of the Bible (Luke 22: 11), when Jesus asks 'where is the herborgerie' where he can eat with his disciples.
host † 1382	Another Wycliffian word for an inn. In his translation of the Acts of the Apostles (28: 23), it would seem he knows the word is new and might be misunderstood, as he immediately glosses it: many came to visit Paul 'to the host, or herbore' where he was staying. As part of the idiom *to be* or *lie at host* the word lasted into the seventeenth century. In Shakespeare's *The Comedy of Errors* (c.1594), Dromio of Syracuse talks about his master's goods 'that lay at host…in the Centaur' (5.1.411).
hostel c.1384	In its sense of 'inn', *hostel* had little use until the nineteenth century, when it was picked up by Walter Scott and other writers. A narrower meaning developed in the sixteenth century ('house of residence for university students'), and this has now entirely replaced the earlier sense, along with the usage (1931) as a shortened form of *youth hostel*.

hostelry *c.*1386	Walter Scott liked to use this word, too, as did Charles Dickens and other novelists, so it became a somewhat literary form. Today, anyone who says they are visiting the local *hostelry* is either being genteel, jocular, or euphemistic (avoiding the more explicit alcoholic connotations of *pub*).
harbergage † *c.*1400	Yet another variant of the 'harbouring' motif, also spelled *herbergage*. It is recorded during the fifteenth century, several times in the alliterative poem, *Morte Arthure* (*c.*1400), as in line 2285: 'Housing and herbergage of heathen kings'.
inn *c.*1400	The word is used several times in the Anglo-Saxon Gospels in its sense of 'dwelling-place', so that it was already well established by the time it developed the sense of a public lodging-place. It entered public linguistic consciousness as part of an idiom when the King James Bible (following William Tyndale) used it as the term of choice for the house where Mary and Joseph were unable to gain lodging (*Luke* 2: 70): 'no room at the inn'.
hostelar † 1424	A Scots variant of *hostelry* (above), also found in *hosteler-house*. It is sporadically recorded in later centuries.
host-house 1570	The name seems to have been used chiefly for the inns where farmers and other country workers stayed on market days. It was common in North Country dialects of England. The term has taken on a new lease of life in the USA, where a newspaper article (*The Bulletin*, Bend, Oregon, 17 August 1986) on the growing bed-and-breakfast service industry reports agencies 'that match screened guests with host houses and owner-occupied inns'.
fondaco 1599	The first of the exotic-sounding inn-names from abroad, arriving in English from Arabic via Italian – whence the alternative spelling-pronunciation *fondego*. A century later, the word appears again as *fonduk* (1704), and a further century on (1826) as *fonda* in Spanish-speaking countries. John Henry Newman, writing to his sister from his lodging in Syracuse, Italy (27 April 1833), refers to 'The landlady of the fondaco'.
auberge 1615	This name for a traditional French country inn has figured regularly in travellers' tales since the seventeenth century, and has now gone well beyond them. It has been used to name innumerable restaurants around the English-speaking world, and has even become a hit record. *Auberge* (from singer-songwriter Chris Rea) reached the top of the British album charts in 1991. The word has an etymological connection with *harbour*.

sporting house 1615	I suppose this just about qualifies as a member of this semantic field, though its *OED* definition as 'especially a house of ill repute' suggests it sits more comfortably in the company of words from a different domain in the taxonomy. (It is in the *HTOED* category *brothel* as well.)
albergo 1617	Another distant connection with *harbour*, like *auberge* (above), but in Italy this time. The word has not travelled as widely as *auberge* – and as far as I know has never named a musical hit – but it is routinely used (usually without italics) in modern English-language travel books.
rancho 1648	The Spanish American word for a hut or shed built to house travellers, which eventually went up in the world as the name of a roadhouse or inn. Notwithstanding the tautology, there are now several Rancho Inns in the USA as well as an El Rancho hotel chain. There's also an El Rancho BBQ restaurant in Clapham, London. As mentioned in the above introduction, it isn't always clear whether names like this are being thought of as English or Spanish – and the same uncertainty affects other business names below (*posada, meson, gasthaus*).
posada 1652	Another Spanish term, used across the Spanish-speaking world. In its first recorded uses, the writers feel the need to gloss it – 'a common posada or inn' ... 'the inside of a Spanish posada (or inn)' – and this usage is echoed in such modern names as La Posada Inn or Hotel Posada. The word comes from Spanish *posar* 'rest, lodge'.
public house 1655	To British eyes, this term is completely out of place in this list, as it could only mean a pub or tavern, where lodging would be either impossible or an unpalatable prospect – as Arabella affirms (in Thomas Hardy's *Jude the Obscure*, 1895, Part 6.6): 'I cannot endure going to a public house to lodge.' Not so to American eyes, where historically food and lodging is primary, and alcohol licensing secondary.
inn-house † 1694	A single *OED* citation illustrates this unusual compound, in a letter written by nonconformist clergyman Richard Frankland from the village of Rathmell in North Yorkshire. The usage is probably local. There is an Angel Inn House in Tollerton, 50 miles away.
livery tavern 1787	A US term for an inn which has facilities to look after horses as well as people. This function may now be obsolete, but the name lives on in several restaurants.

roadhouse 1806	Whether you can lodge at the places in this list depends to some extent on which century you are living in. Roadhouses originally provided accommodation for travellers 'on the road' – on the edge of a town or in rural areas. But increasingly in the twentieth century, such places became (in Britain) public houses catering chiefly for motorists, and (in the USA) places where, as one writer put it (1972) 'you could dine, dance, and drink'.
meson 1817	A Spanish loanword (from the same Latin root that gives us *mansion*), used in Spain, Mexico, and the south-west USA for an inn or boarding house. These days, the word is often seen in a Spanish-speaking country as a name for an upmarket hotel (as in the Hosteria La Meson in Ecuador) or motel (such as the El Meson Lodge in New Mexico).
tambo 1830	The word has arrived in English from Quechua (where *tampu* is a wayside inn) via Spanish. It is known in Peru and neighbouring Andean countries, meeting the needs of travellers following the Inca trail and other important mountain routes. 'We stopped, at four, at the tambo of Acchahuarcu' writes an explorer in an account of a journey made in 1854.
gasthaus 1834	The German equivalent to *guest house* (above). Today the name will be encountered well outside German-speaking countries. Visit the University of Wisconsin-Milwaukee, for example, and you can eat in The Gasthaus.
estalagem 1835	The Portuguese form of the 'hostelry' motif, known in Portugal, the Canary Islands, Brazil, and other Portuguese-speaking territories. The term has been thoroughly Anglicized. An 1875 travel guide to Portugal writes of the 'two estalagems' in a town, and in 2010 a tourist writes online about going on 'an estalagem-organized walk'.
locanda 1838	An Italian inn. A painting by the seventeenth century artist Johannes Lingelback (in the Royal Collection, London) is called 'Figures before a locanda with a view of the Piazza del Popolo, Rome'.
temperance inn c.1849	As the name suggests, an inn where no intoxicants are available. There were several hundred in Britain during the nineteenth-century temperance movement, but the only one surviving today is in Sedbergh, Cumbria: The Cross Keys Temperance Inn (a National Trust property). They don't sell you alcohol, but you can bring your own.

sala 1871	In northern India, a Hindi word (from Sanskrit *sala*, 'house') for a traveller's inn. The word also appears in *dharamsala* for a pilgrim's rest-house – seen also in the name of the city in Himachal Pradesh where the Dalai Lama resides, *Dharamshala*.
bush-inn 1881	A traveller's inn in Australia, whose function is neatly recorded in an account of a coach-ride in novelist Rosa Praed's *Policy and Passion* (1881, ch. 4): 'At intervals the driver paused before a bush inn, of which, at long distances apart, there were several standing solitary among the trees, to change horses, call for the mail, or give the passengers an opportunity of descending for refreshment.' The oldest continuously licensed pub in Australia, in New Norfolk, Tasmania, is called The Bush Inn.
ryokan 1914	A traditional Japanese country inn – literally, a 'travel hall'. The Anglicization of the word is relatively recent. In 1955, a newspaper's travel column advises visitors to Japan 'to make a point of spending some time in ryokan'. In 1970, a similar column talks about 'ryokans'.
pousada 1949	This Portuguese word has become a collective noun for a type of inn administered by the government. A report in *Good Motoring* (1976) comments: 'Hotel prices vary enormously but the State-owned pousadas are good value.'
B and B 1961	The abbreviation for 'bed and breakfast' (also *B&B*) is relatively recent, though the concept is much older. *Bradshaw's Railway Guide* in 1910 advertises 'Bed and breakfast from 4/-' [four shillings]. In *Our Two Englands* (1936, ch. 10), the journalist James Lansdale Hodson is impressed by a sign he has seen on his travels: '"Bed, breakfast and garage" – a new form which the historian should make a note of.'

2 Hotel

hotel 1687	These days, hotels can be virtually any size, but the original idea was to provide larger buildings with more facilities than in other forms of temporary lodging, such as inns. The distinction was often blurred. In John Ash's *Dictionary of the English Language* (1775) we see *hostel* glossed as 'An inn, an hotel'. And *hotel* was early used as an upmarket name for a very much downmarket establishment. James Beresford (in volume 2 of *The Miseries of Human Life*, 1807) is scathing about some of the lodgings he has experienced: in a dialogue on 'miseries of watering places' he talks about 'groping your way to the inn – (I beg pardon – *hotel*) – as the only hole in which you can pig for the night'.

hotel garni 1744	Literally, 'furnished apartment' – *garni* is French for 'furnished' – an upmarket term for a hotel that supplies only 'bed and breakfast' (above). George Eliot, in an 1858 letter, describes them as 'places where you get lodgings and attendance and coffee and nothing else'.
lodge c.1817	The term originally (thirteenth century) referred to buildings of a relatively small size, such as huts and summerhouses, even including arbours, tents, and other temporary dwelling places. In the fifteenth century, it grows: we see it used for solid houses in wild places (as when out hunting), and soon after for a house at the entrance to the grounds of a mansion. Finally, in the nineteenth century, we see it moving to the top of the social scale, as an acceptable residence for the upper classes. Lady Russell, in Jane Austen's *Persuasion* (c.1817), lives in Kellynch Lodge. Today it's most often used as the second element in the name of a house or hotel, and connotes high rather than low living.
gasthof 1832	A German hotel, usually a step up in size and cost compared to a *gasthaus* (above). The folklorist Rachel Busk, in *The Valleys of Tirol* (1874, ch. 3), describes the principal inn of Zell as claiming 'to be not merely a *Gasthaus*, but a *Gasthof*'.
temperance house † 1833	When George Borrow gets to Beddgelert (in *Wild Wales*, 1862, ch. 46), he stops for refreshment at a *temperance house*, asks for ale, and is offered tea instead. He refuses, and is about to leave when the lady of the house emerges with a bottle. He comments: 'I tasted it; it was terribly strong. Those who wish for either whisky or brandy far above proof, should always go to a temperance house.'
temperance hotel 1837	There are now several places around the world calling themselves *temperance hotels*, but in most cases abstinence has been replaced by moderation. As the Temperance Hotel in South Yarra (Victoria, Australia) puts it: 'DJs, live music and designer decor combine with a premium alcohol selection to create a Mecca for the modern lush.'
railway hotel 1839	A hotel situated next to a railway station in Britain would very likely be called The Railway Hotel, or given the name of the local railway company, such as the Midland or Great Western. In the larger towns and cities it was usually a Victorian red-brick pile with a high-ceilinged lobby offering elegant accommodation to the better-off traveller. Most have long since disappeared, or been turned to alternative use, but a few have been renovated and remain as hotels, such as the Midland in Morecambe and the Queens in Leeds.

parador 1845	This Spanish word for an inn or hotel can be found in any Spanish-speaking country, but its reference varies from luxury hotels (such as the government-owned *paradores* of Spain) to simple town or country inns. The contrast can be seen in a *Time* report (6 November 1989) about Puerto Rico: 'New hotels are popping up all over...from multi-million-dollar sports resorts to *paradores* (simple country inns).'
palace hotel 1870	A term for a very grand hotel, which seems to have been first used in the USA, where there was a nineteenth-century vogue for calling luxurious things 'palaces' (as with *palace steamers* and *palace cars*). Today, top-range hotels continue to invite the description, and several use the term as part of their name, such as the Copacabana Palace in Rio de Janeiro or the Bellevue Palace in Bern.
metropole 1890	A *metropole* was at first (sixteenth century) a chief town of a country or district, and had some use as a common noun for a luxury hotel; but it came to be mainly used as a proper name for individual hotels. The earlier use is seen in a memoir by the founder of the Salvation Army, William Booth (*In Darkest England and the Way Out*, 1890, ch. 6), where he describes a better class of accommodation for those who are improving their prospects as 'a superior lodging-house, a sort of POOR MAN'S METROPOLE'.
Ritz 1900	The name of the Swiss hotelier, César Ritz, whose first luxury hotel opened in Paris in 1898. The London Ritz followed in 1906, and the name then became used for a chain of similar hotels. Their opulence led to the use of *Ritz* as a common noun, though retaining its capital letter ('The place is not exactly a Ritz', 1908; 'In the world of hostels, this is the Ritz', 2002), and even generated an idiom, *to put on the Ritz* ('make a show of wealth, behave ostentatiously').
Trust House 1903	The notion of confidence and reliability implicit in the word *trust* (since the thirteenth century) took an unexpected turn in the nineteenth century, when it was used in the commercial world as the name of a type of trading association. Trust Houses was a company founded in 1903 to restore the traditional high standards of old coaching inns and public houses, eventually forming a chain of hotels. Since 1970 the company has been known as Trusthouse Forte, but the use of the original name as a generic noun remains, as seen in a 1972 *OED* citation from Michael Delving's novel, *A Shadow of Himself*: 'I...looked up hotels. There was a Trust House there, the White Swan.'

motel 1925	A blend of *motor* and *hotel* – a roadside hotel catering chiefly for motorists. It's unusual to find an adjectival usage in this semantic field, but we do see this one in an article (from *Punch*, 1 December 1965) where the writer describes Britain as being 'thinly motelled'. In the same article, the writer conveniently (from my point of view) summarizes the lexical choices: 'They call themselves motor lodges, motor courts, motor hotels, even tourtels and autotels, but motel is the word that blisters the night sky of the American suburbs.' He probably could have added *motor inn* (not recorded until 1967).
residential 1940	Chiefly used in Australia, this is a shortened form of *residential hotel* (1865) – a building where you can rent an apartment with the option of using dining and service facilities. A typical example of usage is in this newspaper report from the *Canberra Times* (30 September 1940): 'He went to the aid of two women against a gunman in a residential in South Brisbane last night.'
welfare hotel 1952	A controversial development in New York City in which rundown hotels (such as the Martinique) were taken over as accommodation for the homeless. The practice was at its peak in the 1970s and 80s, but the notorious conditions which developed in these buildings led to a policy change by the end of the decade, so that the term is now found only with reference to its historical context.
botel 1956	A hotel catering for boat-owners – a blend of *boat* and *motel*. Originally a US term, botels are now found anywhere water-parking is available, and even on the water itself, for it is now possible to take a 'botel cruise' (1962), with the ships themselves being referred to by the name.
floatel 1959	Any building that can provide accommodation and float at the same time could in principle be called a *floatel* or *flotel*, and that is how the term was first used. It was also applied to boats operating as hotels and to the accommodation facilities on offshore drilling rigs. Since 1983, *Floatel* has become proprietary usage in the UK as a registered trade mark.

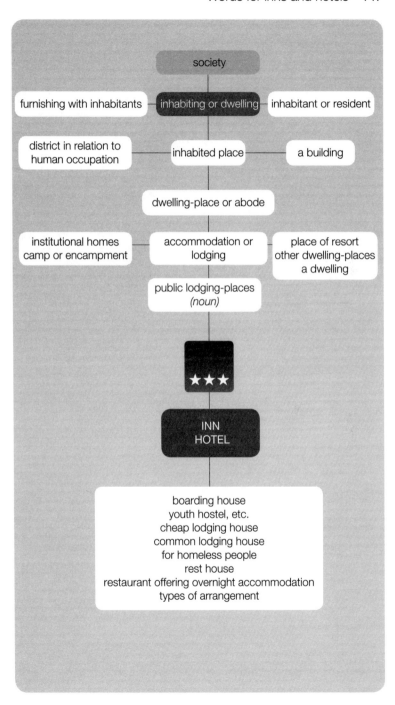

10

From *meretrix* to *parlor girl*

WORDS FOR A PROSTITUTE

In the semantic field of prostitution, the lexical contrast between men and women is truly remarkable: the *HTOED* lists just ten items under the heading of 'male prostitute'; under 'prostitute' [i.e. female] there are 170. This shows gender imbalance at its most noticeable – and a recurrent theme of gender denigration. A modern reader looks with disbelief at times at the attitudes underlying some of the terms that have been used. But for a lexicologist, this area of vocabulary provides a fascinating insight into the way people invent words to cope with a socially sensitive domain. The various semantic subcategories for 'prostitute' are shown in Wordmap 10. This chapter explores only the general nouns used to express the notion.

One fact stands out straight away: the proliferation of words in the period between 1550 and 1700, which cannot be explained as solely an artefact of lexicographic method. Very few items are recorded before the mid-sixteenth century. They include two of the longest-standing words (*whore* and *strumpet*) as well as two of the most widely used adjectivals (*common* and *public*). But in the following 150 years we see the emergence of no less than 69 expressions – just under half of the entire list below. That's a new term appearing every two years. Few other semantic fields illustrate such a rate of growth (but see Chapter 14).

The main reason is the character of the writing that was appearing at the time, with plays reflecting everyday life in an unprecedented way, and the creativity of the writers. Playwrights such as Robert Greene, John Fletcher, and Thomas Dekker figure repeatedly in the list as first recorded users – though whether the occurrence of a word reflects personal linguistic creativity or simply a recognition of an already-existing usage is impossible to say. Compounds such as *hell-moth, land frigate, fling-dust, carry-knave, mar-tail, night-shade,* and *man-leech* feel like the former. *Traffic, trug, croshabell, occupant, pagan, community,* and *venturer* may well be the latter. In modern times, *protisciutto* is definitely the former (a Beckettism).

Directness or euphemism

The linguistic history of prostitution is the story of a few basic terms, a largely male-orientated search for vividly descriptive synonyms, and a class-orientated search for euphemistic alternatives, as people tried to avoid anything resembling a direct description. The basic terms are *prostitute* itself (with its abbreviations, such as *pross, pro, prostie*), along with the earlier *whore, strumpet,* and *punk,* and variations on *streetwalker* (*walk-street, flagger, night-walker*), *girl* (*street girl, girl of the pavement, working girl*), and *woman* (*bordel-woman, public woman, strange woman, common woman, town-woman*).

The descriptive terms are all very physical. The most obvious category uses the place to refer to the person; so we find general locations (*brothel, stew, bulker, barber's chair*) as well as named localities (*Winchester goose, Whetstone whore*). Attributes of the person are used: body parts or appearance (*buttock, quiff, broad, tail* – and the rhyming *brass nail*), clothes (*curtal, waistcoateer, visor-mask, shawl*), and disease (*fire-ship, queen's woman*). Actions provide a major theme, either explicit (*jumbler, turn-up, tweak, twigger, treadle, screw, hooker*) or implied (*horizontal, receiver general, twopenny upright*). The money that changes hands is, surprisingly, little mentioned, apart from the lexical set relating to *hackney*. Attitudes vary, from associations of dirt and waste at one extreme (*drab, drivelling, scupper, slag, mud-kicker*) to those of sweetness and luxury at the other (*marmalade-madam, lady of pleasure*). The generic use of first names is a recurrent theme, right down to the present day: *moll* (Mary), *doll-common* and *dolly-mop* (Dorothy), *mob* (Mab), *mawks* (Maud), and *Suzie Wong.*

The euphemisms are of various kinds. Several are ordinary domestic words (*miss, aunt*) given a second meaning, or work-related words (*professional, model, night-trader, market-dame, customer*). Animals occasionally appear (*cat, polecat, night-worm, loose fish, horse-breaker, soiled dove*). An ingenious solution was to turn to other languages, especially French (*pute, fille de joie, cocodette, cocotte, poule de luxe*). And for those with a more literary or academic bent, classical mythology and folklore provided elegant alternatives: Cyprus, the home of the goddess of love, produced *Paphian, Cytherean,* and *Cyprian,* and there were the alluring *nymph* and *mermaid,* which are as unexpected a pair of euphemisms as we are ever likely to encounter in this semantic field.

Timeline

meretrix OE	The origin is the Latin verb *merere* 'earn as pay' – a verb that was used for several occupations, including prostitution. It led to *merit* too. After its use in Old English, there is a long gap before it surfaces again in the sixteenth century, as part of the fashion to use Latinate expressions, and it continues to be used occasionally in literary or scholarly writing.
whore *c.*1100	The surprising thing about this ancient word, which appears in all the Germanic languages, is that it arrives in English so late. Old English already had several words, such as *forligerwif* (adulterous woman), *myltestre* ('harlot'), and *portcwene* ('woman of the town'), so perhaps *hore* wasn't needed – or perhaps it was known earlier and was simply not recorded. An Old Norse influence is suspected. Its initial *w* is an even later arrival, reflecting a sixteenth-century trend to add the letter to words beginning with *ho-*. (The same thing happened to *whole* – from *hole*.)
strumpet *c.*1327	The origin is unknown, but there is no doubting the popularity of the word, especially in the Middle Ages and in Early Modern English. It was affected by the fashion for abbreviations in the seventeenth and eighteenth centuries (*strum*, 1699). Today it has a literary, light-hearted, and often comical tone, but its archaic feel was challenged by its use as a film-title in a 2001 film directed by Danny Boyle. There have also been regular attempts to reclaim and revitalize the word – as seen in the periodical *Strumpet*, whose brief (according to the website) is 'uniting lady comix stars of the future from the US and UK in one cartoony passage'. The founders explain: 'We like the saucy, timeless quality of the word.'
common *c.*1330	When this word arrived from French, it was evidently felt to be very useful, for it came to be used in all sorts of contexts (political, legal, agricultural...), both as noun and adjective. Probably for this reason, the word is not often found on its own, in its meaning of 'prostitute', but is spelled out as *common woman* (1362), first recorded in one of Wycliffe's writings. This use of *common* carried through into the nineteenth century, where we also find *common prostitute* (1875), and is still occasionally encountered as an intensifying word. For example, an episode of the US television series *Public Disgrace* (27 November 2009) was called 'Common Whore'. Related words include *commoner* (*All's Well that Ends Well*, *c.*1605, 5.3.197) and *public commoner* (*Othello*, *c.*1604, 4.2.75), both from Shakespeare.

pute † c.1384	A French word that turns up in Wycliffe's translation of the Bible, where in chapter 6 of the Book of Baruch we read of the way the priests of Babylon take gold and silver from their gods which they give 'to pute in bordel house'. Only a single later use is known, in a literary translation, but there have been variants, such as *putanie* (1566). A similar use of *putain* (c.1425) had a twentieth-century revival, never thoroughly Anglicized, usually being printed in italics, as in this 1992 quote from the *New Yorker*: 'I am not the son of some *putain*!'
bordel woman † c.1386	A *bordel* is an old word for a place of prostitution. We find both *bordel house* and *bordel woman*.
brothel † 1493	A *brothel* was originally a person – a wretch or scoundrel: John Gower (1393) writes of 'a brothel, which Micheas hight [is called]'. By the end of the fifteenth century it was being used for a prostitute. The first recorded usage talks of going 'to a brodelles house'. Then an interesting change took place. As the spelling suggests, *brothel* and *bordel* were very close in sound. People began to talk of a *brothel-house*, which was then shortened to *brothel*, to give the modern usage. And *brothel*, for the person – along with the variant form *brouthell* (c.1510) – gradually fell out of use.
public woman c.1510	A similar development to *common woman* (above). The influence of French (*femme publique*) is evident, as in English the expression sometimes appears with the adjective after the noun: the first recorded use is in a translation, where we read 'I am as a woman public full of injuries'. The expression with the adjective before the noun is still found in historical writing: a 1994 journal article is headed 'Public virtue and public women: prostitution in Revolutionary Paris'.
drab † c.1533	One of the most famous early uses of this word is in Shakespeare's *Macbeth* (1606, 4.1.31), where one of the witches talks about a 'birth-strangled babe, ditch-delivered by a drab'. It was one of the 'three dangerous D's' listed by the arithmetician Edward Cocker (1675): 'Drink, Dice, and Drabs'. Today, the noun has the more general sense of 'dirty or untidy woman', with the dominant usage being adjectival ('dull, lacking colour').
cat † 1535	The first of the slang animal names for a prostitute, which seems to have survived, as a cant usage, into the eighteenth century.
strange woman † 1535	A biblical description, first used by Myles Coverdale in his translation of the Book of Proverbs (ch. 2): 'That thou mayest be delivered also from the strange woman…'

lady of pleasure c.1550	A euphemistic application of the phrase 'lady of', known in such earlier expressions as *lady of the house, lady of honour*, and *lady of the lake*. It would be followed in later centuries by *lady of easy virtue* (1766) and – in the USA – by *lady of the evening* (1924).
stew † 1552	Long before we got to know *stew* as a kind of food, it was used for a heated room, especially a place where you could take a hot bath. As such places soon came to be used for immoral purposes, *stew* then developed the meaning of 'brothel', usually in the plural (*the stews*), reflecting the way several such houses would come together in a neighbourhood. In the sixteenth and seventeenth centuries, the word was used for a prostitute, as well as some derivatives (such as *stewpot*, c.1613), so we find such examples as 'he had a notorious stew sent him' (1650); but this personal application was soon replaced by other expressions.
causey- paiker † c.1555	*Paiker* was a Scottish word for someone who walks about – a streetwalker, and hence a prostitute. A *causey* was a street or path which had been paved in some way, often with cobbles. (*Causeway* is related.) So a *causey- paiker* was literally a 'street-walker' (see below). It was still being used in the early twentieth century, but is probably obsolete now.
nymph 1563	Semi-divine spirit maidens emerge in English storytelling at the end of the fourteenth century. By the middle of the sixteenth, the word had become a euphemistic and often humorous substitute for a prostitute, and expanded in various ways, such as *nymph of delight* and *nymph of Billingsgate*. Much later (1828), French influence is seen in the expanded expression *nymph of the pavé* ('pavement').
drivelling † 1570	A single *OED* citation in a vocabulary list glosses this word as a 'drab' (see above). It seems unlikely that this usage comes from *drivel* ('spittle from the mouth'); a more plausible origin is the earliest meaning of this word: 'drudge' or 'dirty person'.
punk † c.1575	An etymological mystery. The *pu-* onset echoes *pute* and *public* (above), but where this word came from is unknown. Its original meaning regularly surprises people who come across it in Shakespeare (he uses it four times) and find it difficult to rid themselves of the association with the 1970s subculture associated with punk rock music (Chapter 14). It seems to have been a genteel usage, judging by a comment made by George Peele (see *croshabell* below).

hackney † 1579	Almost as soon as *hackney* arrived in the fourteenth century for an everyday riding horse, it came to be used for a 'hired horse'. The long-term effect of this would be the *hackney carriages* and *cabs* of later centuries. But in the sixteenth and seventeenth centuries, the notion of payment led to the term being used for prostitutes. The root *hack* led to other forms, such as *hackster* (1594), and in the nineteenth century was used without a suffix in this sense.
streetwalker 1591	One of the commonest terms, in regular use since the sixteenth century. It was also used for anyone whose work involved walking in the street, and who would find themselves described in the same way – sometimes with not a little discomfort, because of the semantic overlap. Organizers of an online site in 2013 got some ribald reactions when advertising for people to help police at a local carnival, using the heading 'Street Walkers Wanted'.
traffic † 1591	A single *OED* citation, from the playwright Robert Greene, shows that the usage wasn't widespread, as he feels he has to gloss it: 'These traffics (these common trulls I mean) walk abroad.'
trug † 1592	Another usage first recorded in Robert Greene, along with *trugging-house* and *trugging-place*. It might have been an adaptation of *truck*, in its sense of 'trade, barter', and indeed in a 1631 *OED* citation the word is actually spelled in this way. It turns up again in the eighteenth century in *trugmallion* (1715), where the second element is unclear, though possibly related to *malkin* (see *mawks* below).
stale † 1593	A *stale* was originally (early fifteenth century) a decoy bird, used to entice other birds into a net. It was later applied to people used as a lure, especially among the criminal fraternity (such as for a thief's accomplice), and this included a prostitute so employed. A more emphatic form, often used to describe any woman believed to be unchaste, was *common stale*.
polecat † 1593	A type of weasel (or skunk, in American English), one of the first names to be applied to both sexes, in the context of sexual promiscuity. It evidently took some time for the word to settle down in this sense, as it is glossed in a 1607 *OED* citation: 'London polecats (their wenches I mean)'.
mermaid † 1595	In the sixteenth and seventeenth centuries, the alluring charm of this mythological creature led to its use for a prostitute. Pantilius Tucca uses it in Thomas Dekker's *Satiromastix* (1602, 4.2): 'A gentleman or an honest citizen shall not ... sneak into a tavern with his mermaid.'

croshabell † c.1598	The word is known from playwright George Peele's *Merrie Conceited Jests*. In one of his stories he talks about the different words for a courtesan, and provides us with a rare instance of semantic and stylistic commentary: 'in England, among the barbarous, a Whore; but among the Gentle, their usual associates, a Punk: but now the word refined being latest, and the authority brought from a Climate as yet unconquered, the fruitful County of Kent, they call them *Croshabell*, which is a word but lately used, and fitting with their trade, being of a lovely and courteous condition'.
occupant † 1598	Another single *OED* citation, used by playwright John Marston in *The Scourge of Villanie*, illustrating the continuous invention of words at this time for describing a sensitive area of the lexicon.
Paphian 1598	Paphos, a city in Cyprus, was believed to be the birthplace of Aphrodite or Venus, the goddess of love. Paphian, accordingly, became a literary adjective describing acts of sexual desire, licit or illicit. John Marston uses it for a prostitute in *The Metamorphosis of Pigmalion's Image* (1598), but it seems not to have caught on – until Byron and other nineteenth-century writers rediscovered it. It remains in literary and historical use. As a writer in a Louisville newspaper put it (1990): 'Every once in a while you'll hear someone refer to a prostitute as a paphian.'
Winchester goose † 1598	The expression was used during the seventeenth century both for a type of venereal disease and for a prostitute. It appears there were many brothels using premises in Southwark that were under the jurisdiction of the Bishop of Winchester, and their occupants were labelled accordingly.
pagan † 1600	An unusual euphemism for a prostitute. The first recorded use is in Shakespeare's *Henry IV Part 2* (c.1598), where Prince Hal describes Doll Tearsheet as a *pagan*.
hell-moth † 1602	Samuel Rowlands uses this vivid expression in the dedication to his prose essay *Greenes Ghost Haunting Conie-Catchers*. Inveighing against the 'innumerable harlots and Courtesans' living in London, he asks: 'is there not one appointed for the apprehending of such hell-moths, that eat a man out of body & soul?' In the nineteenth century, *moth* appears again: a slang dictionary (1896) defines it as 'a prostitute, a fly-by-night'.

customer † c.1603	As with *commoner* (see *common* above), a Shakespearian usage, and found in the same two plays. In *Othello* (c.1604, 4.1.118), Cassio is horrified when Iago suggests he might marry Bianca: 'What? A customer?' And in *All's Well that Ends Well* (c.1605, 5.3.288), the King tells Diana: 'I think thee now some common customer'.
moll † 1604	A pet-name for *Mary*, which became a conventional nickname for a prostitute in seventeenth-century London. As Sir Alexander Wengrave puts it, in Thomas Dekker and Thomas Middleton's *The Roaring Girl, or Moll Cutpurse* (1611, 2.2), 'For seek all London from one end to t'other | More whores of that name than of any ten other'. *Molly* developed similarly in the nineteenth century, and is still used in this way in parts of Ireland.
prostitution † 1605	The name of the occupation was extended by some Elizabethan dramatists to the name of the persons involved. John Marston, for example, talks about 'an impudent prostitution' in his play *The Dutch Courtesan* (1605, 1.1).
community † 1606	Another general noun adapted to the person, used in the seventeenth century. Playwright George Chapman in *Sir Gyles Goosecappe* (1606, 1) refers to 'one of these painted communities'.
miss † 1606	This shortened form of *mistress* is known today as a traditional title for a girl or an unmarried woman who has no other honorific or professional title; the earliest recorded instance of this sense is 1667. But from around the beginning of the seventeenth century, the word was being used, along with *mistress*, as the name for a woman other than a wife with whom a man was having a long-lasting sexual relationship. The diarist John Evelyn gives us a clue about the time scale. On 9 January 1662 he goes to see the play *The Siege of Rhodes*, in which he talks about the actress Elizabeth Davenport, who became the mistress of Aubrey de Vere, the twentieth Earl of Oxford: 'the Earl of Oxford's Miss (as at this time they began to call lewd women)'.
night-worm † 1606	An isolated usage. Samuel Daniel in his play *The Queenes Arcadia* (1606, 1.3) talks about 'bed brokers' and 'night wormes'.

prostitute 1607	The verb seems to have arrived first, with *OED* citations from 1530, 'to offer oneself for sex': language scholar John Palsgrave translates French *je prostitue* as 'I prostitute'. Then the adjective arrived, 'engaging in promiscuous sexual activity': lawyer Thomas Norton complains about contemporary crimes, such as 'the prostitute abuse without regard of chastity' (1569). Only at the beginning of the seventeenth century do we find examples of the noun, which would become the default term for the semantic field. There was initially some vacillation between its use for any promiscuous woman and for one receiving payment for services. There were also associated meanings which look surprising to modern eyes, such as the use of the word to mean 'person entirely devoted to another': a 1624 dedication to a nobleman ends 'Your Highness most Humble and devoted prostitute'. But the modern sense was established by the end of the seventeenth century, had already extended to include boys (1654), and would soon extend to include men (*male prostitute*, 1761).
pug † 1607	The origins are unclear. It might be a development of *pug* as a term of endearment (see Chapter 7) or it could be a variant of *punk* (above). In Randle Cotgrave's French/English dictionary (1611), the two are treated as synonyms: 'a soldier's pug or punk'.
venturer † 1607	A single *OED* citation, from Thomas Dekker and John Webster's *Westward Ho*, and a related usage in Shakespeare's *Cymbeline* (*c.*1611, 1.6.123), where Giacomo talks of 'diseased ventures', suggests that this may have been a literary creation. Presumably the notion of 'risk' lies behind it.
curtal † 1611	Soon after *curtal* ('horse with its tail cut short') first appeared in English (1530), it was being applied to people as a general term of derision – especially to rogues who wore short cloaks and to women who wore short skirts.
jumbler † 1611	The various senses of *jumble* ('stir up, mix together, flounder about') made it an obvious slang term for sexual intercourse, and, by extension, for a professional practitioner. This sense seems to have died out by the eighteenth century, and would not have affected the Victorians who went to the first *jumble sales* (1898).
land frigate † 1611	A purely literary creation, by Laurence Whitaker – one of a series of rhyming couplets, assigned to different letters of the alphabet, at the beginning of Thomas Coryat's travelogue, *Coryat's Crudities*: 'Here to his land-frigate he's ferried by Charon,	He boards her; a service a hot and a rare one'.

walk-street † 1611	An unexpected reversal of the more common *streetwalker* (see above). It is recorded just once in Randle Cotgrave's dictionary, as one of the translations of French *bateur de pavez*.
doll- common † 1612	The name of a character in Ben Jonson's *The Alchemist*, which by the end of the seventeenth century was being used in a generic way, as Thomas Otway does in his play *The Atheist* (1684, 5.1): Theodoret harangues Porcia: 'What, be a Doll-Common, follow the camp!'
turn-up † 1612	The word appears in a list of synonyms for *whore* in a popular Italian/English phrase book called *The Passenger*. It is the only recorded instance to date.
tweak † 1617	A seventeenth-century word, presumably related to the verb *tweak* in its sense of 'pull in'. One normally tweaked the nose, but an early *OED* citation shows that it could also refer to lips, meaning 'press together'.
fling-dust † c.1625	Another literary creation: John Fletcher, this time, in his comedy *The Wild-Goose Chase* (4.1). Lillia-Bianca describes Mirabel as 'an English whore, a kind of fling-dust, | One of your London light o'loves'. Some time later (1679), *fling-stink* was used in the same way. The idea seems to be that the dust (or street smell) rises up as one walks the streets.
mar-tail † c.1625	John Fletcher again, in his comedy *The Chances* (4.2). The old man Antonio, furious that his courtesan should have stolen his money and jewels, calls after her sarcastically: 'Well, my sweet mistress? Well, my good madam martail?'
night-shade † c.1625	A word known only from Francis Beaumont and John Fletcher's comedy, *The Coxcombe* (2.2). When Viola appears, a tinker says 'here comes a night-shade', and his associate Dorothy adds helpfully 'A gentlewoman whore'.
waistcoateer † c.1625	Waistcoats arrived during the sixteenth century – the normal garment for a woman (a man would wear a doublet) – and remained in fashion for about a century. A 1688 *OED* citation illustrates its fall from grace: a waistcoat is described as 'an habit or garment generally worn by the middle and lower sort of woman'. *Waistcoateer*, as a name for a low-class prostitute, was one of the consequences. It remained in use into the twentieth century, with modern writers including James Joyce.
twigger † c.1627	One of the meanings of *twig* in the sixteenth century was 'do something vigorously' – a meaning still heard in many regional dialects. Farmers called ewes that were prolific breeders *twiggers*. A slang adaptation to this semantic field soon followed.

carry-knave † 1630	A line in poet John Taylor's writing introduces three expressions at once: 'Our hireling hackney carry knaves, and hurry-whores'. *Hackney* is well attested (see above). The other two expressions remain isolated instances.
night trader † 1630	There are two recorded examples from the seventeenth and eighteenth centuries. Both add a clarifying expression (*night trader in the street*), presumably to help make a distinction with other kinds of people who traded at night. The expression later shortened to *trader*, and developed variants, such as *she-trader* (1682) and *public trader* (1693).
meretrician † 1631	An echo of Anglo-Saxon times (see *meretrix* above): a classical loan which evidently appealed to upper-class sensibilities. The related adjective, *meretricious*, is in Johnson's *Dictionary*, glossed as 'whorish'.
treadle † 1638	A term from spinning. As the *OED* definition puts it: 'a lever worked by the foot in machine and mechanical contrivances, usually to produce reciprocating or rotary motion'. No academic explanation required here.
mob † 1655	A very different sense from the modern usage – a slang shortening of Latin *mobile vulgus* ('fickle crowd'). The prostitute sense is an adaptation of the similarly used *mab*, which was a common familiar form of a female first name (*Mabel*).
girl *c.*1662	Despite the ambiguity with other everyday senses, this word has always been popular in this semantic field. The ambiguity wasn't there at the outset, as it appears in set expressions such as *girl of the game*, *girl at ease*, and *street girl*. But by the eighteenth century, *a girl* and *the girls* were being used without further gloss.
aunt † 1663	A seventeenth-century term for a bawd or procuress, which was sometimes also used for those procured. *Aunt* was frequently given other meanings at this time, as indeed it still is (*Aunt Sally* in fairgrounds, *Aunt Edna* in the theatre, *Aunt Emma* in croquet, and the disbelieving *Aunt Fanny*).
night-walker 1670	A combination of the elements in *streetwalker* and *night trader*. In the twentieth century it became a regular expression in legal contexts. A 1982 law report reads: 'The person arrested was not in fact a common prostitute or night-walker.'
fire-ship † 1672	The allusion is to the heat generated by venereal disease. Fire-ships had been used in naval warfare since the time of the Spanish Armada (1588).

visor-mask † 1672	According to the satirist Thomas Brown in his *Amusements Serious and Comical* (1700), 'a whore is known by a vizor-mask' – a mask used to conceal or disguise the face. The usage is a nice example of synecdoche (the part used to describe the whole). *Visor-mask* is known only from the seventeenth century, but the variant *vizard-mask* (1672) has *OED* citations into the nineteenth.
buttock † 1673	A fairly obvious slang semantic extension of the anatomical meaning (used in English since the fourteenth century), recorded during the second half of the seventeenth century.
marmalade-madam † 1674	The first known reference to marmalade is 1480, and a century later we see its figurative use for anything that suggests a cloying or superficial sweetness (as it still is today – John Steinbeck writes of 'a passage of clarinet marmalade' in his *Russian Journal*, 1949). We find seventeenth-century writers talking about 'marmalade lips', a 'marmalade eater' (for someone daintily brought-up), a 'marmalade lass', and then a 'marmalade madam'.
town-woman † 1675	*Town* became a popular alternative to *street* in this semantic field at the end of the seventeenth century, and has retained its attraction ever since. Later developments include *town miss* (1749), *woman of the town* (1766), *girl of the town* (1819), and *lady of the town* (1982), though the *OED* citations are unlikely to be a good guide to real usage, which must have overlapped a great deal.
mawks † 1677	*Malkin* was a female first name, not used today – a diminutive form of *Mal*, which in turn was a pet-name variant of *Maud*. At some point in the thirteenth century the name came to be associated with servants and country girls, and developed negative associations of untidiness and sluttishness. In regional speech the 'l' was dropped, so that we find *mawkin*, abbreviated as *mawks*, and it is this form which had a short-lived use into the eighteenth century as a word for a prostitute.
Whetstone whore † 1684	Whetstone Park was a lane between Holborn and Lincolns Inn Fields, 'famed' (as a 1699 canting dictionary put it), 'for a Nest of Wenches'. John Dryden uses the derived expression in his translation of Ovid's *Art of Love* (1684, Book 2, Elegy 19): 'Let him who loves an easie Whetstone Whore,	Pluck leaves from Trees, and drink the Common Shore'.
man-leech † 1687	Charles Sedley, in his comedy *Bellamira, or The Mistress* (4.1), calls a prostitute a 'man-leech, that suck'st their marrow and their money'. The expression isn't recorded otherwise.

bulker † 1690	A *bulk*, known from the late sixteenth century, was a framework projecting from the front of a shop on which goods could be displayed. Passers-by would steal from it (hence *bulker* came to mean 'a petty thief') and people could sleep on it. In Nathaniel Bailey's *Universal Etymological English Dictionary* (1790) we see *bulker* defined as 'one that would lie down on a bulk to any one'.
nocturnal † 1693	The adjective, meaning 'of or relating to the night', is known from the fifteenth century. The derived noun was used for anyone 'out at night', and usually referred to people with criminal or suspicious intentions. Its use in relation to prostitution seems short-lived.
fille de joie 1705	An example of the use of French ('girl of delight') to provide a genteel English euphemism. It is still in use.
market-dame † 1706	This expression, for a woman who works in a market, was always derogatory, but an early implication of promiscuity seems not to have outlived the eighteenth century.
barber's chair † 1708	Shakespeare, in *All's Well that Ends Well* (c.1605, 2.2.16), has the Clown talk about 'a barber's chair that fits all buttocks'. In 1632, we find Richard Burton, in *The Anatomy of Melancholy*, using a simile: 'a notorious strumpet, as common as a barber's chair'. So it was only a matter of time before we find the object used for the person. In a translation of Rabelais (1708) we read of 'bonarobas, barbers' chairs, hedge-whores'.
screw † 1725	This slang term has no subsequent recorded use until the twentieth century, when it became widespread as a name for any sexual partner, especially one where the intercourse is hasty and casual. It then left this semantic field behind.
Cytherean † 1751	Like *Paphian* (above), a euphemistic adaptation of a name from classical mythology, Cytherea, sometimes used for the goddess of love herself (Aphrodite, Venus) and sometimes for one of her votaresses. It seems not to have been widely used.
street girl 1764	A further development of *streetwalker* (above). In the nineteenth century it was also used (along with *street boy*) for young people who were forced to earn a living by doing menial outside jobs; but it retained its sexual connotations into the present century, as an *OED* citation from the short-lived men's magazine *Jack* (2002) illustrates: 'His hatred of prostitutes began after he was cheated and humiliated by a local street girl.'

kennel-nymph † 1771	An unusual neologism used only by Tobias Smollett in *The Expedition of Humphry Clinker* (in a letter to Sir Watkin Phillips, 10 June). Tim Cropdale is described as someone who 'during the heats of summer... commonly took his repose upon a bulk [see *bulker* above], or indulged himself, in fresco, with one of the kennel-nymphs, under the portico of St Martin's church'.
loose fish † 1809	Another isolated expression, used by Benjamin Heath Malkin in his translation of *The Adventures of Gil Blas of Santillane* (Book 3, ch. 7) where the narrator talks of 'girls in a servile condition of life, or those unfortunate loose fish who are game for every sportsman'.
receiver general † 1811	A piece of clever wordplay, the original term referring to a public official in charge of government revenues. It appears in the *Lexicon Balatronicum* ('for jesters'), where a certain patronizing tone is unavoidable, reflected in the subtitle: *A Dictionary of Buckish Slang, University Wit, and Pickpocket Eloquence*.
Cyprian † 1819	An inhabitant of Cyprus, famous in ancient times for the worship of Venus/Aphrodite. It was a popular euphemism for a prostitute in the nineteenth century.
dolly-mop † 1834	*Dolly* (a familiar form of the pet-name for *Dorothy*) was a very negative term for a woman in the eighteenth and nineteenth centuries – quite the opposite from the positive sense it acquired in American English in the early twentieth. '*Dolly*, a slattern' says an 1828 book on Yorkshire dialect simply. With *mopsy* and related words already being used as terms of endearment (Chapter 7), the compound *dolly-mop* was an inevitable slang coinage.
hooker 1845	A slang extension of a much earlier word for a thief who snatches something away by means of a hook – such as by pushing it through an open window to pick up household objects. Although chiefly used in American English, it increasingly came to be heard in Britain.
tail † 1846	Another example of synecdoche (the part becoming the whole). *Tail* has long (fourteenth century) been slang for the male or female sexual member. In the nineteenth century, along with *flash-tail* (1869), it seems to have been mainly used for a prostitute, but in the twentieth it broadened to include a woman involved in any kind of sexual relationship.

horse-breaker † 1861	The history of this word provides one of the best etymological stories in this book. In the mid-nineteenth century, Hyde Park was the centre of fashionable horse-riding. A local livery stable owner arranged for Catherine Walters, a well-known London courtesan, to advertise his horses by riding them in the park. She became known as 'the most celebrated hooker on horseback', and not only did the stable-owner's business boom, other upper-class courtesans then decided to do the same thing. The *Times* (28 June 1861) called them *pretty horsebreakers*.
professional † 1862	Folklore describes prostitution as 'the oldest profession', but the use of *professional* as a noun, meaning 'someone engaged in a paid occupation, opposed to *amateur*', is known only from the early nineteenth century. Social reformer Henry Mayhew, in *London Labour and the London Poor* (1862), explicitly distinguishes prostitutes who are amateurs from those who 'devote themselves to it entirely as a profession'.
flagger † 1865	This is *flag* in the sense of 'flagstones' – flat slabs of stone that can be used to make a pavement. *Flagger* ('street-walker') seems to have been local police slang of the period, judging by the sole *OED* citation, which is from a Police Report: 'She wasn't a low sort at all – she wasn't a flagger as we call it.'
cocodette † 1867	A French word for a fashionable courtesan, which became known in England, along with *cocotte* (originally, a child's name for a hen), during the mid-nineteenth century. The words proved attractive to those who, when finding it necessary to talk about such matters, nonetheless wished to distance themselves as much as possible from the everyday expressions in this semantic field.
queen's woman † 1871	In 1864, a Contagious Diseases Act was passed, whereby female prostitutes were required to attend regular medical check-ups, and if found to be infected with venereal disease, were confined for treatment in 'lock hospitals'. This being the reign of Queen Victoria, the slang phrase *queen's women* soon appeared. It did not last long. As men were not required to be dealt with in the same way, the Acts were increasingly felt to represent unacceptable double standards and to be a violation of human rights, and after a vigorous campaign were repealed in 1886.
soiled dove † 1882	An expression that emerged in Australia and later in North America. As a Sydney slang dictionary (1882) put it: 'the "midnight meeting" term for prostitutes and "gay" ladies generally'. The dove is here being seen as a symbol of innocence and purity.

joro 1884	The fascination with things Japanese in the late Victorian era brought with it words belonging to this semantic field. In an 1884 travel book on Japan, *joros* are glossed simply as 'prostitutes', and distinguished from *geishas*, glossed as 'female dancers and singers'. However, the latter was often loosely used in the same way.
horizontal † 1888	A French expression which became fashionable slang in England for a while, also as *grand horizontal* (for the leading courtesans), probably because the meaning was more transparent than in the case of *cocodette* (above). An analogous sexual usage was already being heard in the USA, with people talking about 'horizontal refreshments'.
girl of the pavement 1900	An echo of the seventeenth century *girl of the town* (see *town-woman* above), and a literal equivalent to *nymph of the pavé* (see *nymph* above). The expression would only be encountered in historical writing today.
pross 1901	A colloquial abbreviation of *prostitute*, which arrived at the same time as *prossie*, later also spelled *prozzy*. The fortuitous identity with the shortened form of *professional* (above) led to a third form emerging after the First World War. As Eric Partridge put it, in his *Dictionary of Slang* (1937): '*pro* – a prostitute whose profession is body-vending: as opp[osed] to a notoriously or very compliant "amateur".' A further abbreviated variant developed in the USA: *prostie* (1926).
pusher 1901	A piece of services' slang that hasn't survived, due mainly to the emergence of the later (1928) sense of someone who sells drugs illegally. In the early decades of the twentieth century, though, it was quite common as a label for a prostitute, and contrasted with a *square pusher* ('a girl of good reputation', as an 1890 slang dictionary glossed it).
split-arse mechanic 1903	Another piece of services' slang, but recorded only once, in a 1903 slang dictionary. The term *split-arse* (or *split-ass*) continued to be used in other contexts, such as referring to a showy and reckless flying stunt.
white slave 1913	The source is the notion of subjugation implicit in the word *slave* – a girl who has been trapped into prostitution. The expression is first recorded in this sense in the introduction to suffragette Christabel Pankhurst's *The Great Scourge*. There was nothing new about the collocation, as it had been used in other political and social contexts since the eighteenth century.

broad 1914	A well-known piece of American slang, thanks to its widespread use in crime novels and other popular literature. There was an uncertain boundary between its use as a general term for a woman and its application to prostitution. An article in the journal *American Speech* in 1928 shows the fuzziness, defining *broad* as 'a plump, shapely girl', adding that the word 'sometimes carries a disparaging moral significance'.
shawl 1922	An Anglo-Irish term, illustrated in the *OED* by a single citation from James Joyce's *Ulysses* (part 2): drunken Bob Doran ends up 'in a shebeen in Bride street after closing time, fornicating with two shawls'.
quiff 1923	The type of head-covering known as a *coif* seems to have led to the use of *quiff* for a lock of hair plastered down on the forehead, and in the 1950s for a different style in which a piece of hair is brushed upwards and backwards from the forehead. The link with a sexual sense is unclear, but dates from the seventeenth century (when *quiffing* was one of the slang ways of referring to sexual intercourse). Probably the association with hair (of the head, of private parts) accounts for it.
prostisciutto 1930	A piece of wordplay from Samuel Beckett, who in *Whoroscope* blends *prostitute* and *prosciutto* to represent a woman regarded as an item on a menu.
brass nail 1934	This is Cockney rhyming slang for *tail* (above). As usual with such rhymes, the expression is shortened to its first element. Frank Norman, in his memoir of prison life, *Bang to Rights* (1958, ch. 10), talks of an 'old woman who was a brass on the game'.
mud kicker 1934	A similar usage to *fling-dust* (above), referring to any prostitute who seeks business on the streets.
scupper 1935	The origin is uncertain, perhaps from *scoop* ('pick up water'), but it has since the fifteenth century been used, usually in the plural, for an opening in a ship's side on a level with the deck to allow water to run away. Germaine Greer, in *The Female Eunuch* (1970), sees a link between this sense and a view of 'women as receptacles for refuse'.
poule de luxe 1937	*Poule* (also used for a hen) has long been colloquial French for a girl or young woman, and *poule de luxe* ('luxury') for a call girl. It seems to have had a literary use, with little sign of Anglicization, appearing in italics or inverted commas.

Tom 1941	The origins are unclear. Australian slang has *tom-tart* as a rhyming-slang phrase for a sweetheart (1882). As a word for a prostitute, both as *Tom* and *Tommy*, it may hark back to earlier uses of *cat* (above). Eric Partridge gives it a semantic gloss, 'a masculine woman of the town'.
twopenny **upright** 1958	*Twopenny* as a disparaging epithet ('paltry, of little value') dates from the sixteenth century, heard in such expressions as *not care a twopenny* and *not give a twopenny damn*. An *upright*, as a noun, refers to several kinds of vertical things, such as pianos and goalposts. The first *OED* citation illustrates the combination of these two notions: in *Balthasar* (ch. 2) Lawrence Durrell, describes 'a tart of the Waterloo Bridge epoch, a veritable Tuppeny Upright'.
slag 1958	*Slag* is originally a piece of waste matter, produced during the process of melting metals, and known in this use from the sixteenth century. In the twentieth century, it was increasingly transferred to people in various disparaging senses. Any petty criminal might be called a slag, as might a coward or a prostitute.
scrubber 1959	The jazz singer George Melly tells the story of this word in a short passage in his memoir *Owning Up* (1965, ch. 14): 'I understand that in the beat world it has become debased and now means a prostitute. In our day this was not the case. A scrubber was a girl who slept with a jazzman but for her own satisfaction as much as his.' But *scrubber* had a much earlier use in Australian slang, meaning a person or animal who lived in the wooded countryside. Novelist Berkeley Mather, in *Snowline* (1973), makes the link, relating it to 'a mare that runs wild in the scrub country, copulating indiscriminately with stray stallions'.
slack 1959	The almost simultaneous arrival of *slack* and *slag* (above) suggests there may be a phonetic link between them. Alternatively, the use of the word in this semantic field could come from *slacks* – informal trousers worn by women, which were for many years frowned upon in certain sections of society as improper dress.
yum-yum girl 1960	*Yum-yum* arrived in the 1880s as slang for any delightful sensation, especially when eating food, and achieved popular recognition as the name of a maiden in Gilbert and Sullivan's *Mikado* (1885). Love letters were being called *yum-yum* in navy slang of the Second World War, and by the 1960s the expression was being applied to prostitutes.

Suzie Wong 1962	The name of the leading character in R. L. Mason's novel, *The World of Suzie Wong* (1957), led to a flurry of usage in the 1970s, especially for women who consort with visiting servicemen. The application soon went far beyond the original location, Hong Kong, but faded as the novel (and the 1960 film) left the public eye.
model 1963	An *Observer* article (3 November 1963) identifies the salient feature of this usage: '"Company director" and "model" are useful euphemisms for those who appear in dubious court cases.' The inverted commas are usually required, unless the context is explicit, for without them there would be a total confusion with those involved in the world of fashion modelling.
working girl 1968	The expression emerged in the USA during the 1960s. As with *model* (above), inverted commas are usually needed to identify the special sense, as in this *Chicago Sun-Times* article (26 March 1984): 'U.S. Prostitutes has estimated that thousands of "working girls" will travel to San Francisco for business generated by the convention.'
pavement princess 1976	Another US slang expression, defined in Lanie Dills's *The 'Official' CN Slanguage Dictionary* (1976) as a 'roadside or truckstop prostitute'.
parlor girl 1979	A *parlor girl* was the name for a *parlourmaid* in the USA. It developed its new sense in the 1970s, along with *parlor house* (for a brothel). The word was originally French (thirteenth century) – a room in a convent or monastery for receiving visitors. The semantic contrast could hardly be greater.

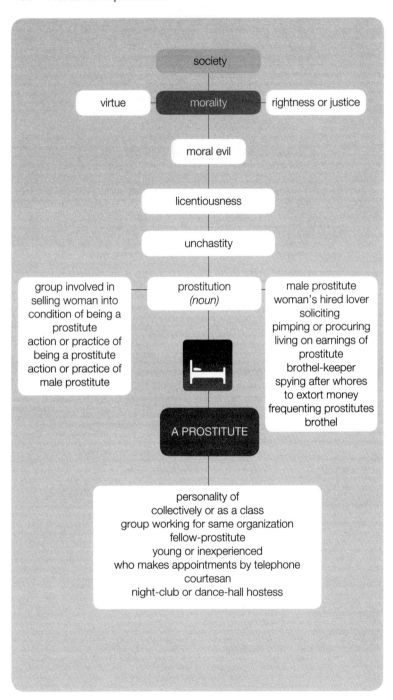

11

From *mint* to *dosh*

WORDS FOR MONEY

English has a huge vocabulary for talking about money – over 2,500 items are classified in this section of *HTOED* – but much of it is of relatively recent origin. Looking at the opening category, general words for 'money' used as a noun, we see only three from Anglo-Saxon times, and only thirteen from the whole of the Middle English period to 1500, with some said to be rare. Then the pace quickens: 33 items between 1500 and 1800, a remarkable 38 from the nineteenth century, and a further 19 items from the twentieth.

It evidently took a while for a general notion of 'money' to be expressed in words. At first, the names of individual pieces of money were used for the more general concept, in much the same way that we still do today when we talk about *saving the pennies*, meaning 'saving money'. The entries on *mynit*, *silver*, *scat*, *penny*, *argent*, *sterling*, *spanker*, *mopus*, and *posh* illustrate this trend from Anglo-Saxon times to the present day – and they are of course included in other *HTOED* categories dealing with specific items or sums of money. Gold shillings and silver pennies were in use in early English society from around 600, but 'commodity money' was also important, especially for low-value exchanges, in the form of cattle, sheep, horses, and other items of special value. Entries such as *fee*, *cattle*, *good*, *shells*, *rhino*, *cole*, *pay dirt*, *dough*, and *bread* show how words moved from their original senses to become a colloquial way of talking about money as a whole. Not all of the items were indigenous to Britain: merchants and sailors trading in Africa, the Americas, and the Far East would have brought news of the way cowrie shells and rhinoceros horns were often used as money. Objects made from these materials had special rarity value in England. It is easy to see how people could be attracted to using their names as street slang for conventional coinage.

The general term is surprisingly late: the first recorded use of *money*, a loanword from French, is not until the early fourteenth century. Before this the only comparably general words in the list were *spense* and *spending*, both expressing the functional notion of what can be done with money. At the same time, words arrive to express a negative view of money: the influence of the Bible is apparent in the way money is seen as a corrupting influence, and several demeaning words are evident thereafter (*muck, Mammon, filthy lucre, trash, scruff, dust, stuff*). A few words illustrate a scholarly strand of innovation, showing the influence of Latin (*pecuny, sinews of war, pecuniary*), and a professional strand is apparent too (*cash, lsd*). Later, in the nineteenth century, talking about money is affected by the desire to avoid the vulgar. This was a period when there was huge sensitivity over niceties of expression. Mrs Gaskell has her narrator in the opening chapter of *Cranford* state as one of the rules of the town: 'We none of us spoke of money, because that subject savoured of commerce and trade.' Other terms had to be found instead. Jane Austen's Marianne Dashwood, in *Sense and Sensibility*, talks about having 'a competence'. And we see the expressions *the necessary* and *the needful* developing a general sense to allow people to talk about their financial situation in a jocular or indirect way.

Later developments

The dominant feature of the lexicon of money, especially from 1800 on, is downmarket. Two-thirds of the words for money in this section of *HTOED* are slang. Slang always presents a problem to the etymologist, because of its transient and colloquial character. It rarely appears in writing; and when it does, its origins are often obscure. The etymology of several words in the timeline (*darby, kelter, steven, brads, scads, jack, scratch, moolah, dosh*) is unknown or unclear, and often one can do no more than hazard a plausible source for a usage. Fortunately, in other cases it is possible to be more confident. Virtually every distinctive feature of money seems to have motivated a slang usage. Coinages have been especially fruitful in relation to its substance (*brass, gilt, iron, pewter, tin, stiff*), colour (*white, ochre, rivets, cabbage, lettuce, green, rust*), and showy character (*gingerbread, ribbin, shiny, snow*); but we also see words related to its size (*grig*), shape (*potatoes*), and sound (*jingle*), as well as to where it is kept (*pogue, poke*) and to how we look after it or use it (*stumpy, splosh, coin*). The presence of the criminal world is never far away in money slang, and is very much to the fore in *bustle, rent, soap, boodle*, and *oil*.

Why does the word-list represent such an explosion of money slang after the 1700s? It's not as if people didn't use slang before that. Rather, it's a reflection of the way society was taking a fresh interest in slang. Dictionaries of cant, dialect, and everyday usage began to be compiled from the end of the seventeenth century, and after a period of being deprecated in the eighteenth, flowered in the nineteenth. There developed a fascination with the language of the 'lower' sections of society, and this was reinforced by the way novelists incorporated it into their writing, Charles Dickens being the prime illustration. In *Sketches by Boz*, Mr Barker talks of passengers who have 'forked out the stumpy'; in *The Old Curiosity Shop*, Mr Swiveller demands 'a reasonable amount of tin'; in *Nicholas Nickleby*, Mr Mantalini talks about making some 'bright, shinking, clinking, tinkling, demd mint sauce'. For lexicographers, the nineteenth century is a goldmine for slang, and many of the quotations supporting this section of the *OED* come from the novels, where money has such an important role to play. The novels, in turn, played their part in introducing the slang into the general public domain.

Wider perspectives

The money timeline displays other aspects of English cultural history, especially of the interaction between English-speaking people and people with different language backgrounds as new worlds came to be explored: *goree* and *Spanish* from the period of empire-building in Africa and the Caribbean; *California* and *wampum* from opening up America; *hoot* from Maori in New Zealand. Old worlds are present too in the form of loanwords from German (*gelt*), Spanish (*dinero*), Romani (*lour, posh*), and Yiddish or Hebrew (*shekels, oof, mazuma*). Many of the new words that entered English from around the globe were to do with trade – *cotton, amber, camphor, syrup, lemon, tarragon...* – and it is not surprising, accordingly, to see a corresponding growth in the colloquial lexicon of money.

The timeline also captures another important trait of English vocabulary: the way people readily play with the language in forming new words. Especially interesting are the examples of jocular adaptation (*ackers, loot*), abbreviation (*mon, moo*), wordplay (*mint sauce, spondulicks*), and effete archaism (*ducat, doubloon*). There are also some little-known instances where Cockney rhyming slang forms a part of the etymology (*sugar, bees and honey, lolly*), including one case (*oscar*) which shows that this kind of word-creation travelled well beyond the sound of Bow Bells, as far as the Antipodes. But when we think of the Londoners who were among the earliest British arrivals in Australia, the transportation of rhyming slang is perhaps not so surprising.

Timeline

mynit † OE	One of the earliest words known in English, found in the *Corpus* glossary: *nomisma* ('piece of money') is glossed as *mynet* – a word that would later evolve into *mint* – and a general sense of money or gold soon developed. It became colloquial during the sixteenth century, and was slang by the nineteenth. We see it in regional speech too: in Mrs Gaskell's *Mary Barton* (1848), Margaret tells Mary to 'take some of the mint I've got laid by in the old tea-pot'.
silver OE	The metal seen as a valuable medium of exchange, along with gold; later used as a general term for 'money', especially in Scotland. Robert Burns gives Tam a telling-off for drinking on market day 'as lang as thou had siller' (*Tam o'Shanter*, 1791, line 24).
fee † OE	*Fee* originally referred to cattle or other livestock, as well as goods and possessions generally; and so, 'wealth, riches'. Hrothgar offers Beowulf *feo* if he will kill the monster (*Beowulf*, line 1380). It was common in Middle English.
scat † 1122	Pronounced 'shat', a silver coin, sometimes used to mean 'money in general', especially in early Middle English. We see the general sense still in modern German *Schatz* 'treasure'.
spense *c.*1225	Related to *expense* and *spend*: 'that which may be spent'. In John of Trevisa's translation of Ranulph Higden's *Polychronicon* (1387), we read that 'the duke was prayed of the emperor for to take costage [expenses] and spence for the way'. The term is still used in parts of northern England to mean 'pocket-money'.
penny *c.*1275	From naming a small-value coin, *penny* broadened its sense to mean 'any piece of money', and thus 'any amount of money'. The old use is still heard today in such phrases as *a pretty penny* or *we need every penny we can get*.
sum of pence † *c.*1290	An early expression for an 'amount of money'. During the Middle English period it was replaced by *sum of money*.
spending † *c.*1290	Very popular in the fifteenth century to mean 'that which may be spent', or 'means of support'. People would talk about 'losing their spending' or 'giving some spending'. *Ready money* we would say today.
money *c.*1325	The collective term for all coins and notes arrives surprisingly late, as a loanword from French. When in 1694 the Bank of England began to issue banknotes, it was sometimes used for coins only. Samuel Johnson writes in a letter (20 September 1777) about sending someone 'money or Bankpaper'.

muck † c.1325	Money seen as sordid or corrupting. The associated words tell the story. A character in Edmund Spenser's *The Faerie Queene* (1590, Book 3, Canto 10) is contemptuous of the way 'minds of mortal men are muchel marred, | And moved amiss with massy muck's unmeet regard'. In William Rowley's comedy *A Match at Midnight* (1633, 1.1) the usurer Bloodhound tells everyone that he has 'given over brokering, moyling for muck and trash'. Joseph Wright found it still being used in this sense in Lancashire and Yorkshire in the early twentieth century.
cattle † c.1330	Originally used in the general sense of property or wealth, but then meaning 'money', especially capital (as distinct from interest). 'All her cattle then was spent save twelve pence' is the first recorded usage, in the medieval romance *Amis and Amiloun*. *Cattle* in the sense of 'livestock' is later, fifteenth century.
white † c.1374	An early slang term, referring to the colour of silver (as opposed to the red or yellow of gold). In *Troilus and Criseyde* (1384, Book 3), Chaucer condemns those who call love a madness, and promises that 'They shall forgo the white and eke [also] the red.' Later, *small whites* would be shillings; *large whites* half-crowns (value 2 shillings and 6 pence).
reason † c.1382	A biblical use by Wycliffe referring to income or revenue, used in both the singular and the plural. In Matthew's Gospel (18: 23), the kingdom of heaven is likened to a king 'that would put reason with his servants' (i.e. settle accounts); and in the first book of Maccabees (10: 40) King Demetrius offers the Jews 15,000 silver shekels 'of the king's reasons'.
worth † 1400	A single *OED* citation shows this word used in the sense of 'money as opposed to goods'. It comes from the medieval religious poem *Cursor Mundi* (line 5393), at the point where the people of Egypt are suffering from famine and have 'neither worth nor ware [money or merchandise]' to get food.
good † c.1400	*Goods* had a singular in earlier English: *a man of good* was a man of property. Especially in the sixteenth century, people would talk about something *costing a great good* – a large sum of money.
pecuny † c.1400	A French loan, ultimately from Latin *pecunia*, 'money', and retaining this sense in English, with the stress on the first syllable. 'Its poecunie that makes the souldiers merry', says a writer in the seventeenth-century news-sheet, *The Moderate Intelligencer*. The word was still being used in Scotland in the nineteenth century.

argent † *c.*1500	Originally, silver coin, but soon generalized to any kind of money, as in modern French. It is included in Bailey's *Dictionary* of 1742, glossed as 'silver or coin', but no such meaning is recorded in Johnson's *Dictionary* a decade later.
gelt 1529	This Germanic word for 'money' arrived in English as a general term: army pay was often described as *gelt*; *bare gelt* was 'ready money'. But the word lost status, and was already being included in canting dictionaries in the seventeenth century. It is the oldest slang term still quite widely used today.
Mammon † 1539	The biblical name of the devil was often used as the personification of greed, and is still used in that way. As a general term for 'money', it seems to have survived well into the eighteenth century. The satirist Edward Ward writes in *The Wooden World Dissected* (1707): 'While his Mammon lasts, he's a mad Fellow'. Dr Johnson glosses it as 'riches' in his *Dictionary* without comment.
scruff † 1559	A contemptuous term for money, following the general sense of this word to mean 'rubbish'. John Knox, in *The History of the Reformation of Religion in Scotland* (1559, Book 1), inveighs against ministers who 'spare not plainly to break down and convert good and stark [solid] money … into this their corrupted scruff and baggages of hardheads and nonsunts [Scottish coins of the period]'.
the sinews of war 1560	The phrase is from Cicero's *nervi belli pecunia infinita* ('unlimited money is the sinews of war'). It became a popular expression for the cost of maintaining a conflict. Churchill adapted it, talking about *the sinews of peace*, in 1946.
sterling 1565	The English silver penny (a 'coin with a star'), dating from Norman times, was a respected currency, and this prestige is still reflected in the expression *pound sterling* (i.e. 'pound of sterlings'). The sense of 'genuine money', as opposed to counterfeit, is used metaphorically by Shakespeare's Polonius, who describes Hamlet's approaches to Ophelia as 'not sterling' (*Hamlet*, *c.*1600, 1.3.107).
lour 1567	A slang word for 'money', used especially by peddlers and beggars, also spelled *lower*, and in the eighteenth century sometimes as *loaver*. It is probably from Old French *louier* 'reward', but perhaps also influenced by Romani, where *loor* meant 'plunder'. Counterfeit coins were being called *gammy lower* in the nineteenth century.

will-do-all †
1583

A single *OED* citation suggests that this is probably an idiosyncratic use with a biblical origin: in *Ecclesiastes* (10: 19), we read that 'money answereth all things'. The point is made by pamphleteer Philip Stubbes, in his *Anatomy of Abuses* (Part 2.1). Theodorus asks why there can be a long delay before a sentence of death is carried out. To allow people to evade justice and obtain a reprieve, replies Amphilogus: 'Sometimes it cometh to pass by reason of (will do all), otherwise called money, and sometimes by friends, or both.'

shells †
1591

A cant term for 'money', especially in Elizabethan England. Richard Greene talks of a farmer who lost his purse: 'lining and shells and all was gone'. The origin probably lies in sailors' tales of the use of shells as currency in many parts of the world.

trash †
1592

A contemptuous term for 'money', along with other objects viewed as rubbish. In Shakespeare's *Julius Caesar* (1599, 4.3.26) Brutus harangues Cassius about selling their honours for bribes – 'for so much trash'.

cash
1596

From French *casse*, *cash* came into English to mean 'a box for money' and almost immediately the meaning transferred to the coins that were the contents. It became the standard term for 'money' in book-keeping, but in other usage remained colloquial.

brass
1597

Earlier used for copper or bronze coins, but then a slang and dialect term for 'money in general'. It is still used today, especially in the north of England. 'No breeding, no brass | No kinship, no class,' sings Mrs Fairfax in the musical based on Charlotte Brontë's *Jane Eyre* (2000).

gilt
1598

It is a short semantic progression from adding a layer of gold to an object to the extra value associated with that object, and thus to a general concept of 'money'. In *A Mad World, My Masters* (1605, 2), Thomas Middleton has Follywit pun: 'Though guilt condemns, 'tis gilt must make us glad.' The usage was slang by the nineteenth century.

counter †
1599

From *counterfeit*, a dismissive term for debased coins, and thus applied contemptuously to any kind of money. In Shakespeare's *Julius Caesar* (1599, 4.3.80), Cassius is condemned by Brutus for not sending him much-needed money to pay his legions. Brutus insists that he would never be so covetous as 'To lock such rascal counters from his friends'.

pecuniary †
1604

One of the scholarly ('inkhorn') terms introduced into English during the sixteenth century, from Latin *pecunia* 'money', first used as an adjective, then as a noun, usually in the plural. People would talk of *pecuniaries*, meaning 'money matters' or 'financial resources'. Robert Cawdrey, compiler of the first English dictionary, includes it in his *Table Alphabeticall* (1604), glossing it as 'coin'.

dust †
1607

This word was given several colloquial extensions of meaning in the seventeenth century, such as *raise a dust*, *kick up a dust* ('make a disturbance'), and *down with the dust* ('put your money down'). It was slang a century later: in *The Adventures of Ferdinand Count Fathom* (1753, ch. 24), Tobias Smollett has Sir Stentor boast about having 'more dust in my fob [money in my pocket], than all those powdered sparks put together'. It is probably obsolete now.

cross and pile †
1625

This expression described the figure of a cross stamped on one side of a coin, with the pile being the reverse side. It was occasionally used to mean 'coins' and thus 'money in general'. A quatrain in Longfellow's poem *Friar Lubin* (c.1856) shows it was still being remembered over 200 years later: 'To mingle, with a knowing smile, | The goods of others with his own, | And leave you without cross and pile, | Friar Lubin stands alone'.

rhino
1628

Slang for 'money', also heard in the phrase *ready rhino*, very likely from *rhinoceros*, because of the great value of the animal's horn. It was especially popular in the USA and Ireland, but is only occasionally heard today.

grig †
1657

The origin is obscure, but probably related to words that meant 'something smaller than normal', as it is used with reference to dwarfs, small eels, crickets, and suchlike. In money, it was a tiny sum, a 'farthing'. Someone without money was *not worth a grig*; and if you had *no grigs* you had no money at all.

spanker †
1663

Originally a gold coin, then in the plural as a slang term for 'money' until the eighteenth century. It is related to *spanking*, as an adjective applied to things that were especially fine or showy. In 'Triplets upon Avarice' (c.1680), Samuel Butler describes the avaricious person: 'And tho' he can produce more Spankers | Than all the Usurers and Bankers, | Yet after more and more he hankers'.

cole
1673

Another case of a valuable object (coal) generating an extended sense in slang, first recorded in a canting wordlist. It led to the idiom *to post/pay the cole* ('to pay down the money').

darby 1682	A slang word for 'ready money', used chiefly in the seventeenth century. The origin is obscure, but there may be a link with *Darby's bands* (also, *Father Darby's bands*), a rigid form of bond which kept a debtor in the power of a money-lender. *Darbies* was slang for handcuffs. The usage may simply be a personification, though some think that *Darby* was the name of a noted money-lender.
gingerbread 1699	The highly decorated shapes made from ginger-flavoured cakes led to the word being applied to things that were attractive and showy. (The *bread* ending is a popular etymology, due to a misunderstanding of the unfamiliar final syllable of Latin *gingiber* 'ginger'.) It was eventually used as slang for 'money': if you *had the gingerbread*, you were well off.
goree † 1699	Probably sailors' slang from Fort Gorée on the African Gold Coast. They called a gold coin an *old Mr Goree* or *Gory*, and the term caught on for a while among the criminal fraternity.
mopus 1699	A small-valued coin, pronounced 'moh-puss'. In the plural, it was slang for money (as in German *Möpse*): people would talk about 'having the mopusses'. It is especially heard in dialects from Lancashire across the Midlands to Lincolnshire. The etymology is unclear, but it is probably a development of a Germanic word for 'bread'.
ribbin † 1699	Another word first recorded in a 1699 canting dictionary, probably a development from *riband* and *ribbon*. If 'the ribbin runs thick', there's plenty of money – and conversely, the ribbin can 'run thin'.
bustle † 1763	Recorded instances of this word meaning 'ready money' all seem to be in criminal contexts. The usage probably comes from the way thieves and beggars would confuse their intended targets by pretending to be in a hurry – *on the bustle*. The word was evidently unfamiliar to the courts in its first recorded usage, in the Proceedings of the Old Bailey in London, for it needed a gloss: 'He had got the bustle (meaning the cash) in his pocket.'
necessary 1772	In the phrase *the necessary*, short for some such expression as 'the necessary funds', and often pluralized: 'have you got the necessaries to buy it?' It feels like a typical eighteenth-century euphemism, allowing the upper classes to avoid having to talk directly about 'filthy lucre'.

stuff 1775	A slang usage, especially in the phrase *the stuff*, as in *hand over the stuff* = 'give me the money'. When, in Richard Sheridan's *The Rivals* (1775, 1.1), Thomas meets Captain Absolute's servant, Fag, and hears of Lydia Languish, he asks him: 'But has she got the stuff, Mr. Fag; is she rich, hey?'
needful 1777	Used in the phrase *the needful* – another eighteenth-century euphemism. 'Needy men the needful need', says *The Comic Almanack* for 1836.
iron 1785	A further example of a metal used as a slang word for 'money'. In the twentieth century in the USA, *iron man* became slang for a dollar, and in Australia for a pound.
Spanish † 1788	A slang usage, especially in the phrase *the Spanish*, meaning 'ready money'. It is a shortened form of the various expressions reflecting a period when ships from Spain brought wealth back to Europe – *Spanish coin*, *Spanish gold*, *Spanish doubloons*. A sporting magazine in 1811 talks about someone 'extracting the Spanish from all his sporting acquaintance'.
ducat 1794	A gold coin in many European countries from the fourteenth century onwards, and used in the plural rather self-consciously in Britain as a colloquial synonym for 'money'. It's heard today especially in theatrical slang, where people recall the usage of Shakespeare's Shylock in *The Merchant of Venice* (c.1597).
kelter 1807	A dialect word for 'money', of unknown etymology, used especially in the northern counties of England, with some usage further south; also spelled *kilter*. In the *English Dialect Dictionary* there's a verb use too, recorded in Shropshire: 'I've bin out kelterin' all day' (= 'collecting money').
dibs 1812	Probably a shortening of *dibstones*, an alternative name to *dabstones*, a children's game in which an object such as a pebble was thrown (*dabbed*) to strike another. In card games, the word was also used for the counters players employed as a substitute for money.
steven 1812	Slang for 'money', heard especially in boxing; also spelled *stephen*. It is perhaps a popular adaptation of the name of a Dutch coin, the *stiver*, used in various idioms in the nineteenth century, such as 'I don't care a stiver', meaning 'I don't care at all'.

pewter † 1814	Another instance where a metal (a grey alloy of tin) is used for 'money', especially when the coins are silver – and especially when used with reference to prize-money. The first recorded use is in a Jane Austen letter (30 November), referring to her brother: 'Tho' I like praise as well as anybody, I like what Edward calls Pewter too.' Pewter was seen as valuable in country houses, and often displayed ornamentally.
brads † 1819	Probably a slang extension of a word for a type of nail, especially used for copper coins (to *tip the brads* was to be generous), but it could also be a reverse pronunciation from *darby* (above). In a different use, between 1914 and 1928, £1 notes were issued that came to be called *brads*, after Sir John Bradbury, Secretary to the Treasury.
pogue 1819	The extension of a slang word for a bag, purse, or wallet. A *pogue-hunter* was a pickpocket. The word probably derives from *poke*, 'pocket'. In Michael Crichton's *The Great Train Robbery* (1975, ch. 7) we read: 'It was the stickman's job to take the pogue once Teddy had snaffled it, thus leaving Teddy clean, should a constable stop him.'
hoot 1820	*Utu* is a Maori word meaning 'reward' or 'payment'; so in New Zealand English slang it came to be used for 'money', to begin with spelled *hutu* or *hootoo*, and then shortened. It crossed the sea to Australia by the end of the nineteenth century. A quotation from 1970 in the *New Zealand Listener* says 'I hadn't heard that word for money in years', but it is still listed as colloquial in the *New Zealand Oxford Dictionary* (2005).
rent 1823	A natural slang extension of the word for 'payment for use of property', but mainly used in relation to money derived from criminal activities. Around the turn of the nineteenth-century, a *rent-collector* was a highwayman.
stumpy 1828	British slang for 'money', also found as *stump*. To *stump up*, meaning 'pay out' was coming into use at the same time. The logic is 'tree-stump' > 'dig a stump up by the roots' > 'find money from one's resources'. *Fork out* developed similarly.
posh 1830	A shortened form of a Welsh Romani word for 'halfpenny'; then used for coins of small value, and then for 'money' as a whole. The later development of meaning from 'money' > 'moneyed' > 'stylish' led to the modern senses of *posh*.

l.s.d. 1835	The colloquial abbreviation of 'pounds, shillings, and pence', taken from book-keeping. The *L* replaced the pound symbol £. The *d* originally stood for *denarius*, Latin for 'penny'. The expression is still heard in the UK, even after the arrival of decimal currency.
tin 1836	Small silver coins in the eighteenth-century, when worn down through use, resembled pieces of tin: a writer of the time talks about 'tin-like sixpences'. The coins went out of use in 1817, but a general sense of *tin* meaning 'money' or 'cash' developed during the nineteenth century.
mint sauce 1839	One of the more unusual colloquial adaptations of an everyday expression, thanks to the pun available with *mint* (above). *Mint drops* developed a similar use in the USA. In Charles Dickens's *Nicholas Nickleby* (1839, ch. 34), Mr Mantalini asks Ralph Nickleby to exchange some bills for some 'bright, shining, chinking, tinkling, demd mint-sauce'.
ochre † 1846	The tint of gold coins led to this slang use for 'money in general'. 'Pay your ochre at the doors', says Master Kidderminster in Charles Dickens's *Hard Times* (1854, ch. 6).
rivets 1846	A slang development very similar in origin to *brads* (above), but rarely heard today: 'copper nails' > 'copper coins'. 'So you got a bit of rivets to speculate?' asks a character in James Curtis's *You're in the Racket Too* (1937, ch. 18).
California † 1851	The gold rush in California began in 1848, and within a few years the name of the state was being used in British slang. The anonymous author of the dining guide *London at Table* (1851, Part 1) names some West End restaurants, observing 'Some "California", as the fast young men of the day term "money", is necessary for these houses.' Later in the nineteenth century, a *Californian* was slang for a type of gold coin.
dough 1851	An ancient Germanic word, which became a popular slang term for 'money' during the nineteenth century in the USA. By the end of the century it had spread into Canada, Australia, and Britain. Early British twentieth-century users include Arthur Conan Doyle and P. G. Wodehouse.
rust † 1858	British slang, from the rust colour of old metal, and thus applied to coins. There is just one *OED* citation: 'There's no chance of nabbing any rust (taking any money)', says Billy Fortune to his companions in author-journalist Augustus Mayhew's *Paved with Gold* (Book 3, ch. 5), with the gloss suggesting that the usage was likely to be unfamiliar to his readers.

dinero 1856	A slang adaptation of the Spanish word for 'money'. It was originally an Americanism, but gained wider use through contact with American films.
shiny † 1856	In the phrase *the shiny*, a slang expression for 'money', referring to the sheen of gold and silver. Similarly, *shiner* was used in the eighteenth century for a gold or silver coin. The word developed a general sense in the plural (*a load of shiners*).
spondulicks 1857	One of the weirdest American slang coinages for 'money', spelled in a variety of ways, and usually used as a plural form in the phrase *the spondulicks*. The etymology is said to be 'fanciful' by the *OED*, but Eric Partridge felt there was a link with Greek *spondulikos*, from *spondulos*, a species of shell used in early commerce.
scad 1858	This was originally used in the USA as a slang word for 'dollar', which developed a general sense of 'money', usually in the plural, *scads*. It then broadened further to mean 'large amount of money' and then 'large amount of anything', in which sense it arrived in colloquial English everywhere during the twentieth century.
soap 1860	US slang for 'money', especially in a criminal context such as bribery, where the link with the meaning of flattery (*soft soap*) is evident.
sugar 1862	Why *sugar*, of all foods, as a slang word for money? It was the first element of a piece of Cockney rhyming slang – *sugar and honey*.
coin 1874	A slang use of the noun in the singular to mean 'money' (as opposed to coins), as in 'I haven't the coin to do it'. There is a related verb use, heard in 'they're coining it'. It was popular in Victorian England as a sporting expression: *to post the coin* was 'to deposit money as a bet'.
filthy lucre 1877	An expression first found in Tyndale's Bible and then in the King James Bible, in the sense of 'dishonourable gain', eventually becoming a self-deprecating reference to 'money in general'. It was so common that by the nineteenth century it could be shortened to *the filthy*. In *If I Were You* (1931), P. G. Wodehouse has Freddie saying: 'Just trying to make a bit of the filthy.'
pay dirt 1882	A mining term from the 1850s, referring to ground containing ore that can be profitably extracted. It was soon extended to mean 'profit', 'success', or 'money in general'. Idioms include to *hit* or *strike pay dirt*. A similar term from the same period was *pay gravel*.

boodle 1883	US slang for 'money acquired or spent illegally', from an earlier use where it referred to counterfeit money. As a verb, it retained a sense of 'bribe' into the twentieth century, but as a noun it soon lost its criminal connotations.
shekels 1883	A silver coin of the Hebrews, which passed into general English via Jewish use. It's especially used in the expression *rake in the shekels*.
oil 1885	American slang for 'money used to bribe or corrupt'. A story in *Detective Fiction Weekly* (1935) has a character say: 'She didn't take care of her protection directly, that is, she didn't slip the oil to the cops herself.' It is a natural extension of the usual meaning of *oil* as a liquid that makes things run smoothly. There are several related idioms, such as *oil the knocker* ('tip the porter') or *oil up to* someone ('attempt to bribe').
oof 1885	London East End slang for money, probably a shortened form of *ooftish*, from Yiddish *gelt afn tish* 'money on the table', when playing cards. In the early 1900s, *oof-bird* described a wealthy person, and *to make the oof-bird walk* was to circulate money. It lies behind the nickname of P. G. Wodehouse's character, 'Oofy' Prosser, the millionaire friend of Bertie Wooster.
mon 1888	In US slang, a shortened form of *money*, and reinforced by such expressions as 'no mon, no fun'.
jack 1890	US slang for 'money in general', which eventually crossed the Atlantic. In the 1950s it surfaced meaning 'five-pound note', from Cockney rhyming slang (*Jack's alive = five*). But the association with money goes back a long way: in the seventeenth century, a *jack* was a cant word for a farthing.
splosh 1890	London shopkeeper slang for 'money', from the way well-heeled customers were said to *splosh* or *splash* money about. If you bet heavily in a race you were said to be *sploshing it on*.
bees and honey 1892	Cockney rhyming slang for *money*, often shortened to *bees*. 'A skipper's life ain't all bees and honey,' says one of the sailors in the pseudonymous L. Luard's account of North Sea life, *Conquering Seas* (1935, ch. 3).
spending-brass 1896	An occasional use, along with other expressions, such as *spending money* and *spending income*. There is a strong dialect influence, as illustrated by Yorkshire novelist James Keighley Snowden in *The Web of an Old Weaver* (1896, ch. 4): 'He had a great deal more "spending-brass" nor I could handle.'

stiff 1897	Nineteenth-century slang for a 'promissory note' or a 'bill of exchange' (because often written on a piece of stiffened paper). It was later used for a 'forged bank-note', and then for 'money in general', as in to *make one's stiff* ('make one's fortune'). The father of the extravagant child Peter Goole bemoans his fate: 'He wrang his hands, exclaiming, 'If | I only had a bit of Stiff | How different would be my life!' (Hilaire Belloc, *New Cautionary Tales*, 1930.)
wampum 1897	American Indian beads that served as currency, eventually being used as a jocular term for 'money' in American colloquial speech. The usage was never very frequent, and tends to be avoided in the era of political correctness.
mazuma 1900	US slang from Yiddish *mezumen* 'ready money', which spread to Canada and Australia through a mixture of American forces abroad, films, and fiction. Thanks to his early use of *mazuma* (1913), Hopalong Cassidy gets his name into the *OED*.
cabbage 1903	US slang for 'money' of any kind, but especially banknotes, through the green colour of dollar bills. The link is clearly indicated in Jack Black's autobiographical novel *You Can't Win* (1926, ch. 15): '"You carry this head of cabbage, Kid," passing me a pack of greenbacks'.
lettuce 1903	Another US slang word for 'paper money', motivated by the colour of a vegetable. The first recorded usage is by Karl Edwin Harriman in his collection of Illinois short stories *The Homebuilders* (1903): 'Unroll that bunch of lettuce you got in your mit and count out thirty-five bucks.'
jingle 1906	Australian and New Zealand slang for 'money'. A *jingle-boy* was a coin, such as a sovereign, and also referred to someone who had a lot of money jingling around in his pockets.
doubloon 1908	A rather self-conscious use of the Spanish gold coin to mean 'money in general'. Freddie's Aunt Constance 'keeps an eye on the doubloons' in P. G. Wodehouse's *Leave it to Psmith* (1923).
scratch 1914	US slang, especially referring to 'paper money' of the genuine kind (as opposed to counterfeit *slush*). The word later crossed the Atlantic: *Private Eye* in 1980 talks about 'putting even more scratch into the bulging wallets of the lawyers'.

green
1917

Slang for 'paper money', first in the USA, and then elsewhere in countries that issued green-coloured currency. Green £1 notes were first issued in Britain in 1917. The word is used both as a singular and a plural (*hard-earned green/greens*). Associated expressions are *greenbacks* and the *green stuff*.

oscar
1917

Australian and New Zealand rhyming slang for 'money' ('cash'), from the name of the Australian-born actor Oscar Asche (1871–1936). His career was made in London, but he became a household name in Australia following a hugely successful tour in 1909–10.

snow
1925

British slang for 'silver money' – in old coinage: sixpences, shillings, two-shilling pieces, half-crowns. It came to be less used after the arrival of decimal currency in 1971, and may now be obsolete.

poke
1926

Slang for a roll of banknotes, and thus for 'money in general'. It derives from the American use of *poke* to mean a wallet or purse, which in turn comes from a small bag worn on the person in Elizabethan times. Touchstone, in Shakespeare's *As You Like It* (c.1600, 2.7.20) draws 'a dial from his poke' (= 'a watch from his purse').

potatoes
1931

US slang for 'money', especially dollars; but in *Uncle Fred in Springtime* (1939) we see P. G. Wodehouse talking about 'two hundred potatoes', where the word means 'pounds'. It probably relates to the nineteenth-century use of *potato* to mean something excellent (as in 'that's the potato'), with an allusion to the round shape of coins. It seems to be a separate development from what happens in Cockney rhyming slang, where *potato* is used for *shilling* (from *potato-peeling*).

moolah
1937

US slang for 'money', also spelled *moola* and *mullah*, and later (1941) shortened to *moo*. It soon spread to Canada, Australia, and Britain, probably through its use in the armed forces. The origin is unknown, though there may be a figurative link with *mool* 'soil ready for working, crumbs', widely used in British and Irish dialects.

ackers
1939

British slang, first used by armed forces in Egypt. Evidently troops would use the word dismissively to refer to Egyptian piastres, and it then became a jocular usage for any sort of 'money'. A character in H. R. F. Keating's murder mystery *Is Skin Deep, Is Fatal* (1965, ch. 19) 'can't offer a great deal in the way of ackers'.

lolly 1943	The usual abbreviation for *lollipop*, which was Cockney rhyming slang for a *drop* ('money given as a tip'). Its use was popularized by alliteration in such expressions as 'lots of lovely lolly'.
loot 1943	The first recorded usage in the sense of 'money' identifies it as Scottish slang for 'pay', which spread rapidly through use in the armed forces. Usage is often jocular, in such expressions as 'hard-earned loot'.
poppy 1943	British shopkeeper's slang for 'money', possibly from the Australian usage of *tall poppy* to mean a person with high income. It had a great deal of media coverage as a result of the economic policy of New South Wales premier Jack Lang in 1931: 'taxing the tall poppies'.
bread 1952	Originally US slang for 'money', deriving from the natural extension of *bread* to mean 'livelihood' (1719). Given the much earlier use of *dough* (above) in this sense, it is a little surprising that this use of *bread* isn't recorded until the 1950s. But it soon became used colloquially worldwide.
dosh 1953	British slang for 'money'. The origin is unknown, but many suggestions have been made, such as a blend of *dollar* + *cash*, or a variant of *doss*, 'get a cheap bed for the night', with the meaning narrowed to the cost involved.

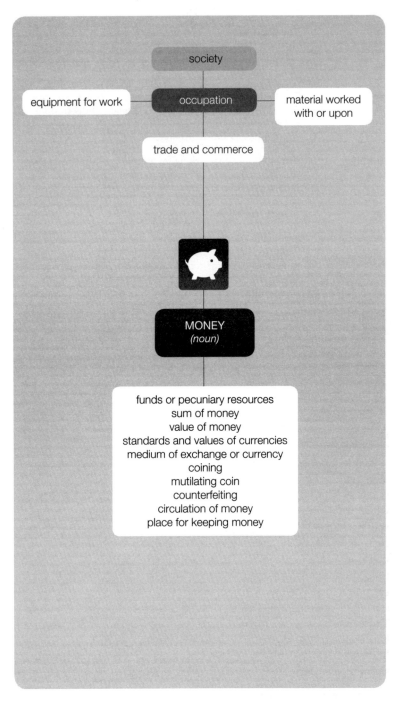

society

equipment for work — occupation — material worked with or upon

trade and commerce

MONEY
(noun)

funds or pecuniary resources
sum of money
value of money
standards and values of currencies
medium of exchange or currency
coining
mutilating coin
counterfeiting
circulation of money
place for keeping money

12

From *smolt* to *untempestuous,* and *reigh* to *ugly*

WORDS FOR CALM AND STORMY WEATHER

Bad news always wins, when it comes to the lexicon. In 2008, as part of an investigation for an advertising company, I went through a concise dictionary to identify words that expressed a sentiment that was positive (e.g. *wonderful, splendid, a bargain*) or negative (e.g. *atrocious, terrible, a mess*). There were 1,771 items under positive and 3,158 under negative: almost twice as many. With weather, the ratio goes up. There are 23 items describing 'calm weather' in the semantic fields discussed below and 49 describing 'stormy weather'.

People love talking about the weather, especially (and stereotypically) in Britain, so we might expect a wide vocabulary. In fact, the range is not so great, presumably because there are only so many ways in which we can talk about something that we routinely experience every waking moment. The regional dialects show some interesting items, such as *smolt, lithe, lown, wair,* and *coarse.* Otherwise, it is a very literal-minded semantic field. A small number of words are frequently used and adapted: *still, calm, settled; stormy, wild, rough.* Even the poets seem at a loss. The literary uses for 'calm' tend to be very derivative – *stormless, calm-winded, unwindy, calmy, untempested, untempestuous.* Those for 'stormy' are more adventurous (*rugged, broily, boisterous, blusterous, unruly, rufflered,* and the scholarly *oragious* and *procellous*), but even here we see pedestrian adaptations of basic words (*stormish, stormful, tempestuous*).

It's always interesting to compare two small areas of the lexicon that are in a clear semantic relationship – here, oppositeness – as it shows how one lexical set depends on the other. The direction of dependence is easy to see: 'calm' is defined by reference to 'stormy' – *stormless, unwindy, unstormy, untempested, untempestuous* – and not the other way round. English has no instances of *calmless* or (with reference to weather) *unstill* or *unserene*, and when we do come across a derivative term (such as *unsettled*), the meaning is weaker than 'stormy'. The norm, evidently, is bad weather. We are impressed when there is 'no storm', and create derived neologisms accordingly.

Bad weather has its own motivation. We like to talk about the severity of a storm, especially if we are about to experience it or have just experienced it. So we find ominous words (*trouble* and its derivatives, *ugly*) alongside words that compete with each other for degree of severity (*wild, broily, turbulent, tempestuous*). The wind, it seems, has a separate place in our linguistic psyche (*rough, boistous, blusterous, rufflered*). Living on the western edge of North Wales, I can understand that.

Timeline

1 Calm	
smolt OE	*Smolt* and *smylt* are how the Anglo-Saxons described weather that was fair, fine, or calm. A millennium later, the word was still being used in regional dialects in England and Scotland. 'The sea is smoultin', they would say in Norfolk, when the sea calms down after a storm.
lithe c.1275	Bede tells us in his *Reckoning of Time* that the name of the month of June is *Ærra* ('early') *Liða* and July is *Æfterra* ('later') *Liða*, because in those months the winds are gentle and the sea is calm. *Lithe* had a range of meanings in Old English, such as 'soft', 'gentle', 'mild', and 'serene'. Calm weather continues to be referred to as *lithe* in several northern British dialects.
still 1390	The original meaning, 'motionless', was very early applied to water and weather where there was no wind to cause noise or commotion. Wordsworth captures the sense in his play *The Borderers* (1795, 2.25), when the villain-hero Oswald visits a churchyard: 'The moon shone clear, the air was still, so still	The trees were silent as the graves beneath them'.

smooth † *c*.1402	*Smooth* has continued in use in relation to the sea – people readily talk of 'smooth water' and 'having a smooth passage' – but not in relation to the weather. In Middle English, we find wind being described as 'smooth', and the usage continued into the eighteenth century. The narrator of a sea-voyage in 1700 reports 'We had a smooth gale of wind at west.' It is an obsolete collocation today.
peaceable † *c*.1425	These days we describe people and their towns or countries as *peacable*. We no longer talk of 'peaceable weather' (1450), 'peaceable winds' (1500), or a 'peaceable night' (1859).
calm *c*.1440	Whenever *calm* is used, there is an implied contrast with 'not calm' – a wind or storm that has been or could be. Often the contrast is explicit. In the Book of Jonah (ch. 1), in the King James translation, sailors frightened by 'a mighty tempest' cast Jonah into the sea so that 'the sea may be calm'.
serenous *c*.1440	A single *OED* citation from Palladius' *On Husbandry* refers to a 'pleasant and serenous' land. The adjective never found favour, and was soon (1508) replaced by *serene* for weather that was clear, fine, and calm. The modern application of *serene* to a person who is untroubled in mind or whose countenance displays an inward calm comes much later (1640). Weather isn't often described as *serene* today, other than in literary contexts. But journalists like it, especially when there's a nice rhyme: 'Serene weather expected for Boston after Irene' ran a website headline following the August 2011 hurricane.
lown *c*.1450	This word for calm weather can still be heard in parts of northern England, southern Scotland, and Ireland. People talk of the wind being *lown* or *lownd* (i.e. lowered). The *English Dialect Dictionary* has many examples of the way the word has been used: 'a lown sunny day', 'a fine lown day', 'a very lownd night'.
stormless *c*.1500	The first of a series of words that define 'calm' as an 'absence of storm'. The *OED* citations suggest that its use was fostered by the opportunities it presented for alliteration: 'stormless seas' (1605), 'stormless summer' (1819), and Algernon Swinburne's 'sunless and stormless in all seasons of wind or sun' (1867).
calm-winded † 1577	John Grange, in his fictional allegory, *The Golden Aphroditis*, is the sole *OED* source for this compound: 'Making as heavenly a noise as doth an arbour of nightingales in a calm-winded night'.

unwindy 1580	This coinage is likely to have been used far more often than its two *OED* citations suggest, being the kind of colloquial coinage one often hears with *un-*. Charles Dickens uses it in a creative way in *The Haunted Man and the Ghost's Bargain* (1848), describing a 'sun-dial in the corner, where the wind was used to spin with such unwindy constancy'.
calmy † 1587	A word whose extra syllable makes it an ideal choice for poets wanting to make up the metre of a line. We see it in Edmund Spenser's *Faerie Queene* (1590, Book 2, Canto 12), 'it was	A still and calmy bay', and in Alexander Pope's translation of Homer's *Odyssey* (1726, Book 15), 'Six calmy days and six smooth nights we sail'.
sleek † 1603	The physical senses of *sleek* (hair, skin) have come to dominate its use, making obsolete the old collocations with sea and sky. The apothecary Gallipot illustrates the earlier usage in Thomas Middleton and Thomas Dekker's *The Roaring Girl* (1611, 3.2): 'After a storm the face of heaven looks sleek'.
pacific 1633	The favourable winds and calm sea encountered by explorer Ferdinand Magellan led to the name *Pacific Ocean* (1521), and the usage became general in relation to the sea, and later to the weather as a whole. The day at Grantchester was evidently perfect when Rupert Brooke wrote about 'The Old Vicarage' (1912): 'Great clouds along pacific skies'.
settled 1717	Both good and bad weather can be *settled* – maintaining itself without change or break – but when we talk of *settled weather* we usually mean 'calm and fine'. A gardening dictionary of 1731 offers advice about planting 'towards the latter end of May, when the weather appears settled and warm'. Not in 2013 in the UK, it wasn't!
unstormy 1823	Lord Byron is the sole *OED* citation, in *The Age of Bronze* (1823), in an ironic comment on two famous rival politicians of his time (Pitt and Fox), buried next to each other in Westminster Abbey: 'How peaceful, and how powerful is the Grave	Which hushes all! A calm, unstormy wave	Which oversweeps the World'.
untempested † 1846	Another literary use, occasionally encountered in the nineteenth century. In Rolf Boldrewood's novel *A Colonial Reformer* (1890, ch. 19), Ernest Neuchamp rises early to find a cloudless day, 'perfect as a poet's dream of the serene untempested heavens of the isles of the blest'.

placable † 1858	Nathaniel Hawthorne, in his diary account of his French and Italian travels (25 May 1858), experiences a violent wind in Assisi that nearly blows his hat away: 'the wind blew in momentary gusts, and then became more placable till another fit of fury came'. It was an unusual usage: the word was normally applied to people and their moods.
untempestuous 1864	Another neologism from Algernon Swinburne (see *stormless* above), this time from *Atalanta in Calydon* (1864, line 400): Althaea describes her sister's sons as 'gracious heads | Like kindled lights in untempestuous heaven'. Although lacking citations, the coinage remains a natural one, so the word is probably still being used from time to time.

2 Stormy

reigh † eOE	An important word for a seafaring nation, a blend of words that meant 'stormy' and 'wild'. In *Beowulf* (line 548), the Anglo-Saxon hero tells the story of the bad weather he encountered during a swimming-match in his youth: 'Hreo wæron yþa' – 'rough were the waves'. He might also have said *hreohful* ('rough-ful'), *scurfah* ('shower hostile'), or *ystig* ('tempestuous').
stormy c.1200	The word most often used for weather characterized by high winds, heavy rain, and other violent disturbances. Expressions such as 'stormy day', 'stormy weather', and 'stormy winter' are all recorded in the 1300s. *Stormish* (c.1430) and *stormful* (1558) were equivalent forms favoured by some writers. Thomas Carlyle (1834) liked *stormful*, along with *stormfully* and *stormfulness*.
wild c.1250	In Shakespeare's *King Lear* (c.1608, 2.4.303) Cornwall counsels Gloucester: 'Shut up your doors, my lord; 'tis a wild night.' Soon after (3.2.1), Lear tells us what *wild* means in a famous scene-opener: 'Blow, winds, and crack your cheeks! Rage! Blow!'
trouble † c.1374	*Trouble* is no longer used as an adjective, but in Middle English we find several examples. Chaucer is one who talks of 'the trouble wind' (in his translation of *Boethius*, c.1374, Book I, Metrum 7). *Troubled* (c.1425), *troublous* (1482), and *troublesome* (1560) were also used in the same way, but only *troubled* has retained some use in relation to weather. 'The sky was dark and troubled', reports Lord Macaulay in his *History of England* (1855, Book 4, ch. 20).

rough *c.*1400	The word is very close in form and meaning to *reigh* (above), though it has a different origin. One would hardly be able to distinguish between a reigh and a rough day, however.
rude *c.*1439	The modern meaning of 'impolite' has made the application to weather almost obsolete, apart from in a few established phrases, such as 'rude blasts' or 'rude winds'. A US news report in 2003 talks of countries enduring 'many a rude winter'.
boistous † 1470	In 1361, writes John Hardyng in his verse *Chronicle* (1470, ch. 184), 'Specially the wind was so boistous, | The stone walls, steeples, houses, and trees | Were blow down in diverse far countries'. By the end of the sixteenth century, *boistous* had begun to be replaced by *boystrous* (1594), later spelled *boisterous*. The meaning of *boisterous* has since then gradually narrowed, so that these days it is usually heard only with reference to people, having lost its negative associations in the process ('good-natured exuberant behaviour').
wair † *c.*1480	A rare Scottish usage, meaning 'wild, stormy'. Poet Robert Henryson provides the only *OED* citation, in his translation of Aesop's *Fables*, with 'wicked winds of the winter wair'.
tempestuous 1509	The word has always been popular as a more vivid alternative to *stormy*. In 2013, the online fashion news site *Fashionista*, reacting to a serious storm heading for New York, ran a series of storm-inspired fashion photographs. They headed it: 'Stormy weather: Our Favorite Tempestuous Editorial and Campaigns'.
blusterous † 1548	The word has been largely replaced by *blustery* (1774) – which is a hundred times more frequent (according to a Google search) – but not entirely. A weather report for Chicago (*Chicagoist*, 21 May 2012) was headed: 'Today's Weather: Blusterous'. And a writer on Facebook in 2011 complains of the 'blusterous gusterous weather'.
rugged 1549	It was perhaps the hard, plosive consonants (*g*, *d*) that made this word appeal as a synonym for 'stormy'. It certainly had some influential users in the literary domain, such as Myles Coverdale, who is the first recorded user in a translation of Erasmus (1549, 'none so rugged a winter') and John Milton in *Lycidas* (1638, 'every gust of rugged wings'). There was also a variant, *ruggy* (1577), common in regional dialects. These days the expression most often heard is 'rugged weather'.

turbulent 1573	Today, more used in relation to states of mind or political affairs; formerly, often used to describe very rough sea and very bad weather. In Shakespeare and Wilkins's *Pericles* (*c.*1609, 3.2.4), Cerimon comments that it has been 'a turbulent and stormy night'. It has indeed. In the previous scene, King Pericles has railed against the 'deafening, dreadful thunders' and 'nimble, sulphurous flashes'.
rufflered † 1582	A single *OED* citation from Richard Stanyhurst's translation of Virgil illustrates this word. He talks about the 'south wind's rufflered huffling' – two words that onomatopoeically suggest blustery, blowy weather.
oragious † 1590	From a French word (*orageux*) meaning 'tempestuous'. The word must have appealed to the Latinate temperament of the sixteenth century, but there is only one *OED* citation, from the poet John Burel, and his use there is clearly prompted by the need for a good rhyme: 'The storm was so outrageous, | And with rumblings oragious'.
broily † 1593	*Broils* were disturbances, quarrels, and general turmoil. Poet Richard Carew applies the notion to the weather in his translation of Tasso (Canto 4): 'storms of broily whistling'.
unruly 1594	A literary usage, first recorded in Shakespeare's poem *The Rape of Lucrece* (1594, line 869): 'unruly blasts wait on the tender spring'. It was perhaps his usage – it turns up again in *Macbeth* (1606, 2.3.51, 'The night has been unruly') and in *Henry IV Part 1* (*c.*1597, 3.1.27, 'unruly wind') – that made it appeal to later writers.
procellous † *c.*1629	Another classical borrowing (Latin *procellosus* 'stormy'). The American usage anthologist C. C. Bombaugh (1875), in *Gleanings for the Curious*, discusses 'English words and forms of expression', and puts a question to lexicographers. 'Odd words are to be found in the dictionaries. Why they are kept there no one knows; but what man in his senses … would talk of a stormy day as procellous …?' None today, I suspect.
coarse 1774	The first recorded usage was in *The Gentleman's Magazine* ('Bright morning, coarse midday, wet evening'), but the usage was not sufficiently established for Samuel Johnson to notice it in his *Dictionary*. It seems to have become dialectal very quickly all over England and Scotland, and then travelled abroad.

ugly
1844

A late development of *ugly* to refer to the sea (1744) and sky (1844), in such expressions as 'an ugly black sky' and 'an ugly night'. The implication is usually serious, but J. Henry Harris in *Our Cove: Victorian Life in a Cornish Fishing Village* (1900, ch. 2) is more cautious: 'You know the weather is going to be "ugly", which means anything from tricky to downright bad.'

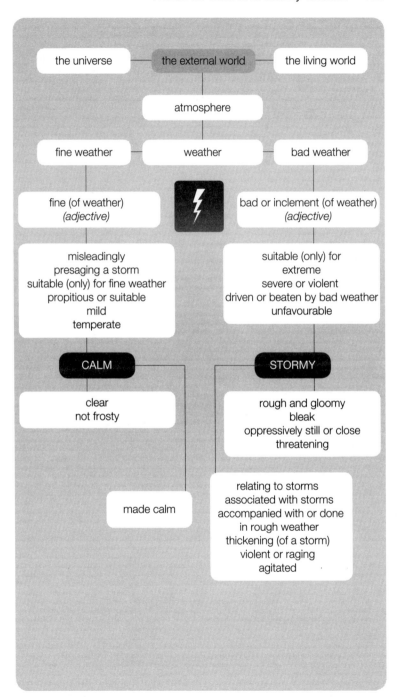

the universe — the external world — the living world

atmosphere

fine weather — weather — bad weather

fine (of weather)
(adjective)

bad or inclement (of weather)
(adjective)

misleadingly
presaging a storm
suitable (only) for fine weather
propitious or suitable
mild
temperate

suitable (only) for
extreme
severe or violent
driven or beaten by bad weather
unfavourable

CALM

STORMY

clear
not frosty

rough and gloomy
bleak
oppressively still or close
threatening

made calm

relating to storms
associated with storms
accompanied with or done
in rough weather
thickening (of a storm)
violent or raging
agitated

13

From *ealda* to *geriatric*, *bevar* to *poppa stoppa*, and *trot* to *old boot*

WORDS FOR OLD PERSON, OLD MAN, OLD WOMAN

I chose this topic to illustrate the need to look at both a vertical (see Chapter 4 and Chapter 5) and a horizontal (see Chapter 12) semantic relationship in order to understand the broader structure of a semantic field. We see a general category, 'old person', divided into the antonyms 'old man' and 'old woman'. We might therefore expect the higher category to be semantically neutral with respect to the gender division below it, but this is to ignore historical social realities. Although I've illustrated from both male and female examples of usage in the entries, the *OED* citations repeatedly show 'old person' words used with reference to men, reflecting the traditional bias of a male-dominated vocabulary. *Ancient*, for example, has seven citations, six of them male.

Dictionaries hold a mirror up to society, in the words they contain, and thesauruses do too. If there is a social imbalance in society, as there has long been in the case of words relating to age and gender, the semantic fields in the lexicon will inevitably reflect it. A simple count of the number of items in a field, however, does not tell the whole story. The *OED* listings show almost twice as many terms for 'old woman' (52) as 'old man' (29), which might suggest that women are well represented in English vocabulary. But when we examine the character of the individual words, we obtain a very different picture.

Attitudes to age

In the beginning, words in the general category are pedestrian (*old, older, oldster, oldie, ancient*), with the occasional exaggeration (*antediluvian, prediluvian*) and literary idiosyncrasy (*emerit, pelt, elderling*). But the general tone is one of respect – of reverence, even – as is argued by social historian David Hackett Fischer in *Growing Old in America* (OUP, 1978). This is understandable, given that so few people reached old age: in 1790, less than 2 per cent of the population were older than 65.

From the end of the eighteenth century, there is a noticeable inter-generational shift in attitude, which Hackett puts down to the general revolutionary spirit of the times. Old people controlled society, in politics, religion, economics, and property ownership. Any revolt against 'the establishment' would carry with it a reaction against age itself. As Hackett says in his introduction, 'The people of early America exalted old age; their descendants have made a cult of youth.'

The change was reflected in many ways. Elderly people lost their seats of honour in churches and meeting-houses. New laws forced early retirement. Clothing and hair fashions flattered the young rather than the old. Children were less often named after old people. The image of old people also altered, as their numbers grew. Many descended into poverty, living in a way that appalled younger people. In 1940, over two-thirds of Americans over 65 were receiving some sort of charity. Homes for old people developed. A similar picture is painted by nineteenth-century novelists in Britain.

All this is reflected in *HTOED* vocabulary. The lexicon of respect that we find in earlier centuries (*old, oldster, ancient*...) is replaced by one of contempt (*relic, old fogey, wrinkly, crumbly, geriatric*). *Fogey* makes a perfect illustration of the shift, for it was originally an admiring nickname for a wounded soldier. And when we examine the gender divide, we see this shift even more dramatically.

Attitudes to gender

The earlier lexicon for 'old man' is full of 'purr-words' (to use semanticist S. I. Hayakawa's term for words that have positive associations), including several elegant loans; *beaupere, vieillard, Nestor, old sire, vecchio, ageman, antiquary, grandsire, elder, patriarch*. The associated words in the *OED* citations are also generally positive: *noble, wise, good, venerable*. Literary idiosyncrasies aside, there are just a few 'snarl-words' (conveying negative associations), such as *pantaloon, hag*, and *crone* – and it is notable that the last two were used of women first. Later terms tend to be ambiguous with respect to sentiment: *codger*, for example, could be purr or snarl, depending on the way it is said and the context in which it is used.

When we look at the emerging female lexicon, we see a reverse picture. Although there are several early purr-words (such as *grandam, beldam, aunt*, and *patriarchess*), these are far outnumbered by snarl-words, which are there from the outset, and make their presence increasingly felt as the millennium proceeds (*trot, carline, hag, crone, old witch, mackabroine, runt, harridan, grimalkin, old trout, tab, bag, crow, old boot*). The animal names are notable – no sign of these with men. And hardly any display the attitudinal ambiguity we see with male names: *grannie* and *ma* are exceptions. For old-fashioned respect, we have to look to other cultures, such as the Caribbean (*mama*) and South Africa (*tante, tannie*).

The future

The entries below stop in the later twentieth century, but we must expect the lexicon in this semantic field to develop further as the next century unfolds. The new system of social relations which emerged after the 1950s has already resulted in attempts to provide attitudinally neutral forms of expression, such as *OAP* and *senior citizen*, and we must expect to see further neologism in the general category, as society emphasizes the opportunities (as opposed to the difficulties) of later life. The *University of the Third Age* (*U3A*) is an illustration of a positive expression that could in time generate its own lexicon. A photograph of a Christmas party on an Australian U3A website in 2004 is captioned: 'Happy U3Aers'. It begins!

New social attitudes result in linguistic change, and even the old vocabulary can be affected. Several of the formerly divisive words are increasingly being used across the age and gender gaps. The Google search exercise I report below (see *old crow*) shows that several female snarl-words have now crossed the gender divide, such as *old trout, old boot*, and *old bag*. Similarly, the age divide is breaking down: expressions such as *old bean* and *old geezer* are heard these days about anyone older than the speaker, or perceived to be older. And there is increased reciprocity as people accommodate to each other: my son Ben calls me *old bean*, and I do the same to him.

In the two subcategories, the expectation is that the most demeaning terms will become less used, avoided in written standard English and in speech reduced to the status of slang. They are out of place in a world where age discrimination is increasingly outlawed, where we are alert to the need for medical and social provision for the elderly, and where gerontology (first recorded in 1903) is now a respected branch of medicine.

Timeline

1 Old person	
old eOE	Old English *ealda* was often used in the singular to mean 'an old person', with a first recorded use in King Alfred's translation of St Gregory's *Pastoral Care* (ch. 25): 'Ne dreata ðu na ðone ealdan' ('Do not rebuke the old one'). The usage has come down to us, usually with *the*, to mean 'old people as a class': a typical contrast is 'the old' versus 'the young'. However, since the late nineteenth century in Australia and New Zealand, there has been a colloquial plural for old persons, especially parents. A report in the *Sydney Morning Herald* (18 September 1982) talks about teenagers who 'try to avoid hassle with the olds'.
older c.1450	A single *OED* citation from late Middle English suggests that this use of the comparative form to mean 'old person' never caught on. Rather, the comparative was used to mean anyone superior in age or rank, so that (for example) 'second graders are olders, kindergartners are youngers' (1997). But the word seems to have achieved a new lease of life in recent US usage, judging by this citation from a 2001 newspaper: 'As older people age and become what some people call "the older olders" ...'
ancient † 1502	Most uses of *ancient* as a noun meaning 'old person' have a man in mind; but Samuel Richardson gives us a clear female reference in his epistolary novel *The History of Sir Charles Grandison* (1753, Book 6, Letter 9). Lady G gushes to Miss Byron, 'Excellent Mrs. Shirley! Incomparable woman! How I love her! If I were such an excellent ancient, I would no more wish to be young, than she has so often told us, she does.'
antediluvian 1684	The word literally means 'before the deluge' – the Flood referred to in the biblical Old Testament. The noun here is a piece of hyperbole, suggesting that reaching a very great age is tantamount to existing before the Flood. Since the eighteenth century, it has increasingly been used negatively, referring to anyone (not necessarily of great age) who is incapable of seeing things in a modern way. *Prediluvian* (1690), though far less used, has had a similar history.
emerit † 1710	The word is usually an adjective, meaning 'superannuated', and was normally used as a contemptuous epithet. In the eighteenth century it wasn't at all nice to be called *an emerit*.

pelt †
1757

Another demeaning word, likening an old person to the withered appearance of a dried animal skin. In the letter-series by Richard and Elizabeth Griffith, *A Series of Genuine Letters between Henry and Frances* (1757, Book 1, Letter 16), the writer gets very cross with Fanny, describing her as 'a diabolical miserable pelt of an old maid'. The word was probably more widely used than this single *OED* citation suggests.

oldie
1799

The first of a series of colloquial substitutes for 'old person', though at first simply referring to someone of any age who is 'older than oneself'. The term received a fresh lease of life in 1992 with the launch of *The Oldie* in the UK – a magazine which, although read by many who under no stretch of the imagination could be described as 'old', is chiefly associated with those who (as one of its slogans said) need to 'buy it before snuff it'.

relic
1832

When referring to an old person, the usage can be either derogatory or respectful. Walter Scott (in *Tales of my Landlord*, 1832) illustrates the negative use, describing someone as 'an old relic of the wars, stuffed full of conceit'. Mark Twain in the *Buffalo Express* (21 August 1869) uses it in a more positive way, referring to an old man he met in a forest as a 'noble relic'.

oldster †
1846

The analogy is with the well-established *youngster* (first recorded in 1589), and is usually contrasted with it, as in an article in *Harper's Magazine* (January 1883): 'The carriages appeared for the oldsters, and the youngsters went on foot.' But the earliest usage of the word (1818) is nautical, referring to a midshipman who has served for over four years.

old fogey
1848

Anyone thought to be old-fashioned or having antiquated ideas would be called a *fogey* or *fogy* (1790). The word seems to be of Scots origin – services' slang for an invalid soldier (1785) or army pensioner – though in an even earlier use in Scotland (1494), *fog* was a word for moss or lichen (and thus likely to be covering something old). Used with self-reference by a person, the expression *old fogey* can be humorous and self-effacing. Used about someone else, the force is invariably that of an insult.

elderling †
1863

A literary use with a single *OED* citation – from Mark Lemon, the founder-editor of *Punch* magazine, in his novel *Wait for the End* (ch. 19): 'The two elderlings began to lament their situation.' The couple, earlier described as 'two elderly ladies', have left a theatre, found it to be raining, and need a carriage to get back home.

the Ancient of Days 1937	A biblical name for God, which Rudyard Kipling uses as a jocular description of a very old person, in the opening chapter of *Something of Myself*: 'Once I remember being taken to a town called Oxford and a street called Holywell, where I was shown an Ancient of Days who, I was told, was the Provost of Oriel.'
senior citizen 1938	A euphemism for an elderly person, especially one past the age of retirement, which supposedly avoids the demeaning associations of other descriptions, such as 'old age pensioner'. The usage began in the USA but is now widespread.
OAP 1942	A chiefly British abbreviation for 'old-age pensioner', very common in the mid-twentieth century, but often considered 'politically incorrect' in an age when people are not considered to be 'old' but 'chronologically challenged'.
wrinkly 1972	A slang substitute for 'old person', especially one who is so old that they are incapable of serious activity; also spelled *wrinklie*. The label is variously used, with a variety of attitudes that run from jocular to insulting, and with considerable uncertainty over the age range. An article in the *Times* (31 August 1978) refers to a teenager who 'reserves "wrinklie" for the 60-year-old generation', whereas her parents are 'oldies' (see above).
crumbly 1976	Even older than a *wrinkly*; also spelled *crumblie*. The body, evidently, is now falling to bits – and also the mind, as the label is often used for someone considered to be senile. As with *wrinkly*, the effect it conveys depends very much on the attitude held by the user. In a *Daily Mail* article (4 October 2006) headed: 'Crumblies: NHS workers accused of dehumanizing older patients', the context is plainly demeaning. By contrast, an article in the online magazine *Wartime Housewife* (19 March 2010) had a strongly positive tone: 'Three cheers for the crumblies! In praise of old people'.
geriatric 1977	The technical name of the branch of medicine that deals with the health of older people (*geriatrics*, 1909) quickly developed an associated adjective and noun, but there was no demeaning sense until the 1960s, when a sense of 'old and senile' emerged. The associations are almost always negative today.

2 Old man

old man eOE	The oldest, and still the most common appellation for 'a man who is past middle age'. We might think this would be a sufficient description, but the range of items below indicates otherwise.
bevar † c.1275	*Bever* or *biver* has long been widely used in regional dialects in England and Scotland to mean 'shiver, tremble'. In Scotland, a *bever hair* (c.1500) was a 'trembling old man' – the *hair* element related to *hoary*.
beaupere † c.1300	An elegant, polite term of address from French ('good' + 'father') for anyone considered to be a father or elderly father-figure. There are no *OED* citations after the early seventeenth century.
vieillard † 1475	Another French loan, from *vieille* ('old'). It was a standard name, judging by its use in the title of a French treatise by Simon Goulart on old age, which appeared in English in 1621: *The wise vieillard, or old man. Translated out of French into English by an obscure Englishman, a friend and favourer of all wise old-men.* It also appears later as *velyard* (c.1529).
Nestor c.1510	A Homeric hero famed for his age and wisdom, who came to be used proverbially in many languages. 'God give us joys and Nestor's days' is an early example, where the expression means 'give us long life'. As a separate noun, meaning 'old man', it has both singular and plural use: 'the Nestor of English science' (1983), 'aged Nestors tottered along' (1817).
hag † c.1529	This insulting label for an 'ugly old woman' (see below) generalized to men in the sixteenth century, with a citation as late as 1698, when the Scottish minister Robert Blair describes himself in ch. 12 of his autobiography as 'an old hag'. The word later reverted to its original female use.
old sire † 1557	An expression that achieved some use in the second half of the sixteenth century. The first recorded use is in a poetry anthology, where Nicholas Grimoald (in 'Methodorius' mind to the contrary') draws a contrast between youth and old age: 'Young bloods be strong: old sires in double honour dwell.' In the early twentieth century, *old sir* had a similar use as a term of address.

vecchio *c.*1570	An isolated use in the sixteenth century of this Italian word for 'old' is followed by a lack of citations until it surfaces again in the twentieth. In a 1944 letter, George Bernard Shaw describes himself as 'a vecchio, nearly eightyeight and a half'.
ageman † 1571	A single *OED* citation in a legal context illustrates this unusual formation: 'Wm. Walker is an ageman and broken in labour'. The source is a court deposition from Durham, so there may be a regional factor in its use. I thought that would be the end of this lexical story, until I encountered *AgeMan*, a registered trade mark for a suit (developed in Germany) that a young person can wear to experience the physical limitations that many elderly people have to cope with. It weighs 10 kilos, has a helmet that muffles hearing, a visor to restrict vision, padded gloves to reduce the sense of touch, and knee and elbow pads to restrict movement. I take the point (without a suit).
antiquary † *c.*1571	The meaning of 'student or collector of antiquities' came at around the same time (1587) and soon became standard, supplanting the short-lived use for a 'man of great age'. Edmund Campion, in the opening chapter of his *History of Ireland* (1571) describes Ruanus the Giant as a 'noble Antiquarie', which seems reasonable, as he was reputedly 2,041 years old.
grave-porer † 1582	A single literary citation from Richard Stanyhurst's translation of Virgil (Book 4) describes a 'bedrid graveporer old sire' – someone who is so old that he is looking towards his grave.
grandsire *c.*1593	This old word for 'grandfather' (or, in Scotland, 'great-grandfather') was occasionally used for any grandfather-like old man. Shakespeare uses it twice in this way: Hamlet quotes lines in which King Priam is called a grandsire (*Hamlet*, *c.*1600, 2.2.462), and Petruchio addresses Vincentio as 'good old grandsire' (*The Taming of the Shrew*, *c.*1593, 4.5.50).
huddle-duddle † 1599	Another literary usage, recorded only in the opening paragraphs of Thomas Nashe's *Lenten Stuff*. In a passage of great vivacity, he describes the old men who rejected Homer as 'dull-pated penny-fathers . . . greybeard huddle-duddles and crusty cum-twangs'. *Huddle* was being used as a word for 'miserly old person' at the time; *duddle* was a verb meaning 'confuse'. The combination made a fortuitous rhyme.

elder †
1600

The word was occasionally used for 'old man', even into the nineteenth century, but was overtaken by its more specialized uses in various political and religious settings. There was also a shortened form, *eld*, which appealed to poets: Samuel Taylor Coleridge, in his visionary poem 'The Destiny of Nations' (1796) talks of 'a tottering eld'.

pantaloon
1602

In early Italian theatre, a *pantaloon* (1592) was a character representing the older generation, typically a foolish old man dressed in a bizarre costume. The word had hardly arrived in English when it was being used by the dramatists for a 'feeble old man' – most famously by Shakespeare in the 'seven ages of man' speech from Jaques in *As You Like It* (c.1600, 2.7.159): 'the lean and slippered pantaloon'.

cuff †
c.1616

Slang for 'old man' – especially a miserly one, as the collocation *rich cuff* is common – probably related to *cove*, *cuffin*, *chuff*, and other slang words for 'man'. The label, often reinforced by *old* (as in a 1699 dictionary illustration: 'a pleasant old cuff'), is sometimes contemptuous, sometimes jocular.

crone †
1630

A word that was originally used for 'old woman' (see below), similar in use to *hag* (above), and later occasionally extended to men. Richard Brathwait, in *The English Gentleman* (1630, page 255), includes in his definition of 'a gentleman': 'He wonders at a profuse fool, that he should spend when honest frugality bids him spare; and no less at a miserable crone, who spares when reputation bids him spend.'

dry-beard †
1749

Two eighteenth-century *OED* citations support this usage for 'old man with a dry or withered beard'. 'Well said, old dry-beard', says a character in the opening act of David Garrick's satire *Lethe* (1749).

codger
1756

The origin is obscure, but it may be a dialectal variant of *cadger*, an itinerant countryside dealer, applied to any elderly man. It usually has a jocular or whimsical use, and often appears in the form *old codger*. One of the early issues of the US periodical *Salmagundi* (20 March 1807) spells out some typical associations: 'A gouty old codger of an alderman'.

patriarch
1819

Originally a religious term referring to a bishop, or a ruler of a biblical people. In the nineteenth century, its use was extended to any 'venerable old man', especially the oldest man in a community or the oldest living representative of a profession. In Paul Gallico's novel *Foolish Immortals* (1953), we read of a place 'called the country of the patriarchs because of the great age of many of the inhabitants'.

oubaas
1824

A South African word for an elderly owner of a house, farm, or business (Afrikaans *oud* 'old' + *baas* 'master, boss'), which was later extended to refer to any elderly white man, and often used as a title or term of address. The Johannesburg *Sunday Times* (30 May 1982) has someone asking for 'Oubaas Wilkinson, the veteran who fought in the Boer War'.

pop
1844

A variant of *papa* 'father', heard colloquially in several variants, such as *poppa*, *pops*, and *pop*. In the USA, it came to be used as an informal title for an old man, especially one well known in a local community. A famous instance was Andrew J. Seeley, who lived in a cabin on a Hudson River creek for decades: his *New York Herald* obituary (18 February 1915) described him as 'the aged boatman of the Spuyten Duyvil and known to everyone in that vicinity as "Pop" Seeley'.

tad
1877

The origin may be an abbreviation of *tadpole*, applied colloquially in the USA both to a very young or small boy or ironically to an old man. The latter meaning usually needs to be made clear by using an adjective (*old tad*).

senex
1898

Latin for 'old man', generally only encountered in literary or scholarly contexts. In Chaucer's *The Miller's Tale*, the story is told of an old carpenter from Oxford who has married a young wife of 18. F. N. Robinson adds, in his commentary on this tale in Chaucer's *Complete Works* (1957): 'The Oxford carpenter is an example of the familiar figure of the "senex amans" [amorous old man].'

poppa stoppa
1944

African-American slang, usually a term of abuse when addressing an old man, but as a name adopted by black media personalities. It was the nickname of at least three US radio disc jockeys in the second half of the twentieth century.

3 Old woman

old wife
eOE

Wife was a general word for a woman before it became the correlative of 'husband', so the use of *old wife* to mean 'old woman' has a long and varied history. We hear an echo of this usage most often today in the expression *old wives' tale* (*c.*1425), where the story being told does not necessarily come from a married women.

trot †
*c.*1375

A disparaging name for an old woman, of unknown origin. In Shakespeare's *The Taming of the Shrew* (*c.*1593, 1.2.78), Grumio suggests that, if all Petruchio wants is a wealthy wife, he need do no more than 'give him gold enough and marry him . . . to an old trot with ne'er a tooth in her head'.

carline c.1375	A word from northern England, ultimately from Old Norse *kerling* 'woman' or 'old woman', a feminine form of the name *Karl*, and usually used in a disparaging way. Spelling/pronunciation variants include *carling* and *carley*. Dialect usage was strong in Scotland, Ireland, and northern England. Robert Burns liked the word, even naming one of his poems 'The Five Carlins' (1789).
hag 1377	*Hags* were originally evil spirits in female form, such as the Furies or Harpies of classical mythology. Witches (not necessarily old) were also called *hags*, most famously in Shakespeare's *Macbeth* (1606, 4.1.47): 'How now, you secret, black and midnight hags?' These senses have now died out, as the meaning broadened and became widely used to include any old woman (and, for a while, man – see above) perceived to be ugly or repulsive.
crone c.1386	The adjectives in the *OED* citations clearly indicate the attitude: crones are *cursed* (c.1386), *crooked* (1572), *old* (1621), *decrepit* (1640), *frugal* (c.1844), *aged* (1795), and *ancient* (1849). In fact it's unusual to find a use of the word without some sort of negative qualifier.
vecke † 1390	The female equivalent of *vecchio* (above), though the early date of the loan suggests a possible origin via French. The first recorded instance is in John Gower's *Confessio Amantis* (Book 1, line 1675), when the young knight Florent looks at the old woman ('this vecke') that he has promised to marry. It appears also as *vekke* and *wekke* in the fifteenth century, but there are no citations thereafter.
mone † c.1393	Another word from *Confessio Amantis* (Book 1, line 1634), in which an old lady is called 'that olde Mone'. It is related to Dutch and German words which mean 'aunt' or 'mother', and is nothing to do with 'moaning'.
old witch c.1430	Samuel Taylor Coleridge sums up his view of old women in a *Table-talk* classification (7 July 1831): 'There are only three classes into which all the women past seventy that ever I knew were to be divided: – 1. That dear old soul: 2. That old woman: 3. That old witch.'
maud † c.1500	A further example (as with *mab* and *moll*, see Chapter 10) of the practice of using a first name for a class of people. In Lewis Wager's morality play, *A New Interlude Entreating of the Life and Repentaunce of Marie Magdalene* (1566), the vice Infidelitie says to Mary: 'In good faith when ye are come to be an old maude,	Then it will be best for you to play the baude'.

mackabroine †
1546

A single *OED* citation suggests the meaning 'old, disobliging woman'. John Heywood's anthology of English proverbs (1546, ch. 6) contains a section about a man 'that hath chosen a divell to his wife', and the woman is described as 'an olde witch, such a mackabroyne'. The origin is unknown, but the first element is probably a short form of *magpie* (*mag* or *mack*), which is recorded in the *English Dialect Dictionary* in dialects all over England with senses such as 'chatterer' and (in Worcestershire, near where Heywood spent his early years) 'a fault-finding woman'.

grandam †
1550

This early French loanword (*grand* 'great' + *dame* 'lady/mother') entered English in the thirteenth century with the meaning of 'grandmother', but later developed the sense of 'old woman'. There is usually a preceding adjective: the three *OED* citations show 'superstitious', 'old', and 'shrivelled'. Colloquial pronunciation led to the slightly later (1597) *grannam*.

beldam †
1580

Another French loanword, but with the direct source being the variant *dam* 'mother' rather than *dame* 'lady'. *Bel*- was being used in Middle English at the time as a kinship term: a *belfader* or *belsire* was a grandfather; a *beldame* or *belmoder* was a 'grandmother'. During the sixteenth century, *beldam* came to be used for any 'woman of advanced years', and was a common way of addressing a nurse. Richard Steele captures the age contrast in a *Tatler* essay (1709, No. 83): 'I am neither Childish-young, nor Beldam-old'.

aunt †
1595

Shakespeare provides the sole *OED* citation for the wider use of this word to mean 'old woman' or 'gossip'. In *A Midsummer Night's Dream* (c.1595, 2.1.51), Puck describes the mischief he performs on 'the wisest aunt, telling the saddest tale'.

patriarchess †
1639

The female equivalent of *patriarch* (above), quite often used in its religious sense ('wife of a patriarch'), but with only one *OED* citation for the meaning 'oldest woman in a community'. A newspaper in 1882 described a centenarian as 'the patriarchess of the district'.

runt
c.1652

Originally an animal term – at first (1549) a small-sized ox or cow, then (1638) an undersized horse, then (1798) the smallest pig in a litter, then (1902) any small or inferior animal. You can see where this is leading...British dialects, especially in Scotland and Northern Ireland, took up the label for an old person, especially a disagreeable woman. But as a term of abuse, it could be applied to anyone, male or female, old or young. Iona and Peter Opie report its use in their *Children's Games* (1969).

harridan 1699	A French word for an old horse (*haridelle*) probably led to this label for 'a haggard old woman; a vixen; a decayed strumpet' (this last expression from Samuel Johnson's *Dictionary*). It was ferociously vituperative when it first appeared, but its force later weakened, especially after it came to be used figuratively. When John Hill Burton reports (in *The Scot Abroad*, 1884, ch. 3) the words of an ambassador taken aback by the formality of the Danish Court – 'that old harridan Etiquette, with all her trumpery' – the tone is almost jocular.
grimalkin † 1798	Another animal name (see *runt* above), this time for a cat, especially an old she-cat. Shakespeare is the first recorded user, as the name of a witch's familiar (*Macbeth*, 1606, I.I.8). A demeaning use of *malkin* we have already seen in another connection (*mawks* in Chapter 10). During the eighteenth century, it came to be used for 'a jealous or imperious old woman'.
mama 1810	For once, a more positive expression, analogous to *pop* (above), used chiefly among people of African-American origin in the USA and Caribbean. People unaware of the convention can misinterpret it, but to address an aged woman as *mama* usually conveys both familiarity and great respect. In other parts of the world, both *maw* (1826) and *ma* (1932) have also been used as familiar forms of address to old women, though lacking the politeness associated with *ma'am* (very common in the USA) or *madam*.
tante 1815	A French loanword (*tante* 'aunt'), used for any older woman who stands in a close relationship to the speaker. In South Africa, it is a term of respect for any elderly woman. As Harold Blore put it, in his autobiographical *An Imperial Light Horseman* (1900): 'If a Boer were to be presented at Court he'd offer to shake hands with Queen Victoria, and address her as "Tante".' A shortened colloquial form also exists, *tannie* (1958), which the South African memoirist Iris Vaughan found endearing (in *The Last of the Sunlit Years*, 1969, ch. 9): 'most Afrikaans children call one "Aunty" or "Tannie", and are most charmingly co-operative'.
granny 1816	The familiar form of *grandmother*, used for 'old woman' (without any kinship implied), can express virtually any attitude, from affection to contempt; also spelled *grannie*. In the nineteenth century – and still regionally today – *your granny!* was a common exclamation of disbelief, in which a word is repeated and derided. In Mark Twain's *The Adventures of Tom Sawyer* (1876, ch. 25) Tom tells Huck that if he goes to Europe he'd see plenty of diamonds 'hopping around'. Huck can't believe it: 'Do they hop?' Tom replies: 'Hop? – your granny! No!...Shucks, I only meant you'd *see* 'em.'

Mother Bunch
1847

The name of an alehouse keeper in Elizabethan London, who is supposed to have lived to a great age. She gave her name to several book titles, usually collections of folk wisdom, and she turns up in places as diverse as Charlotte Brontë – Colonel Dent describes an old gipsy woman as 'one of the old Mother Bunches' (*Jane Eyre*, 1847, ch. 18) – and the *Guardian* (28 December 1964): 'She no more looks like a Mother Bunch than sounds like one', though here the reference is more to girth than age.

dowager †
1870

A French loanword, originally (1530), a woman who has inherited a title after the death of her husband, but eventually extended to any 'elderly lady of dignified demeanour'. It is used in this way by Charles Dickens in *The Mystery of Edwin Drood* (1870, ch. 3): 'the matronly Mrs Tisher heaves in sight...rustling through the room like the legendary ghost of a dowager in silken skirts'. The word became *dowrier* in Scotland (1551), and *douairière* in literary England (1869).

veteraness †
1880

The female equivalent of a *veteran* – someone who has grown old in service (originally for soldiers, 1611). There is just one *OED* citation, in a US magazine, reflecting a military context. Today, if a long-serving woman were to be described in this way, there would be no suffix.

old trout
1897

A derogatory term for 'old woman', with *old* obligatory. Ironically, in the seventeenth century, *trout* was used as slang in a positive way, thanks to alliteration: a confidential friend or servant could be called a *true trout* or *trusty trout*.

tab
1909

A short form of *tabby* (cat), used since the eighteenth century for 'an old maid' (as Francis Grose defines it, in his *Classical Dictionary of the Vulgar Tongue*, 1785). James Redding Ware, in *Passing English of the Victorian Era* (1909) thought the abbreviation to be theatrical slang, but later examples show a wider use. Ruth Rendell, in her suspense novel *One Across, Two Down* (1971), has a character say: 'We've got some old tab coming here...Pal of my ma-in-law's'.

bag
1924

A disparaging term for an unattractive or elderly woman, ultimately a short form of *baggage*, used in earlier centuries (first recorded use, 1601) for a woman (of any age) perceived as good-for-nothing or immoral, or (with an appropriate adjective, such as *saucy* or *artful*) as a playful reference to a young woman. The slang use of *bag* (usually with *old*, when the referent is elderly) began in the USA, but is now widespread.

crow 1925	The animal motif continues, usually in the slang phrase *old crow*, used chiefly for a woman perceived to be ugly. Since the Middle Ages the crow has had a bad press, especially among farmers, and has often been used as a term of insult for both men and women. Usage seems to be changing. In 2013 a Google search brought to light three times more examples of 'He's an old crow' than of 'She's an old crow', and some quite famous males receive the appellation these days.
Skinny Liz † 1940	The *OED* citation illustrates the use of this phrase only as a piece of public-school slang (from St Bees in Cumbria), but – as Eric Partridge comments – this is 'a mere localization of general and widespread *skinny Lizzie*, rudely applied to a thin woman of any age'. It remains a historical idiosyncrasy in this semantic field.
old boot 1958	A theatre review in the *Daily Telegraph* (1 July 1998) captures the tone of this expression well: 'I particularly liked Jean Challis as the much abused old boot of a hostess.' Unlike some other 'old' expressions (such as *old hen*), it does seem to be used only with reference to genuine old age.

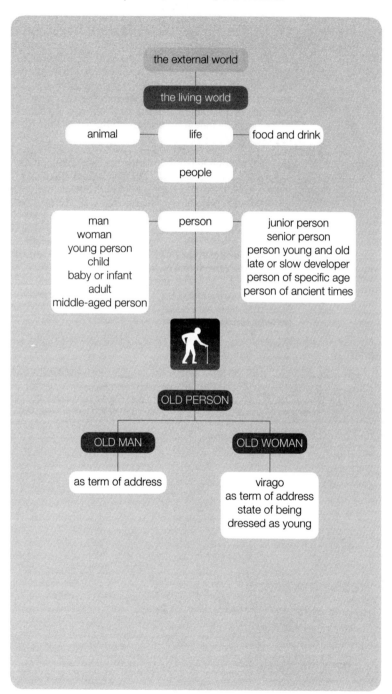

14

From *skiffle* to *grime*

WORDS FOR TYPES OF POP MUSIC

There is a famous story in Middle English, where William Caxton, having encountered the words *eggs* and *eyren* – regional dialect variants of 'egg' – and not knowing which he as a publisher should choose, exclaims in exasperation: 'Lo, what should a man in these days now write: eggs or eyren? Certainly it is hard to please every man because of diversity and change of language.' What he would make of the semantic field of pop(ular) music it is difficult to imagine.

The genre emerged in the late 1950s, with a strong melody and beat, using electric instruments and amplification, intended to have wide appeal and commercial success. It was not the first time music had been called 'pop', but no previous period had evoked such a proliferation of musical labels as this one was about to do. During the 1980s and 1990s, according to the items so far collected by the *OED*, new musical styles were arriving at the rate of one every three months. Between 1960 and 2000 we find 124 terms (ignoring variations, such as *progressive rock* > *prog rock* > *prog*), and there is no sign of the rate decreasing. The lists below show nothing after 2003, but this will change as lexicographers catch up with what is one of the fastest-moving semantic fields in the whole of the English lexicon.

Problems of treatment

The problem facing the lexicographer is not simply one of keeping up with the coverage, but one of treatment. The entries demand a high level of encyclopedic (as opposed to linguistic) knowledge. In this chapter I had to stand on the *OED*'s shoulders to get a sense of the semantic nuances involved (which is why I quote so much from the dictionary). They, in turn, had to stand on the shoulders of the writers who provided the citations. And what sort of thing did they find? Look at what this *Melody Maker* journalist has to say (1989: entry on *house* below):

> In the aftermath of the first waves of Acid and Balearic, clubbers have been offered, in no chronological order, dance music under the names of... Acid jazz, ska House and hip House... There's been the Garage and Techno sounds of New York and Detroit respectively, Belgian New Beat,... and, most recently, Dutch and Italian House. It's enough to confuse even the most dedicated clubber.

If the clubbers get confused, what chance have lexicographers got? Not only are some of these terms yet to be included in *OED* coverage, it makes an accurate and consistent treatment virtually impossible. We repeatedly see commentators on the musical scene throwing up their hands in a Caxton-like way. A journalist for *Wire* (1993: entry on *ambience* below) reviews a concert in which 'Electroacoustic, tape collage, post-industrial, ambient and various polystylistic unclassifiables are weird and sometimes wonderful bedfellows for nearly 75 minutes.' Unclassifiables, says the specialist.

The thesaurus makes us juxtapose entries that an alphabetical system keeps well apart, and it is interesting to see the limitations in definitions when they become neighbours. It quickly becomes plain that a purely lexical definition, in terms of musical notions (instruments, sound effects, techniques), is not going to be enough. At one level, *disco-funk* is easy to define: it is a combination of *disco* and *funk*. What you make of this will depend on how much prior experience you have had of the two genres. Note, I say 'experience', not 'knowledge of the language'. If we leave the dictionary world and enter the encyclopedic, we see the difference immediately. Every genre is identified with reference to the individual musicians, singers, and groups that gave rise to the name. Sometimes individual artists are identified in the literature as being 'the king of' a genre, or the 'founder' of a genre – though such assignations are often hotly debated (giving an etymologist nightmares). Some writers use terms as synonyms (see *pomp rock* below); some differentiate. There may be no word for what people want to say: 'No single term really describes the music of all these bands', says a commentator in relation to *cowpunk*. Attempts to describe a sound inevitably fall far short of the acoustic reality. The only way in which a dictionary could ever bridge the gap would be to provide audio clips as citations – a prospect which (in an online lexicographical world) may actually be not too far off.

Hybrid genres

The problem is especially marked in this semantic field because of all the hybrid genres that exist. This is a world where, in the search for new sounds, anything can be combined with anything. And because each genre is itself an amalgam of several features – different types of instrument, rhythm, vocals, electronic techniques... – the result is a definition that is opaque, because it does not say which features of which genres have come together. *Swingbeat*, for example, is said to combine 'elements of rhythm and blues, soul, hip-hop, and rap music'. To find out which elements, we have to know a lot more. It is often left to individual artists to say what sort of music they perform, and then wait to see if other people agree with them. Genre names are bandied about idiosyncratically, often eccentrically, in a world where a personal lexical innovation can readily become the latest fashion. It is a world where Lewis Carroll's Humpty Dumpty rules: 'When I use a word, it means just what I choose it to mean – neither more nor less.'

One result of all this is a very large category of 'Other' (over 100 items listed below) – always a sign that the taxonomist has thrown in the semantic towel. It is of course possible to see potential subcategories. Ethnicity is one possible criterion, reflected in the distinctive loanwords showing varieties of world music (e.g. *marabi, malombo, dangdut, rai, zouk*). Geographical origin is another, seen in general terms (e.g. *Britpop, Europop, J-pop, Cantopop*) as well as more specific areas (e.g. *Motown, Philly, Liverpool*). Terms such as *alternative rock, New Wave, nu-skool, post-rock*, and *post-punk* show that chronology is important, though with a field as fast-moving as this, it is difficult to keep track. But no single 'obvious' way of classifying stands out. And the taxonomist has the additional problem of having to cope with a situation where fashions change so rapidly. As a commentator says, in relation to *alternative music*, 'so-called alternative music...is now the mainstream'. Still, one does one's best. And if a historical thesaurus cannot throw light on this kind of thing, nothing can.

Timeline

Pop music	
pop 1862	In 1956, the music magazine *Melody Maker* (7 April) introduced a new feature, 'a regular weekly listing of the best-selling "popular" records of Great Britain'. They called it 'Top of the Pops'. *Pop* generated a huge number of collocations: *pop album, band, concert, fan, festival, group, record, single, star* ... But novelist George Eliot was there first. She writes in a letter (26 November 1862): 'There is too much "Pop" for the thorough enjoyment of the chamber music.'
sounds 1955	US slang for any kind of popular music, including jazz. As a *Daily Mirror* article put it (27 August 1968), 'Together cats don't buy records, they buy *sounds*'.
1 Skiffle	
skiffle 1926	A style of jazz music popular in the USA in the 1920s, which in the 1950s developed, especially in Britain, into a style of popular music. The vocal part is supported by a rhythmic accompaniment of guitars or banjos, as well as homemade or improvised instruments such as a washboard and tea-chest bass. This is my era. I still know all the words of Lonnie Donegan's 'Rock Island Line' (a top-10 hit single in 1955), which appears in the aptly named album *King of Skiffle*. The etymology is unknown, but similar-sounding words (such as *skiff* 'touch lightly, move quickly') suggest an onomatopoeic origin.
skiffle music 1948	*Skiffle groups* (or *skiffle bands*) played *skiffle music*. The *Decca Book of Jazz* in 1958 identifies the time frame: 'The phenomenon of skiffle music, peculiar only to Britain as yet, is well under way.'
2 Rock	
rock 'n' roll 1955	A style of music originating in the southern USA, 'characterized by a heavily accentuated backbeat and simple melodies and structures'. A note added to this *OED* definition develops the notion: 'based around a twelve-bar structure, typically featuring an instrumentation of guitar, double bass, and drums, with the snare drum providing the characteristic backbeat'. For those who lived through the era of Bill Haley and the Comets, and thus idolized 'Rock Around the Clock' (1954), piano and saxophone have to be added.

r'n'r 1955	An abbreviation of *rock 'n' roll* (above), used mainly by journalists in writing. It appears in both lower-case and upper-case (*R 'n' R*) forms.
rock 1956	A genre that evolved from *rock 'n' roll* in the mid to late 1960s. As a writer in the US *National Observer* put it (3 November 1968): 'It has been clear for some time that "rock" is getting longer, more sophisticated, more ambitious, restless with chordal limitations and the three-minute format.' Many sub-genres followed.

2A Types of

rockabilly 1956	The word is a blend of *rock* (above) + *billy*, as in *hillbilly*, a person from a remote rural or mountainous area, especially in the south-east USA – an area known for its folk music. The genre combined elements of rock 'n' roll and country music. The US music magazine *Billboard* (16 June 1956) noted 'the wave of "rock-a-billy" imitators of Elvis Presley'.
rockaboogie 1956	Another blend, this time of *rock 'n' roll* and *boogie-woogie* (1928) – a piano style of playing blues with a persistent left-hand rhythm. It was often written as *rock-a-boogie*. Bill Darnel's song 'Rock-a-Boogie Baby' (1956), sung by Diana Decker, was one of the first hits that popularized the genre: it is all about a baby who 'uses boogie to go to sleep | Shakes his little rattle "stead of countin'" sheep'. Even the parents don't understand how it happened.
acid rock 1966	The drug LSD was colloquially known as *acid*, so *acid rock*, popular in the late 1960s and early 1970s, was an obvious usage whenever psychedelic effects were added to rock 'n' roll. As the *OED* definition circumspectly puts it: 'typically featuring extended improvisatory solos, distorted or effects-enhanced guitar sounds, and surrealistic lyrics, intended to evoke or accompany the use of acid'. Eugene Landy sums it up in his *Underground Dictionary* (1971): 'the musical equivalent of an LSD-induced state'.
folk-rock 1966	Folk-music with the kind of strong beat that is heard in rock 'n' roll. Bands that influenced the growth of the genre included The Byrds, The Beatles, The Animals, and The Searchers.
raga rock 1966	Rock music which includes a melody or improvisation in the style of the raga in Indian classical music. *Raga* is a Sanskrit word which, in addition to 'melody', also means 'colour' and 'passion'.

hard rock 1967	A genre which makes a loud, intense, and aggressive sound, thanks to a heavy use of distorted electric guitars, a very strong beat, and harsh vocal effects. A review of a concert by the *Boston Sunday Herald* (26 March 1967) talks of the theatre being shaken by the 'mesmeric hard-rock beat'. A less strident genre came to be known as *soft rock* (1969).
progressive rock 1968	This is 'progress' in the sense of 'intricate (often classically influenced) musical motifs, prominent use of electronic instrumentation, extended compositions, self-consciously intellectual or poetic lyrics, and displays of musical virtuosity'. That *OED* definition sums it up well, but makes no evaluation – unlike a reviewer in the *New York Times* (4 August 1968), who didn't like it, calling it 'musically advanced but emotionally barren. The indulgence of a new, cerebral audience has endangered that raw vitality which was once a hallmark of the rock experience.' It was later (1976) shortened to *prog rock*, and then (1978) *prog*.
jazz-rock 1970	A combination of jazz and rock music – two genres that until the late 1960s had had very little to do with each other. The direction of influence was both ways, with rock bands introducing jazz harmonies and improvization and jazz groups experimenting with rock rhythms and electric instruments.
punk rock 1970	Rock music played in a fast, aggressive, or unpolished manner. In the late 1970s it was characterized by 'a deliberately outrageous or confrontational attitude, energetic (and often chaotic) performance, and (frequently) simple or repetitive song structures' (*OED*). The term was almost immediately shortened to *punk* (1970), which was applied also to the youth subculture that emerged with its distinctive clothing, hair-styles, and body adornment. The etymological link with earlier senses of *punk* (as in Chapter 10) is unclear, but doubtless was influenced by the various street slang meanings of the word, such as 'hoodlum' and 'thug'.
swamp rock 1970	The French-influenced area in southern Louisiana known as Acadiana produced a genre of rock music that was sufficiently distinctive to earn its own name, derived from the wetlands along the coast. Popular in its region, a single *OED* citation suggests a limited awareness elsewhere.

cock rock 1971	A slang description of rock music characterized by the ostentatious male sexuality of the lyrics and performance. *Kitchen Sink Magazine* (2003, No. 19) sums it up, describing Led Zeppelin as the creators of the genre, 'in the hyper-masculine sexuality of their sound, their songs and in the presentation of their actual packages, which were often practically visible through their tight-ass bell bottoms'.
techno-rock 1971	A genre of rock music which makes heavy use of sounds generated or modified electronically, especially using synthesizers. The rock 'n' roll magazine *Creem* (1971, No. 38) described it as 'pushing electronics to their earsplitting limits'.
glitter rock 1972	The *glitter* element refers to the glittering costumes worn by the performers, along with flamboyant hairstyles and make-up, and an inevitable suggestion of sexual ambiguity. The glamorous clothes generated the alternative label *glam-rock* (1974). David Bowie's alter ego, Ziggy Stardust, is one of the most famous personifications.
grunge 1973	*Grungy* (1965) is US slang for anything grimy or dirty – probably an onomatopoeic coinage based on similar-sounding words such as *grubby, grimy, dingy,* and *gungy*. The associated noun was a general term of disparagement for anything unpleasant, so whoever first used the term for a type of rock music characterized by 'a raucous, often discordant guitar sound, lazy vocal delivery, and downbeat, often nihilistic lyrics' (as the *OED* puts it) must have taken a perverse delight in giving the word a positive semantic spin.
pub rock 1974	A genre of fast, blues-based rock music played by small pop groups in British public houses. As *Q Magazine* put it (March 1989), 'Pub rock enjoyed its brief heyday just prior to punk' (see above).
alternative rock 1975	This is *alternative* in its widely used sense of 'presenting something that is not the orthodox way of doing something', as in *alternative lifestyle* and *alternative medicine*. In the case of this genre of rock music, the alternative refers not only to the music, which comprises many styles, but to the way it is heard, associated with output on local radio stations and independent record labels.

AOR 1977	The abbreviation of *album-oriented rock*, a genre characterized by 'long, free-form album tracks rather than short, tightly-structured singles' and where 'a rock backing is combined with softer, more melodic elements and often vocal harmonies'. An important comment is added to this *OED* definition: 'frequently depreciative, with the implication of something slickly executed but bland'. The genre should not take it too personally: it is the fate of most of the names in this semantic field to be talked about in a depreciative way at some point or other.
New Wave 1977	This genre emerged in the late 1970s, 'originally associated with punk rock but typically less aggressive in performance and musically more melodic and experimental, often characterized by spare guitar lines and an edgy vocal delivery' (*OED*). A *Time Out* reviewer was caustic at the outset (17 June 1977): 'If New Wave means anything at all as a description, it means...young bands playing again. For a long time the young bands were just joining the old bands.'
pomp rock 1978	This is *pomp* in the sense of 'bombastic or grandiose in its delivery', with the *OED* adding, 'characterized by prominent keyboards and drums and heavy use of guitar effects'. The online magazine *tvtropes* places it in the middle of a cluster of synonyms in its article on *arena rock*: 'also known as pomp rock, melodic rock, anthem rock, stadium rock [1979 in *OED*] or AOR [see above]', the common feature being songs that appeal to large crowds, to be performed in big stadiums. The article adds: 'it isn't always treated kindly by music critics', reporting their use of negative expressions such as *corporate rock* in the 1970s and *dad rock* (see below) in the 1990s.
Oi 1981	A genre of 'harsh aggressive rock music' which, as an *Observer* article explained (12 July 1981) 'aspires to articulate the grievances of unemployed, poorly housed, disenchanted youth who feel themselves to be harassed by the police'. The *oi* is the interjection normally used to attract attention, especially when the speaker is annoyed or objecting to something.
noise-rock 1982	This is *noise* in the sense of sound that is dissonant or inharmonious, using loud distorted guitars, amplifier noise, feedback, and other deliberately harsh effects. It had a confrontational performance style that sometimes involved the performers destroying their instruments and even, at times, fighting with the audience.

trash rock 1983	Originally a US term (*trash* = British [domestic] *rubbish*), and often referred to simply as *trash*, a genre of rock music 'noted for its raucous sound or throwaway nature'. An entry in the *Urban Dictionary* provides a more subjective take on the 'throwaway' part of this *OED* definition: 'trashy, seedy, campy rock 'n roll with an often androgynous, drunk/ drugged out, and b-movie-obsessed disposition'.
emo-core 1986	*Emo* is an abbreviation of *emotional*, referring to a genre 'derived from hardcore punk music [see above] and characterized by emotional, usually introspective lyrics' (*OED*). *Emotional* means what it says. According to *Thrasher* magazine (1986, No. 74), 'Crowds are said to be left in tears from the intensity'. It was soon (1988) shortened to *emo*.
Goth 1986	The allusion is to the Germanic tribes who once invaded Europe, though the physical appearance of the performers (and their fans) owes more to the dramatic way characters were portrayed in gothic horror movies, with 'dark eye make-up, pale skin colouring, dark clothes, and bulky metallic jewellery'. The musical etymology is from punk rock (above).
rawk 1987	An unusual phenomenon – a humorous pronunciation (of *rock*) given a conventional spelling, and often accompanied by *rowl*. The idea was to reassert what was perceived to be the essence of the rock 'n' roll genre, though performers interpreted this in wildly different ways, and the term came to be used both positively and negatively, according to taste.
grindcore 1989	A genre of 'fast, harsh-sounding rock music, combining elements from heavy metal and punk rock, and typically incorporating loud, distorted noise' (*OED*). *Grind* originally referred to the earsplitting grating sounds made by the clash of weapons. Grindcore fans would say that this was exactly right.
queercore 1991	An aggressive kind of rock music derived from hardcore *punk* (see above), and characterized by lyrics focusing on homosexual issues. *Spin* magazine (1993, No. 48) tried to capture its pugnacious nature: 'fueled by the snotty, rebellious spirit of punk, queercore youth have punctured the stilted air of the "gay establishment" by exposing the clichés and stereotypes present within the gay and lesbian community'.

lo-fi 1993	A coinage based on *hi-fi* ('high-fidelity'), used contrastively in acoustics since the 1950s for sound reproduction that is less good in quality than hi-fi. *Rolling Stone* magazine (14 October 1993) summarized its adoption in rock music: 'minimal overdubs, CD-unfriendly sound and a general disdain for technical perfection'.
dad rock 1994	This chiefly British term (also *Dadrock*, *dad-rock*) is usually used in a mildly depreciative way by young people dismissive of the musical tastes of the older generation, especially when these reflect the original era of rock 'n' roll in the 1960s. The groups themselves seem to attract the label. U2, for example, are described as 'dad-rock dinosaurs' in a 1997 review.
nu metal 1995	This alternative spelling of *new* was first used (1892) to give an eyecatching appearance to the written form of US commercial brand-names, and it greatly influenced the British pop music scene in such expressions as *nu-disco*, *nu-soul*, *nu house*, and (for rock music) *nu metal*. The *OED* characterizes the latter by its 'staccato guitar riffs and typically combining elements of hip-hop (especially in vocal delivery) with heavy metal [see below] and industrial music'.

3 Heavy metal

heavy metal 1973	The 'metal' refers primarily to the materials from which guitar strings are made, such as stainless steel, or a steel core with a metallic wrapping such as nickel. The 'heaviness' resides in the use of considerable electronic amplification for the instruments accompanied by a powerful and usually fast drum beat. The adjectives in the *OED* definition capture its attributes: 'loud', 'vigorous', 'clashing', 'harsh', 'intense', 'spectacular'. Music journalists soon abbreviated it to *HM* (1974) and then (1984) *metal*.

3A Types of

thrash metal 1985	A style of heavy metal music which includes elements of punk rock (above), notable for its fast guitar riffs and strongly aggressive drumming (harking back to the earliest sense of *thrash* for beating corn). The 1980s also saw the name abbreviated to *thrash*.

4 Jamaican

bluebeat 1964	A chiefly British term derived from a brand-name, the *Blue Beat* record label, founded in 1960, which distributed music of Jamaican origin in Britain. The name reflects the main rhythmical characteristic of the music – a strongly accentuated offbeat.

ska 1964	The word is probably onomatopoeic, reflecting the distinctive rapid guitar and piano sounds used in the music. Judging by a Jamaican newspaper (*The Daily Gleaner*, 17 March 1964) it was there before its British equivalent: 'The "Ska" hits London – but they call it Blue Beat.'
rocksteady 1967	A development of *ska* (above), but (as its name suggests) using a slower and more even tempo. Alton Ellis's song 'Rock Steady' (1967) gave the new genre a focus.
reggae 1968	A further development of *ska* and *rocksteady* (above), which in the 1970s became a music of social protest, strongly associated with Jamaican identity, but internationally popular through the songs of Bob Marley. The dominance of the genre, as perceived by the world outside Jamaica, is evident from the succinct definition given by the *Daily Mail* (10 October 1969): 'Reggae, West Indian music'.
dub 1974	*Dubbing*, as an electronic technique, has been around since the 1930s, when a film was provided with an alternative soundtrack (the word is an abbreviation of *double*). Forty years later, we see it used in Jamaica for a piece of recorded music in which (as the *Oxford Times* put it, 13 January 1978) 'the recording is remixed with various electronic effects and alterations – reverberation, feedback, repetition – while keeping the existing bass line throughout'. It surfaces again in the early 2000s as *dubstep* (2002).
skank 1974	The etymology is unknown, though it is difficult to resist a link with *ska* (above). It is a type of reggae (above) supporting a dance style (*skanking*, 1976) in which 'the body bends forward at the waist, and the knees are raised and the hands claw the air in time to the beat' (*OED*).
roots reggae 1976	A type of *reggae* (above) where the song lyrics focus on social and spiritual themes, and hark back to the historical roots of the people in Africa. The links with Rastafarianism are crucial.
dance hall 1982	Another development from *reggae* (also known as *dancehall* or *dancehall reggae*), originating in the dance halls of Jamaica, in which a disc-jockey improvises lyrics over a recording. The often virtuoso performances are referred to as *toasts*, and the activity as *toasting*.

ragamuffin 1986	A fifteenth-century word of uncertain origin, with the first element probably related to *ragged* (in personal appearance) and the second possibly from a French source (one suggestion is *mal* + *felon*, 'scoundrel'); also spelled as *raggamuffin*, reflecting the spelling of the shortened form *ragga* (1990). In Jamaican English, *ragga ragga* is an adjective meaning 'ragged'. Musically, the genre derives from dance hall (above) with the addition of electronic instrumentation and the use of digital technology.
chutney 1989	A food associated with Indian cuisine (the word is from Hindi), which was adapted in Trinidad to describe a fusion of Caribbean rhythms and Indian folk music. The Trinidadian variety of calypso known as *soca* (a blend of *soul* + *calypso*) gave rise to the synonymous compound *chutney-soca*.
bashment 1996	The sense of *bash* 'party' (1948) presumably lies behind this usage, though the earlier (1805) sense of 'heavy blow' is surely involved, given the more aggressive sound and vocal delivery of this genre, a development of dance hall and ragga (above).

5 Other pop music

marabi 1933	A South African term, of uncertain origin (perhaps the name of a township, perhaps Sotho loanwords for 'fly around' or 'gangster'), used for the pop music associated with a working-class culture of the 1930s. A *Reader's Digest* article (1989) describes it as 'a throbbing blend of Christian spirituals, Negro rags, Boer *vastrap* [folk dance, from Dutch *vas* "firm" + *trap* "step"] . . . and traditional rural rhythms and harmonies'.
doo-wop 1958	A style of rhythm-and-blues music sung by vocal groups, originally from the USA, either a cappella or with little instrumental accompaniment. The name reflects the kind of nonsense phrase accompanying the vocal lead.
filk 1959	An unusual coinage, arising from a typographical error that became standard usage. The story goes that an essay by Lee Jacobs was submitted for publication in the 1950s with the title 'The Influence of Science Fiction on Modern American Filk Music'. The essay went unpublished because some of the lyrics it contained were obscene, but the publicity surrounding the case led to the typo gaining wide currency among science-fiction fans. Eventually it was adopted as a name for the kind of music performed at fan conventions, in which the lyrics of traditional songs are rewritten or parodied to reflect sci-fi themes. A new lexical family has emerged as a result (*filk-songs, filk-singing, filk-music*, and the verb *to filk*).

funk 1959	A general slang label for any pop music considered to be *funky* (*OED* originally 'down-to-earth, uncomplicated, emotional', and later 'in, swinging, fashionable'). The root has an unclear etymology, possibly a French dialect word for 'smoke' (hence applied to places where people experienced authentically 'earthy' smells, such as tobacco smoke). Francis Newton in *The Jazz Scene* (1959, ch. 6) is in no doubt, defining funky as 'smelly, i.e. symbolising the return from the upper atmosphere to physical, down-to-earth, reality'.
Liverpool sound 1963	The pop music that came out of Liverpool in the 1960s, associated chiefly with the Beatles. Journalists soon came up with alternative descriptions, such as *Mersey sound* and *Mersey beat* (also 1963) – Liverpool being on the River Mersey.
surf music 1963	A genre of pop music that originated in southern California, associated with surfing and surf culture. Songs typically used high vocal harmonies and contained lyrics about surfing.
malombo 1964	The word is from the South African language Venda, meaning 'spirit'. The drumming and singing that accompanied rites of exorcism and healing became the hallmark of a pop music group that called itself *Malombo*, fusing elements of jazz and African popular music.
mbaqanga 1964	A Zulu word for 'steamed maize bread', adopted by musicians in the townships of Johannesburg as the name for their individualistic fusion of jazz and traditional African styles.
easy listening 1965	A style of recorded music which, as the *OED* puts it, 'is popular without being loud, abrasive, or otherwise demanding'. William Safire was more caustic in a *New York Times* article (7 September 1986): 'the music of the 60's played in the 80's with the style of the 40's'.
Motown 1966	The word is short for *Motor Town*, the nickname of Detroit, a city known for its motor manufacturing. It became the proprietary name for records produced by the Motown record company (founded in 1959), and it was immediately used to describe the blend of soul and pop music performed by its black artists. A separate label, Tamla Records, was introduced at the same time, the name being an adaptation of *Tammy* (from the hit song by Debbie Reynolds in the 1957 film *Tammy*). The sound eventually came to be called *Tamla-Motown* (1968), or simply *Tamla* (1970).

power pop 1967	A genre characterized by, literally, *power*, in its earliest sense of 'strength' and 'energy', as reflected in the *OED* definition: 'loud volume, a strong melodic line with simple rhythms, heavy use of guitars and keyboards, and often sentimental or romantic lyrics'.
Tex-Mex 1968	An abbreviation of *Texan-Mexican*, also written lower-case as *tex-mex*. It refers to the fusion of folk and pop music produced by Mexican-American musicians in Texas, 'characterized by use of the accordion and guitar, and often incorporating elements of Czech and German dance music' (*OED*).
bubble-gum 1969	A dismissive label for any pop music of a bland or repetitive character (reflecting the automatic chewing behaviour associated with bubble-gum); also called *bubblegum pop*. A commercial genre marketed to appeal to teenagers and tweenagers, the name is often used dismissively by older people when talking about the musical tastes of the young.
world music 1969	A very loose generic term for – as a writer in *The Times* put it (24 October 1987) – 'popular music from all over the globe that doesn't already fall into an existing category'. The common feature is the inclusion of traditional folk elements belonging to particular ethnic groups, especially from the developing nations.
MOR 1970	The abbreviation of *middle-of-the-road*: any popular music that appeals to a wide audience, providing melody and harmony and avoiding harsh and aggressive sounds. The term is usually found in relation to the policy of commercial radio stations, where it is used for classical as well as popular music. Listeners who want more challenging styles of music tend to use it pejoratively.
post-rock 1971	A writer in the *Japan Times* (15 January 2003) neatly summed up the features of this reaction to traditional rock music: 'Post-rock's aim was a departure from rock's basic instincts, placing mood and texture over guitar hooks and shrill histrionics. This detour veered through jazz rhythms, ambient minimalism and world pop, often incorporating instruments not normally associated with rock.'
industrial 1972	A genre originating in the USA which incorporates electronic sounds resembling those produced by industrial tools and machinery. As a writer in the *New York Times* (16 August 1992) put it: 'industrial acts...manage to weld grinding, machinelike noises into a dance beat at factory-level decibels'.

Krautrock 1972	The derogatory name for German people (*Kraut*, from *sauerkraut*) received a more positive spin in the 1970s when it described various experimental styles of pop music coming out of Germany. In English, it usually lost its initial capital letter.
Afropop 1974	A very general term, referring to any style of pop music coming from an African country. The use of *Afro-* as a combining-form dates from the 1930s.
punk funk 1974	Another fusion, this time of *punk* and *funk* (above), and including a diverse range of musical styles. The words were sometimes reversed as *funk punk*, though whether this carried with it a semantic shift is one of those questions…
disco 1975	A short form of *disco music*, referring to the style of loud music, with a heavy bass beat, played in discothèques. The earliest *OED* citation for the full form is 1976, but it must have been around earlier, as suggested by *disco-beat* (1965) and *disco-sound* (1975).
P-funk 1975	*Funk* is understandable (see above). The question is: what does the *P* stand for? It could be the initial of one of the groups formed by US singer George Clinton that inspired the genre: *Parliament-Funkadelic*. Or, of the name of the band's hometown (*Plainfield*, New Jersey). Or, most likely, *p* for *pure*, judging by Clinton's words (in the album *Mothership Connection*), 'I want my funk uncut (make mine the P)'. *P* had for several years (at least since 1967) been a slang abbreviation for an illegal drug in its pure form. The name also appears as *P. funk*.
Europop 1976	A general label for the pop music played by groups from continental Europe, 'with simple, usually upbeat melodies and lyrics, often sung in English' (*OED*). Although it has had its hugely popular successes (notably, ABBA), the label is often used dismissively by people in Britain, as when they find little individuality in the entries for the Eurovision Song Contest.
mgqashiyo 1976	A South African genre of pop music featuring female close-harmony groups singing traditional or neo-traditional African songs. The word is from Zulu, meaning 'dance attractively or in a modern style'.
disco-funk 1977	Another fusion: of *funk* with the heavy beat of *disco* music (above). As with other combinations, the styles vary a great deal, from aggressively loud to (as the *Oxford Times*, 6 January 1984, put it, somewhat unexpectedly) 'relaxed'.

hard core 1977	'Any of various forms of popular music (often a variety of an established genre) regarded as particularly extreme, aggressive, or experimental' (*OED*). The term also appears as *hardcore*, and has taken on some of the nuances of other uses of this word (*hardcore pornography*, *hardcore terrorism*), especially in the way it reacts against anything perceived to be populist or mainstream.
alternative music 1978	As with *alternative rock* (above), a genre considered to be outside the main fashions in pop music. The risk, of course, is that after a while the unorthodox loses its novelty. A writer in *Music Week* (27 April 1996) comments on the US scene: 'so-called alternative music...is now the mainstream'.
punkabilly 1978	The continuing search for new genres brought this somewhat unexpected blend of *punk rock* and *rockabilly* (above). A further development was *psychobilly* (1978, a blend of *psycho(tic)* + *rockabilly*), where humorous or grotesque lyrics, often with taboo content, are added to an aggressive performance style.
R & B 1978	The abbreviation of *rhythm and blues* (also as *R and B*, and often without spaces, as *R&B*), but taken in a different musical direction from its use in the early jazz years (1920s on). The 1970s saw a new generation of African-American musicians introduce elements from several of the genres in this semantic field, such as funk and disco (above) and rap and hip-hop (below).
cowpunk 1979	This is a blend of *cowboy* and *punk*, a genre of pop music that combined elements of country-and-western singing with those of punk rock (above). The fusion evidently stretched lexical imaginations, for alongside *cowpunk* we find *techno-country*, *prairie modern*, and other labels. As a writer in the *New York Times* (10 June 1984) reluctantly concluded, 'no single term really describes the music of all these bands' – a complaint that could apply to most of the terms in this semantic field.
dangdut 1979	An Indonesian word, probably onomatopoeic, echoing the pulsing tabla drum beat heard in this music. Although long established in Indonesia, the modern style incorporates Arab and Malay folk elements as well as features of the contemporary international scene, such as synthesizers.
Northern Soul 1979	The 'north' here is the north of England, where there was a fashion in dance clubs to reprise US soul music of the 1960s, especially less-known recordings.

rap 1979	The original sense of *rap* ('blow', 'stroke') suggests an onomatopoeic origin (compare *tap* and *clap*). From the 1950s, it was being used in the USA as a colloquial description of any impressive verbal display, and in the 1980s it became hugely popular as a musical genre (*rap music*, 1981). The words transmuted into rhyming and often improvised lyrics, spoken in a rapid rhythm over a strong instrumental beat. The performance is *rapping* (also 1979).
hip-hop 1979	*Hip* (1904) and *hep* (1908) have long had an association with anything smart, stylish, and up-to-date, and this was probably where the first element of this name came from. The musical genre was defined rhythmically by US writer Steven Hager in his book *Hip Hop* (1984) as 'funky music suitable for rapping; a collective term used to describe rap/graffiti/breaking/scratchin'. The *hop* reflects the movements involved in the associated break-dancing. The resulting reduplication, reinforced by the short-vowel alternation (as in *tick-tock*, *flip-flop*, *wishy-washy* ...), gave the name an appealing ring, and fostered its popularity.
jit 1980	The name of a popular music style originating in Zimbabwe (the word is from the Shona language); also called *jit-jive*. It combines features of traditional African music with a fast dance rhythm (hence the *jive* element, borrowed from early jazz days) and a prominent electric guitar sound.
electro-pop 1980	Any kind of pop music that uses electronically generated sounds. Several versions exist, such as *electro-funk* (1982), *electro-beat* (1985), and *electro-house* (2004), with *electro-music* (1971) a superordinate term. After a while, people would just say *electro* (1983).
techno-pop 1980	As with *techno-rock* (above), any style of pop music which uses sounds generated or modified electronically, and relying greatly on synthesizers. The *techno-* could precede virtually anything, such as *techno-funk* (1990), *techno-house* (1991), and *techno-electro* (2004). It later appeared simply as *techno* (1988), the title of an album that described itself as 'the new dance sound of Detroit'.
trance 1980	Any style of pop music which uses rhythms and sounds that are intended to be hypnotic or trance-inducing. It has classical antecedents (in Steve Reich and Philip Glass).

post-punk
1981

A type of pop music that came after the main wave of *punk* rock (above), influenced by it and yet reacting against it. A music critic in the *New York Times* (22 March 1981) described it as being 'so much more varied and sophisticated, and so much less doctrinaire, than punk music'.

scratch
1982

A musical style, often used in *rap* music (above), in which a record is briefly interrupted while it is being played and manually rotated backwards and forwards to produce a rhythmical scratching effect (*scratch music*, 1983). The term also appears in expressions such as *rap and scratch* or *pop and scratch*.

synth-pop
1982

Synth is a colloquial abbreviation of *synthesizer*. The genre originated in Britain in the early 1980s, characterized by the heavy use of electronic instruments, especially synthesizers.

garage
1983

The original *garage* was Paradise Garage, a dance club in Manhattan, New York City, where the house music was 'influenced by soul, with powerful vocals and a strong emphasis on the lyrics' (*OED*). The groups that came to be called *garage bands* were characterized by an energetic vocal style that harked back to punk rock (*garage punk*, 1985; *garage rock*, 1990), and their music became widely known as, simply, *garage*. Sub-varieties soon emerged, such as *UK garage* (*UKG*) in the early 1990s. Pronunciation note: British *garage* rhymes with *ridge*, not *large*.

karaoke music
1983

A genre that originated in Japan (from *kara* 'empty, void' + *oke* (from English 'orchestra')) in which anyone with sufficient courage sings the words of a popular song to the accompaniment of a pre-recorded backing tape, the whole thing being electronically amplified to an audience; usually shortened to *karaoke*. As anyone who has attended a karaoke evening will readily testify, the quality ranges from the unexpectedly brilliant to the excruciatingly awful.

Latin
1983

This is short for *Latin America* not (regrettably) the Latin language. It is a very general term, including any popular music originating in the countries of Central and South America or those in the Caribbean which relate to that culture (such as Cuba).

Philly
1983

The nickname of *Philadelphia*, which gave its name to a type of soul music that began there, 'incorporating lush strings and horns over a strong smooth rhythm' (*OED*). Derived expressions include *Philly soul* and *Philly sound*.

New Age 1984	Any era of human history can attract this label (first recorded use is 1640), but in the 1970s it came to be associated with a popular alternative culture rejecting Western values and privileging concepts from astrology, ecology, and a range of spiritual movements. In *New Age music* (1985), the name is applied to any style influenced by these ideas, typically looking to 'develop a mood of relaxation in the listener by reproducing [I would add also "echoing"] sounds from the natural world, and by the use of light melodic harmonies and improvisation' (*OED*).
Britpop 1986	A blend of *British* + *popular*. It was a very broad label, referring to the wave of guitar-led pop groups that emerged in the UK during the late 1980s and early 1990s, drawing on specifically British influences, such as the Beatles.
house 1986	The origin is uncertain, but probably derives from the name of *The Warehouse*, a Chicago nightclub which played electronic dance music influenced by *funk* and *disco* (above), and 'typically featuring the use of drum machines, sequencers, sampled sound effects, and prominent synthesized bass lines, in combination with sparse, repetitive vocals and a fast beat'. This sounds precise enough, except that house music (1986) rapidly spread and generated a range of diverse styles, with such names as *deep house* (1988), *hip-house* (1988), *techno-house* (1991), and *acid house* (below), which (according to *Melody Maker*, 14 October 1989, referred to in the Introduction above) were 'enough to confuse even the most dedicated clubber'.
mbalax 1986	A word from the Wolof language ('rhythm'), naming a type of Senegalese popular music based on traditional drumming patterns. Bands use Western instruments alongside or instead of traditional drums (such as the tama).
rai 1986	A genre of Algerian popular music which combines Arabic folk elements with contemporary international styles. *People Weekly* (24 February 1986) called the sound 'space-age Arabic folk music'. The etymology is uncertain: Algerian French *raï*, possibly related to an Arabic word meaning 'opinion, view', as the lyrics often feature anti-establishment themes.
zouk 1986	A pop music genre from the French Antilles combining Caribbean and Western elements, with a strong fast beat derived from traditional drumming. The name is a local creole word meaning 'party'.

bhangra 1987	The name is from Panjabi, referring to a traditional folk-dance of the Punjab. It developed as a genre of pop music among the Asian community in Britain, 'a mix of traditional Asian musics, disco and rock' (as *New Musical Express* described it, 5 September 1987).
dance music 1987	Nothing new about the term, which dates from at least 1861 in its general sense of 'music to dance to'; but in the 1980s it was appropriated in popular culture to refer to a genre 'largely or wholly synthesized, has a repetitive beat, few or no lyrics, and frequently incorporates sound samples' (*OED*). 'The beat goes *boom, boom, boom, boom*, with no real melody line and no relief', said a reviewer in the *Chicago Tribune* (4 March 1987). When shortened to *dance* (1988) the meaning can be opaque to those not in the know.
old school 1987	Any style of popular music regarded as traditional and old-fashioned has been called *old school* (also spelled, subversively, *old skool*). A writer in 1993 calls hiphop 'old school' compared with gangsta (below). Years pass quickly in pop music onomastics.
acid house 1988	*Acid* surfaced in the 1960s as a genre name (*acid rock*, above), and resurfaced in the 1980s for a new style originating in Chicago, characterized by 'a fast beat, a spare, hypnotic, synthesized sound, and a distinctive gurgling bass noise' (*OED*) – 'fantastic squelchy noises which sounded great over a dance beat', as a writer in the *Daily Telegraph* (23 October 2003) put it. Aficionados talk simply of *acid* (1988).
Cantopop 1988	A blend of *Cantonese* and *popular*, written variously (*Canto Pop, cantopop*). The genre originated in Hong Kong, combining Western styles with Cantonese lyrics.
swingbeat 1988	The *OED* definition is a very clear illustration of the hybridity characteristic of this semantic field: 'a form of dance music combining elements of rhythm and blues, soul, hip-hop, and rap music'.
dream pop 1989	A genre of popular music notable for its quiet or breathy vocals and the creation of an ethereal atmosphere. I love the *Buffalo News* description the *OED* lexicographers unearthed (23 August 1992): 'a kind of hazy, hallucinatory music, sort of "Sgt. Pepper" meets the Grateful Dead'.
gangsta rap 1989	A style of *rap* music (above), originating in Los Angeles, 'featuring aggressive and confrontational lyrics centring on the violence of gang culture' (*OED*). The non-standard spelling is an attempt to capture local African-American pronunciation. It soon (1991) shortened to *gangsta*.

J-pop 1989	The *J* is for *Japanese*, and the name is often capitalized throughout (*J-Pop, J-POP*). The term became popular in the 1990s when Japanese journalists began distinguishing popular music from within Japan from that originating elsewhere.
multiculti 1989	A playful rhyming adaptation of *multicultural*, used colloquially in all sorts of multicultural contexts. In the present semantic field, it applies to any style that incorporates musical elements from different cultural backgrounds.
new jack swing 1989	In US slang, a *new jack* is a newcomer, especially to a street gang – the name *Jack* being a long-established (1889) way of addressing a man you don't know. The *New York Times* (24 November 1991) summed up the music genre with a reference to 'Teddy Riley, the architect of new jack swing, which attaches lover-boy crooning to the choppy, electronic beat of hip-hop'. It was soon shortened to *new jack* (1990). When performed by women, the ancient nursery rhyme was remembered in the name *new jill swing* (1990), or simply *new jill*.
noise-pop 1989	A harking back to *noise-rock* (above), but this time with the loud and distorted sound effects (*noise*) combined with a strong emphasis on melody.
Tejano 1989	An American-Spanish name for someone from Texas with a Mexican ethnic background. The musical genre harks back to *Tex-Mex* (above), with which it's often identified, though distinguished to the extent that artists of the 1990s incorporated elements of styles that were not around in the 1960s.
breakbeat 1990	A genre of popular music that takes its name from a syncopated drumming style (as opposed to the regular four-four beat of much dance music). *Time Out* (25 April 2002) memorably described the style as 'sampladelic' – a blend of *sample* ('record sound digitally for subsequent electronic processing') and *psychedelic*.
chill-out music 1990	Any style of popular music that promotes a relaxed mood, usually heard in a setting which is comfortable and quiet. A writer in the *Daily Telegraph* (12 September 1992) opined that 'it has never been more fashionable to sound as though you are heavily sedated'.
indie 1990	The usual abbreviation for *independent*, here referring to any popular music (*indie music*, 1989) produced by independent record labels.

noisecore 1990	A further development of the *noise* and *core* motifs (above). *Time Out* (2 January 2002) describes: 'Martial beats and scouring layers of feedback duke it out with melodic basslines and incisive lead guitar.'
ambience 1991	The notion of *ambient music* dates from the 1970s, referring to any style (such as Brian Eno's *Music for Airports*) that avoids the persistent beat typical of modern pop music and creates a mood of relaxation or contemplation. Alongside *ambience*, hybrids soon emerged, reflected in such names (see above) as *ambient house* (1989), *ambient rap* (1991), *ambient techno* (1994), and *ambient dub* (1995), as well as *ambient* as a solo noun (1993).
baggy 1991	*Baggy* as a noun usually (since the 1960s) refers to loose-fitting shorts, later extended to loose-fitting trousers and other casual clothing. It had a vogue in British pop music in the 1990s 'combining the guitar-based melodies of indie pop with the dance rhythms of Acid House and related genres' (*OED*).
handbag house 1991	Yet another electronic variation on the *house* motif (above). Apparently the name started out as a disparaging description of women dancing with their handbags at their feet, but then ameliorated as the music's 'highly commercial appeal, catchy melodies, and upbeat mood' (*OED*) caught on.
loungecore 1991	A blend of *lounge music* and *hardcore* (above). Given that lounge music – played in a bar, cocktail lounge, and the like – was typically softly melodious and unobtrusive, the combination with elements of hardcore (the total opposite) resulted in one of the most unexpected collocations of this semantic field.
psychedelic trance 1991	A genre of pop music using synthesizers and psychedelic effects, to produce – as a review in an Edinburgh university student newspaper put it (1999) – 'a more transcendental and spiritual kind of music than the average four to the floor'.
shoegazing 1991	'They stare at their feet as they play', said a *Daily Telegraph* reviewer (11 November 1991), referring to a British pop music style where the performers behaved introspectively, standing still and not looking at or confronting the audience in the aggressive manner used by many other groups. The various guitar effects, operated by foot-pedals, reinforced the impression of 'shoe-gazing'.

slowcore 1991	A genre of pop music characterized by 'slow tempos, a sombre, atmospheric, sometimes densely textured sound, and quiet, forlorn vocals' (*OED*). The gloomy lyrical content rather than the acoustic effects led to the synonymous *sadcore*. Descriptions vary and are usually creative, such as 'dirge-disco' and 'chic bored hush-hush'. 'The best thing about slowcore bands', said *SF Weekly* (6 May 1998) 'is that they demand the listener pay attention, The worst thing about them is that sometimes you fall asleep by the third song.'
rave 1992	Those who first used this word in the sixteenth century (for the roaring of the wind) could never have anticipated the way it would develop in the 1960s for a wild 3-D (dance, drink, drugs) party. When held on a large scale, often outdoors, the kind of electronic dance music being played soon took over the label.
jungle 1992	Musical effects echoing jungle sounds have long (since the 1930s) been known in jazz music. The pop music usage seems to be different, though people debate the term's origins. Some ascribe it to the distinctive rhythmical drumming (compare: *jungle drums*); others to the urban focus of the lyrics (compare: *urban jungle*); others to the nickname ('The Jungle') of the Tivoli Gardens in Kingston, Jamaica. The combination of a fast drum track and a heavy, usually slower bass track led to an alternative name, *drum and bass* (1992).
electronica 1993	A general name for electronic music derived from *techno* and *rave* (above), but with a more esoteric or ethereal quality. It is, as a writer in the *Independent* put it (31 November 1993) 'as spooky as it gets'.
trip hop 1994	This is *trip* in the sense of a hallucinatory experience. A slow *hip-hop* (above) tempo is combined with more melodic and psychedelic sounds, with less confrontational lyrics.
nu skool 1997	The converse of *old skool* (see *old school* above), and usually spelled in a similarly subversive way. Virtually anything can be called *nu skool*, as long as a contemporary musical element is incorporated into an established genre.
grime 2003	A genre of pop music that began in east London, 'influenced by UK garage, dancehall, and hip-hop, and typically characterized by a minimal, prominent rhythm, a very low-pitched bassline, and vocals by an MC' (*OED*). *Big Issue* (3 January 2005) observed: 'Grime has reinvented UK urban music in under 12 months.' And there, in a nutshell, is the problem facing the lexicographer of this semantic field.

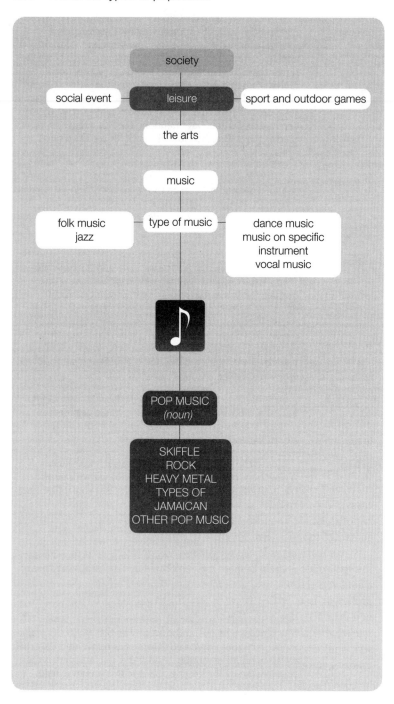

15

From *astronaut* to *Skylab*

WORDS FOR SPACECRAFT

This subject didn't exist 150 years ago, except in the minds of some writers of fiction. And now we have a thesaurus category which, though very limited in the number of items it contains, already has a dozen subcategories, with more in the offing. The interest lies not so much in the vocabulary, which is actually rather pedestrian, but in the insight we obtain into the early stages of development of a semantic field.

The field has actually come from a conflation of two sources: science fiction and astronautics. Several of the terms in the list below were first used by sci-fi novelists and short-story writers, such as *astronaut* (in the spacecraft sense), *spaceship, liner, space flyer, shuttle ship, moon-ship,* and *star-ship.* As repeated use of *ship* illustrates, the chief motivation has been to take words already being used in traditional fields of transport (such as *craft, shuttle, ferry, buggy, fleet*) and adapt them to their new setting. A few words, such as *capsule* and *module,* have transferred from other subjects. There are hardly any loanwords (*lunik* and *sputnik* are the only cases), reflecting the development of space technology by just two nations, the USA and Russia. The lexicon clearly reflects the 'space race' climate of the 1950s and 1960s.

By comparison with the other semantic fields illustrated in this book, the spacecraft domain is singularly unimaginative. If a vehicle lands, it is a *lander*; if it orbits, it is an *orbiter*; if it flies by a planet, it is a *fly-by*; if it probes, it is a *probe.* There is no difference between the fiction and non-fiction worlds here. The only sign of a metaphorical spirit is in *flying saucer,* which was chiefly a media creation out of the various vague descriptions circulating when UFOs were first being discussed. *UFO* itself is unusual, in that the acronym has given rise to a family of related expressions. The English-language media also had some creative linguistic fun with the Russian words, part of a veritable explosion of -*nik* coinages in the second half of the twentieth century. But apart from these, and the short-lived *satelloon*, the linguistic domain of spacecraft shows little of the inventive and playful spirit that characterizes the English lexicon as a whole.

However, it is early days, as the subcategories below suggest: only a few have more than one or two entries. The expectation must be that these will 'fill out' as space technology and exploration proceeds. We are bound to see more types of lifting body, buggy, satellite, and simulator – the latter is already developing fresh applications in the world of computer games, and new collocations here will eventually produce new compounds (as has already happened with types of satellite). There will also be some reassignment of entries among the subcategories, as technological distinctions evolve. We must also expect further blends of the *Spacelab* and *Skylab* type, especially in fiction. Perhaps one day we will see this semantic field boldly going where no other has gone before.

Timeline

Spacecraft in general	
astronaut † 1880	Long before an astronaut became a person (earliest *OED* citation, 1928) Percy Greg in *Across the Zodiac* (1880, ch. 2) has his narrator build a spaceship to visit Mars: 'In shape my astronaut somewhat resembled the form of an antique Dutch East-Indiaman.' The collocations today seem very strange: 'I entered the Astronaut on the 1st August'; 'the first beams of dawn light shone upward on the ceiling of the Astronaut' (ch. 4).
spaceship 1880	The science-fiction readership at the close of the nineteenth century avidly took up the notion of a manned spacecraft. Various fictional notions were being explored, such as Jules Verne's cannon (in *From the Earth to the Moon*, 1865) and H. G. Wells's sphere (in *The First Men in the Moon*, 1901), but *ship* had long been applied to flying vessels, such as navigable balloons (1679), so it soon became the term of choice for a fictional space vehicle.
liner † 1905	Towards the end of the eighteenth century, a regular series of public conveyances (coaches, ships) plying between places came to be called a *line* (as in the 'Cunard Line'), and the ships themselves *liners* (1838). In one of the short stories in Rudyard Kipling's *Actions and Reactions* (1909) a *planet liner* rescues the crew of a damaged freighter. The story is called 'With the Night Mail', and is subtitled 'A Story of 2000 AD'. It reads like an episode of *Star Wars*.

space flyer † 1911	An alternative way of describing a spacecraft, which fell out of use because of its ambiguity: it could also describe the person inside the spacecraft. In the February 1931 edition of *Wonder Stories* (strapline: 'the magazine of prophetic fiction') two people are described as 'old and seasoned space-fliers'.
rocket ship 1925	A *rocket ship* was, originally and literally, a ship armed with rockets (1809). During the 1920s, the term began to be used in discussing possible future spacecraft, and was soon taken up by science-fiction writers. But the 'real world' continued to use it: a *Daily Telegraph* report (15 April 1981) described the first space-shuttle flight as 'the maiden flight of the first re-usable rocketship'.
spacecraft 1929	The term of choice by scientists and technologists when discussing vehicles designed to travel through space. On the whole, *spaceships* are fiction, *spacecraft* (sometimes pluralized as *spacecrafts*) and *space vehicles* (1930) are non-fiction.
ship 1930	The origins of the use of *ship* for aircraft are nicely shown in the first *OED* citation, from the title of one of the collections of papers that Robert Hooke made for the newly founded Royal Society (1679): 'A Demonstration, how it is practically possible to make a Ship, which shall be sustained by the Air, and may be moved either by Sails or Oars'. Fuller expressions such as *flying ship*, *aerial ship*, and *aerostatic ship* followed, with *ship* emerging once again in the twentieth century, at first for aircraft, then for spacecraft.
spacer 1942	An alternative term for either *spaceman* or *spacecraft*, popular among science-fiction writers, but less used today as other meanings of *spacer* have developed (such as in building and medicine).

1 Quality of

space worthiness 1934	The analogy is with *seaworthiness* and *airworthiness*. The term began in science fiction, but by the 1960s had transferred to astronautics, though there is no clear dividing line. 'The Mark II had just received its spaceworthiness certificate from NASA' sounds like fact, but is in fact from John Varley's novel *Red Thunder* (2003).

2 Which can land on a planet

lander 1961	We might expect 'someone/something that lands' to have a history as old as the fourteenth-century verb from which it derives; but there are no *OED* citations before the mid-nineteenth century, when we see it used in the argot of mining. It received a new lease of life in the 1960s when moon landings (and later planetary landings) became a reality.

soft-lander
1961

The distinction between a 'hard' and a 'soft' landing became critical in the 1960s: the various probes and vehicles needed to land slowly without causing serious damage. There is ongoing uncertainty about its spelling: all three possibilities are found – *soft-lander*, *soft lander*, and *softlander*.

3 Which can make repeated journeys

shuttle rocket
1953

The concept of passing to and fro has a long history, starting with weaving in the fourteenth century and proceeding through several types of mechanical equipment until we reach the transport applications with trains (1888), cars (1905), buses (1951), aircraft (1944), and spacecraft. There is just one *OED* citation for *shuttle rocket*. It was soon replaced by *space shuttle* (below).

spaceplane
1957

An article in the *New York Times* magazine (29 January 1978) provides a useful definition: 'designed to take off like a rocket, fly in orbit like a spacecraft, and return to a runway landing like a glider'.

shuttle ship
1959

Another science-fiction usage, here recorded in an issue of the magazine *Amazing Stories* (June): 'Hubbard visited the spaceport...and watched the shuttle-ships come and go.' The usage seems not to have proved popular, for this is the only *OED* citation.

shuttle
1960

A space rocket with wings, enabling it to land like an aircraft and thus be used repeatedly. *Space shuttle* is first recorded in science fiction (1950), and there was evidently some uncertainty when it was first used in a factual domain. The *New Scientist* (5 June 1969) put inverted commas around it when talking about the planned space station: 'NASA has announced the formation of task groups to look into...a re-usable low-cost "Space Shuttle" to relay men and materials to and from the station.' But the scare-quotes were soon dropped, and the expression shortened to *shuttle* as familiarity with the technology grew.

4 To go to the moon

moon-ship
1931

Science fiction first talked of *moon-ships*, and it was picked up by journalists when real moon exploration became a reality. The *Wall Street Journal* (19 August 1963) reported a contract to build an 'Apollo Moonship'.

lunik 1959	The Russian name for their moon rocket, from *luna* 'moon' plus the suffix *-nik* (as in *sputnik* below). The usage generated several humorous formations in the English-language press whenever a device failed to get into orbit, such as *kaputnik, flopnik*, and *stayputnik*.
mooncraft 1962	The term has a double application: some writers use it for a spacecraft bound for the moon; some for the vehicle which traverses the surface of the moon (a *moon buggy* or *moon rover*). These usages were popular when the moon landings were taking place in the 1970s, but are only occasionally heard now. If/when fresh moon missions materialize, they will receive a new lease of life.

5 Laboratories and observatories

space observatory 1952	An astronomical observatory in space, usually one remotely controlled in earth orbit. The expression is often shortened to *observatory*, as long as there is no chance of confusion with the terrestrial counterpart.
probe 1953	A small unmanned exploratory spacecraft which can transmit information about its environment. The term came into use at the same time as *space probe* and *moon probe* (both first recorded in 1958, but probably around several years earlier).
space laboratory 1954	A remotely controlled vehicle in earth orbit equipped as a laboratory. The term has a potential ambiguity, as it could also refer to a terrestrial laboratory that specializes in space research – as in the Mullard Space Laboratory at University College London. The abbreviated form, *space lab* (1955), is less likely to confuse, thanks to *Spacelab*, the name of the device carried into earth orbit by the space shuttle in the 1980s and 1990s. *Skylab* (1970) continued the lexical pattern.
fly-by 1960	A *fly-by* originally (1953) was the American equivalent of what in Britain would be called a *fly-past*, when an event is celebrated by a procession of aircraft overhead. Because of US dominance in space exploration, it was the American term that came to describe a spacecraft making a close approach to a celestial body for the purpose of observation.

6 Spacecraft of specific shape

| **lifting body** 1964 | A wingless spacecraft with a shape designed to produce lift, so that some aerodynamic control of its flight is possible within the atmosphere. The contrast is with aircraft where the lift is obtained from the wings. Although this is the only entry in this subcategory at present, it is probably only a matter of time before technological developments add further lexical items. |

7 Module or capsule

ferry
1951

One of the oldest words to transfer to space exploration, from the conveyance which enables people to cross a waterway (1490) to aircraft (1917) to spacecraft (1951). A *ferry rocket* or *landing ferry* is a module which can be separated from the main spacecraft to allow descent onto the surface of a celestial body.

capsule
1954

Capsule has always had the meaning of a small container of some kind, whether in physiology (1693), botany (1693), medicine (1875), or – now, along with *space capsule* (1954) – astronautics. Here it refers to a small spacecraft, or the detachable part of a larger spacecraft, which can carry astronauts or research instruments on a space flight.

module
1961

This technical way of describing a self-contained component of a larger or more complex system has proved itself in a wide range of fields, such as computing (1963), education (1966), and role-playing games (1979). Astronautics presents a goodly array of modules, but the most famous were undoubtedly the two that received huge publicity during the Apollo moon landings: the *command module* (below) and the *lunar excursion module* – a form that cried out for early abbreviation, and received it in the initialism *Lem* (1962).

moonbug
1963

A colloquial name for the lunar excursion module (above). It needs to be kept distinct from the later (1970) *moon buggy*, which was a small vehicle designed for use on the moon. An early (1971) newspaper account described the first one to be designed as 'a space-craft with wire wheels, telescoping fenders, and chair-like seats'.

landing craft
1969

This term became widely known during the Second World War, describing the shallow-draught naval vessel used to land troops in an amphibious assault. When it transferred to astronautics, it named the section of a spacecraft which made the final descent to the surface of the moon (and later, of any planet).

7A Command module or mother ship

command module
1962

The compartment in a spacecraft containing the personnel and the main controls. Once the descent module (see above) has been jettisoned, what is left is the *command service module* (1969) – the combination of the command module with the module that contains the main engine and other supporting equipment, enabling midcourse corrections, lunar take-off, and thrust to return to Earth orbit.

mother ship 1969	Originally (1890) a nautical term for a ship that escorts or has charge of several other craft. In space exploration, it refers to the spacecraft from which other craft are launched or controlled. The term has proved invaluable to science-fiction writers portraying fleets of alien spacecraft, with the most famous of all movie mother ships appearing at the end of *Close Encounters of the Third Kind* (1977).

8 Satellite

space station 1930	A large artificial satellite intended as a long-term base for astronaut operations. The first recorded reference (1929) actually calls it a 'spatial station', but the present-day term quickly replaced it – as it did *satellite station* (1945), which had a short-lived presence during the 1950s. However, *space platform* (1951) continues to be used, especially when a space station is seen more as a launching point for further exploration.
satellite 1936	The original (1665) meaning of a secondary planet revolving around a larger one easily transferred to the case of a man-made object placed in orbit around the Earth. Today, the term has generated a semantic field of its own, reflecting the various functions such devices perform (see below). The increased awareness of the existence of natural satellites around other planets was probably the motivation for the more explicit phrase *earth satellite* (1949). Similarly, the growth in other contexts for the word *satellite* (such as politics, town planning, anatomy, and computing) motivated the more explicit *space satellite* (1952).
satelloid 1955	The -*oid* suffix has the meaning 'something having the form or appearance of; something related or allied in structure, but not identical', as in *factoid*, *ellipsoid*, and several other scientific terms. What makes a satelloid 'not identical' is that it is a low-altitude satellite that uses an engine to provide the thrust it needs to maintain its orbit.
sputnik 1957	With a capital *S*, this was the first artificial satellite, launched by Russia on 4 October 1957; the name means 'fellow-traveller'. With a lower-case initial, the term was generalized to any unmanned satellite during the 1960s and 1970s, becoming progressively less used as the huge increase in satellites from other nations made the Russian name otiose.
orbiter 1958	A spacecraft that is designed to go into orbit around a celestial body, usually without any intention that it should land. The contrast with *lander* (above) is made clear in a *Daily Telegraph* article (12 November 1971): 'While the Viking orbiter continues to survey Mars from space, the lander will start a robot examination of its surroundings.'

8A Space station used for specific purposes

biosatellite 1957	A satellite that contains living organisms for experimental purposes. The inverted commas captured the novelty of the term when it was first used, as in this report from a Californian newspaper, *The Daily Review* (11 October 1957): 'the Soviet Union shortly will launch a "biosatellite" carrying animals into space'.
communications satellite 1957	A satellite used for telecommunications. The term has led to several new collocations as different types and functions have evolved, such as *geostationary, low-earth-orbiting, broadcasting,* and *reconnaissance satellites,* as well as terrestrial terms such as *satellite radio* and *television.*
balloon satellite 1958	A satellite where the name defines the shape, not the function – resembling a balloon, having been inflated with gas after being placed in orbit. For a while, the media invented a new blend, calling them *satelloons.*
navigation satellite 1960	A satellite that transmits signals for use in navigation. The concept has generated its own set of abbreviations, such as *satnav* ('satellite navigation'), *GNSS* ('global navigation satellite system'), and *GPS* ('global positioning system'). Most remain initialisms, such as *QZSS* ('Quazi-Zenith Satellite System'), but a few end up as pronounceable mnemonics, such as *DORIS* ('Doppler Orbitography and Radio-positioning Integrated by Satellite').
weather satellite 1960	A satellite that observes weather conditions and provides meteorological information. The new collocation here is *polar-orbiting,* along with *geostationary* (see above).

9 Space simulator

space simulator 1956	A training device that replicates the conditions found during space travel, and the interior and behaviour of a spacecraft; also called a *space flight simulator.* The term has broadened considerably in recent years, now including the various simulations of the universe and of space travel (real or fictitious) available for download onto computers or smartphones. The Microsoft Space Simulator (1994) was one of the first, allowing users to visit existing locations (such as the Kennedy Space Center) or futuristic ones (such as the Marineris Base on Mars – a name derived from the *Mariner* spacecraft that observed the planet during the 1960s/70s).

10 Fictional spacecraft	
cruiser 1923	The notion of cruising always suggests a movement to and fro, without having a single destination in mind. The word is related to *cross*, but the *ui* spelling points to the influence of Dutch. Today, the usual association is with pleasure, but in science fiction there can be a more serious intent. In a story in *Best SF* (1958), 'The cruisers carried the colonists to their new worlds.'
star-ship 1934	There was a time when this word largely replaced *spaceship* in the minds of science-fiction television viewers, thanks to the great success of *Star Trek*: 'Captain James Kirk of the star-ship *Enterprise*' (1966). All three written forms – *star-ship*, *star ship*, and *starship* – have been used, but the overwhelming preference today is for *starship*.

10A Fleet of	
space fleet 1931	The term is primarily found in science fiction; but in the political and business worlds the notion is not as far-fetched as it might seem. An article (17 July 2007) in the aerospace industry periodical *Space Daily* (strapline: 'your portal to space') affirms that 'Visionary business leaders...have already begun building space fleets', seeing the commercial potential of space flight on a grand scale.

11 Flying saucer or UFO	
flying saucer 1947	The nickname given to the various unidentified disc-shaped objects that people saw (or thought they saw) in the sky. The term vied with several other descriptions (especially *flying disc*) before the media settled on this one. The shortened version, *saucer* (1947), was also common in press coverage.
unidentified flying object 1950	Once the military began to take the prospect of alien spacecraft seriously, it distanced itself from the popular media by using this more serious-sounding descriptor. Sometimes the *flying* was dropped, when the context allowed it, but the expression as a whole gained ground, and within a few years had been institutionalized in the form of an acronym: *UFO* (1953). Edward J. Ruppelt, the director of a US government project investigating these phenomena, explained (in a 1956 report) how the military preferred the less colourful name because they thought *saucer* was 'misleading when applied to objects of every conceivable shape and performance'.

11A Study of

ufology
1959

An unusual coinage, for acronyms do not usually act as a base for other words. But this one has also led to *ufological*, as well as *ufologist* (below), and the lexicon continues to grow. *Ufologic* appears in the name of a UFO club in Ukraine.

11B Believer in

ufologist
1963

Ufologist has itself become a base for other words, though (as with *ufologic* above) none have yet achieved much use beyond their coining country. We find both *ufologistic* and *ufologistical* (the latter in the name of a Belarussian UFO club), and some enthusiasts already talk of a putative science of *ufologistics*.

12 Takes off and lands like aeroplane

aerospace plane
1962

The category heading is in effect the definition. There is clearly an overlap of usage with the *spaceplane* assigned to category 3 above.

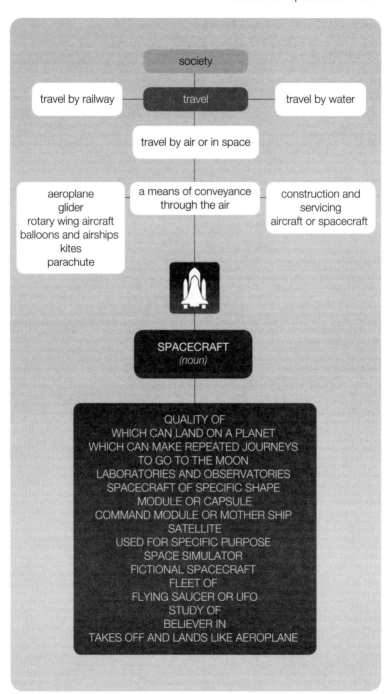

Glossary

alliteration A sequence of words (or stressed syllables within words) beginning with the same sound (e.g. *lolly* at 11: 1943).

amelioration A change of meaning in which a word loses an earlier unpleasant sense (e.g. *old thing* at 7: 1625).

blend A word made by merging parts of two separate words (e.g. *motel* at 9: 1925).

borrowing *see* **loanword**

cant Special vocabulary used by a secretive social group to protect its members from outside interference (e.g. shells at 11: 1591).

coinage *see* **neologism**

collocation The habitual co-occurrence of individual words (e.g. *rich cuff* at 13: 1616 [2]).

comparative A grammatical form used to make a comparison (e.g. *older* at 13: 1450 [1]).

diminutive The form of a word that expresses the notion of 'little', often used as a form of endearment (e.g. *goosey* at 6: 1852).

English The following distinctions are made:

Old English from the seventh to the eleventh century.

Middle English from the eleventh to the fourteenth century.

Early Modern English from the fourteenth to the eighteenth century.

Modern English from the eighteenth century to the present day.

etymology The study of the origins and history of the form and meaning of words.

euphemism The use of a vague or indirect expression in place of one which is thought to be unpleasant, embarrassing, or offensive (e.g. *darn* at 8: 1781 [5]).

intransitive verb A verb that does not take a direct object (e.g. the listing in Chapter 1).

lexical field *see* **semantic field**

lexicography The art and science of dictionary-making.

lexicology The study of the vocabulary (*lexicon*) of a language.

loanword or **borrowing** The introduction of a word from one language or dialect into another (e.g. *meson* at 9: 1817).

syllables in words The following distinctions are made:

monosyllable a word consisting of a single syllable (e.g. *nod* at 6: 1563).

disyllable a word consisting of two syllables (e.g. Chapter 1: Introduction).

trisyllable a word consisting of three syllables (e.g. Chapter 1: Introduction).

neologism or **coinage** The creation of a new word, as a response to changed circumstances in the external world, which achieves some currency within a speech community (e.g. *kennel-nymph* at 10: 1771).

onomastics A branch of semantics which studies the etymology of proper names.

onomatopoeia or **sound symbolism** A direct association between sounds in speech and sounds in the external world.

phonetics The study of human sound-making, transmission, and reception.

plosive A consonant sound made when a complete closure in the vocal tract is suddenly released (e.g. *rugged* at 12: 1549[1]).

semantic field or **lexical field** A network of semantically related items (illustrated by the different chapters in this book).

semantics The study of meaning in language.

sociolinguistics A branch of linguistics which studies the way language is integrated with human society.

sound symbolism *see* **onomatopoeia**

superordinate A higher level of classification in a taxonomy; opposed to **subordinate**.

synecdoche A figure of speech in which the part is used for the whole or the whole is used for the part (e.g. *tail* at 10: 1846).

taxonomy A system of hierarchical classification.

transitive verb A verb which takes a direct object (e.g. *knock off* at 1: 1657).

Further reading and sources

Coleman, Julie. 1999. *Love, Sex, and Marriage: A Historical Thesaurus*. Amsterdam: Rodopi.

Crystal, David. 2003. *The Cambridge Encyclopedia of the English Language*, 2nd edn. Cambridge: Cambridge University Press.

Durkin, Philip. 2009. *The Oxford Guide to Etymology*. Oxford: Oxford University Press.

HTOED online. <http://public.oed.com/historical-thesaurus-of-the-oed> and <http://historicalthesaurus.arts.gla.ac.uk/webtheshtml/homepage.html>.

Hüllen, Werner. 1999. *English Dictionaries, 800–1700: The Topical Tradition*. Oxford: Oxford University Press.

Kay, Christian, Jane Roberts, Michael Samuels, and Irené Wotherspoon. 2009. *Historical Thesaurus of the Oxford English Dictionary*. Oxford: Oxford University Press.

Kay, Christian, and Jeremy J. Smith (eds.). 2004. *Categorization in the History of English*. Amsterdam: Benjamins.

Partridge, Eric. 1984. *A Dictionary of Slang and Unconventional English*, 8th edn., ed. Paul Beale. London: Routledge.

Roberts, Jane, and Christian Kay with Lynne Grundy. 2000. *A Thesaurus of Old English*, 2nd edn. Amsterdam: Rodopi.

Samuels, Michael. 1972. *Linguistic Evolution*. Cambridge: Cambridge University Press.

Wright, Joseph. 1898–1905. *The English Dialect Dictionary*, 6 vols. London: Henry Frowde.

Chronological indexes

As with any thesaurus (see General Introduction), an alphabetical index, organized letter by letter, is an essential aid to quickly finding the location of a word or phrase. To facilitate this process in the present book, the indexes reflect the book's ethos, and are chronological in character, referring to chapters and dates rather than pages: *2: 1300* refers to the entry for the year 1300 in Chapter 2. In chapters where there is more than one chronological listing, reflecting the presence of numbered subcategories, the number of the relevant subcategory is given after the year: *11: 1957 [3]* refers to the entry found in Chapter 11, year 1957 in section 3. *Introduction* refers to the opening essay in this book. *I* refers to the introductory essay in each chapter, preceded by the chapter number: *9: I* refers to the introduction to Chapter 9.

Multi-word items are indexed under their content words: *yield up the soul* will be found under both *yield* and *soul*, and *space platform* under both *space* and *platform*. Grammatical words are ignored in the alphabetical listing: *by jingo* will be found only under *jingo*. Words appearing in citations or *OED* definitions are not indexed, nor is the repeated use of a word if it is mentioned in a chapter introduction.

Chronological index of words

abracadabra 8: 1694
absolutely 3: 1982
account, final/last; go to/make
    one's 1: 1817
accounts, hand in one's 1: 1817
acid (house) 14: 1988 [5]
acid (rock) 14: 1966 [2A]
ackers 11: 1939
acushla 7: 1825
Adcock 6: 1577
adead 1: OE
aerial/aerostatic ship 15: 1930
Afro(pop) 14: 1974 [5]
Age, New 14: 1984 [5]
aged 13: 1386 [3]
ageman/AgeMan 13: 1571 [2]
aggro 2: 1899
airworthiness 15: 1934 [1]
alanna 7: 1825
albergo 9: 1617 [1]
album-oriented rock 14: 1977 [2A]
alcohol, under the influence of 3:
    1879
alive, Jack's 11: 1890
aloft, go 1: 1390
alternative music 14: 1978 [5]
alternative rock 14: 1975 [2A]
ambience/ambient (dub/house/
    rap/techno) 14: 1991 [5]
ancient 13: 1502 [1], 13: 1386 [3]
Ancient of Days, the 13: 1937 [1]
anders-meat 4: 1598 [2]
andren 4: 1691 [2]
antediluvian 13: 1684 [1]
antiquary 13: 1571 [2]
AOR 14: 1977 [2A]
ape-drunk 3: 1592

aplight 8: 1297 [1]
appetite, whet the 4: 1688 [2]
April Gouk 6: 1605
argent 11: 1500
arse 3: 1984
artful 13: 1924 [3]
ass 6: 1578, 6: 1901
ass, as lumpy as an 3: 1810
ass, don't give a rat's 3: 1984
assessment 8: 1859 [4]
astronaut 15: 1880
aswelt 1: OE
auberge 9: 1615 [1], 9: 1617 [1]
aunt 10: 1663, 13: 1580 [3]
Aunt Edna/Emma/Fanny/Sally 10:
    1663
autotel 9: 1925 [2]

bach 7: 1889
back, cut in the 3: 1673
backhouse 5: 1819 [1]
backside 5: 1704 [1]
bad cess to 8: 1859 [4]
bag(gage) 13: 1924 [3]
bagging (-can/-time) 4: 1746 [2]
baggingless 4: 1746 [2]
baggy 14: 1991 [5]
bagpudding 7: 1608
bait 4: 1661 [2]
bait-bag/-poke/-time 4: 1661 [2]
baking 4: 1538 [1]
balloon satellite 15: 1958 [8A]
banana 6: 1965
band, skiffle 14: 1948 [1]
B and B 9: 1961 [1]
bands, (Father) Darby's 11: 1682
banquet 4: 1509 [2]

brass nail 10: 1934
bread 11: 1699, 11: 1952
bread and salt 8: 1575, 8: 1842
breakbeat 14: 1990 [5]
breakfast 4: 1526 [1]
breakfast, second 4: 1775 [2]
breath, lose one's 1: 1596
breath, slip one's 1: 1819
breath, yield (up) the 1: 1290
bright, honour 8: 1819 [1]
bring home 1: 1618
British/Britpop 14: 1986 [5]
broad 10: 1914
broadcasting satellite 15: 1957 [8A]
broils/broily 12: 1590 [2]
brothel/brouthell 10: 1493
bubble-gum (pop) 14: 1969 [5]
bucket, kick the 1: 1785
buff 3: 1858
buffalo 6: 1655
buffard/buffer 6: 1430
buffle/bufflehead 6: 1655
buffy 3: 1858
buggered 3: 1923
bulch(in) 7: 1582
bulk(er) 10: 1690
bulkin/bull 7: 1582
bully 7: 1475, 7: 1548
bum/bumpsy/bumsie 3: 1611
bun 7: 1587
Bunch, Mother 13: 1847 [3]
bung, go 1: 1882
bunny (girls) 7: 1587
bunting 7: 1529
burk 6: 1929
burra khana 4: 1859 [1]
bush-inn 9: 1881 [1]
bustle 11: 1763
butting 7: 1529
buttock 10: 1673
buttons, dash my 8: 1797 [6]
buy it 1: 1825
by-bit 4: 1819 [2]

cab, hackney 10: 1579
cabbage 7: 1840, 11: 1903
cabbage, my (little) 7: 1840
cable, slip one's 1: 1751
cadger 13: 1756 [2]
café complet 4: 1933 [2]

California(n) 11: 1851
call, get one's/the 1: 1884
call home 1: 1618
call to one's reward 1: 1703
calm 12: 1440 [1]
calmy 12: 1587 [1]
calypso 14: 1989 [4]
can 5: 1900 [2]
cancro 8: 1597 [4]
cang/cank 6: 1225
canned (up) 3: 1914
Cantonese/Cantopop 14: 1988 [5]
cap, feather in a 6: 1598
cap, fuddle one's 3: 1656
capot (me) 8: 1760 [4]
capsule 15: 1954 [7]
caramba 8: 1835 [8]
care a darn, don't 8: 1781 [5]
cargo 8: 1607 [4]
carley 13: 1375 [3]
carline/carling 13: 1375 [3]
carriage, hackney 10: 1579
carry-knave 10: 1630
carsey/carsy 5: 1961 [2]
case, closet 5: 1662 [2]
case, crapping 5: 1932 [1]
cash 11: 1596, 11: 1953
cash (in) one's checks/chips 1: 1869
castle, crapping 5: 1932 [1]
cat 10: 1535, 10: 1941
cat, whip the 3: 1582
catch one's death 1: 1488
catch the fox 3: 1611
cattle 11: 1330
causeway/causey (-paiker) 10: 1555
cess to, bad 8: 1859 [4]
chair, barber's 10: 1708
chamber foreign 5: 1297 [1]
champers 3: 1957
change one's life 1: 1546
checks, cash/hand/pass/send/
     throw in one's 1: 1869
chick(en) 7: 1598
chill-out music 14: 1990 [5]
chips, cash/hand/pass/send/throw
     in one's 1: 1869
chips, have one's 1: 1869
Christ 8: 1897 [6]
Christmas 8: 1897 [6]
Christmas, Jiminy 8: 1803 [6]

go home 1: 1618
gold-poll/goldilocks/golpol 7: 1568
goluptious 3: 1937
gomph 6: 1825
gong (-farmer/-hole/-house/-pit)
    5: OE [1]
good 11: 1400
goodness' sake, for 8: 1885
goodyear, what a/the 8: 1555
goof (-ball)/goofer 6: 1916
go off 1: 1605
go off the hooks 1: 1840
goose 6: 1547, 6: 1852, 6: 1916
goose, Winchester 10: 1598
goose-cap/-gabble 6: 1547
goosedom 6: 1547
goosey 6: 1852
go out of this world 1: OE
goree 11: 1699
gorm/gormless 6: 1936
gory 11: 1699
Goth 14: 1986 [2A]
go to glory 1: 1814
go to siege 5: 1400 [1]
go to the deuce 8: 1651 [4]
go (over) to the majority 1: 1687
go up the flume 1: 1865
go west 1: 1532
gowfin 6: 1570
gowk 6: 1605
GPS 15: 1960 [8A]
grandam 13: 1550 [3]
grand horizontal 10: 1888
grandmother 13: 1816 [3]
grannam 13: 1550 [3]
grannie/y 13: 1816 [3]
granny, your 13: 1816 [3]
gravel, pay 11: 1882
grave-porer 13: 1582 [2]
great horn spoon, by the 8: 1842
green(s)/greenbacks 11: 1917
green stuff 11: 1917
green swizzle 3: 1843
grig 11: 1657
grimalkin 13: 1798 [3]
grime 14: 2003 [5]
grimy 14: 1973 [2A]
grind(core) 14: 1989 [2A]
grogged/groggy 3: 1770
groin 2: 1513

ground looks blue, till all the 3:
    1813
group, skiffle 14: 1948 [1]
grub 4: 1857 [1]
grubby 14: 1973 [2A]
grunge/grungy 14: 1973 [2A]
grunyie 2: 1513
gubbins 6: 1916
guest 9: OE [1]
guest house 9: OE [1], 9: 1834
guff/guffin 6: 1570
gump/gumph/gumphead 6: 1825
gungy 14: 1973 [2A]
guzzle 3: 1843

hack(ster) 10: 1579
hackney 10: 1579, 10: 1630
hag 13: 1529 [2], 13: 1630 [2], 13:
    1375 [3]
hair, bever 13: 1275 [2]
half-cut 3: 1673
half-shaved 3: 1818
half-tanked 3: 1893
hammer 6: 1592
Hancock 6: 1577
handbag house 14: 1991 [5]
hand in one's accounts 1: 1817
hand in one's checks/chips 1: 1869
handle 2: 1708
hang/hang it (all)/hanged 8:
    1400 [4]
harbergage 9: 1400 [1]
harbergery 9: 1377 [1], 9: 1382 [1]
harbour 9: 1382 [1], 9: 1615 [1],
    9: 1617 [1]
hardcore/hard core 14: 1977 [5],
    14: 1991 [5]
hard rock 14: 1967 [2A]
harridan 13: 1699 [3]
Harry, by the Lord 8: 1693
hat, stewed to the 3: 1737
have had it 1: 1952
have one's chips 1: 1869
have the death 1: 1488
hazy 3: 1897
heart 7: 1290,7: 1305
heavenly fool 7: 1530
heaven's sake, for 8: 1885
heavy metal 14: 1973 [3]
heels, kick up the 1: 1573, 1: 1785

heels, lay up/tip up/topple up/turn
    up one's 1: 1573
hell, what the 8: 1400 [4]
hell-moth 10: 1602
hen, old 13: 1958 [3]
hence, part 1: 1325
hep 14: 1979 [5]
herbergage 9: 1400 [1]
herbergery 9: 1382 [1]
hi-fi 14: 1993 [2A]
high (as a kite/spirits) 3: 1627
high-flown 3: 1658
hillbilly 14: 1956 [2A]
hilt, up to the 8: 1598
hilts, by these 8: 1598
hip/hip-hop 14: 1979 [5]
hit pay dirt 11: 1882
hit under the wing 3: 1844
HM 14: 1973 [3]
hoary 13: 1275 [2]
hocus-pocus 8: 1825
hoddy-dod 6: 1500
hoddypeak 6: 1500, 6: 1598
hokey, by 8: 1825
hokey(s), by the 8: 1825
hokey farmer/fiddle, by the 8: 1825
home, bring/call/get/go 1: 1618
hon 7: 1375
honey 7: 1375, 7: 1587
honey, bees and 11: 1892
honey-baby/-bun/-bunch/chile/
    -sop 7: 1375
honeycomb/honeysuckle 7: 1375
honk 3: 1957
honker 2: 1948
honkers/honking 3: 1957
honour, lady of 10: 1550
honour, on/upon one's 8: 1460 [1]
honour bright 8: 1819 [1]
hood, by my 8: 1374
hooker 10: 1845
hooks, be/drop/go/pop/slip off the
    1: 1840
hooligan 6: 1929
hoot 11: 1820
hooter 2: 1958
hootoo 11: 1820
hop 14: 1979 [5]
hop, trip 14: 1994 [5]
hop off 1: 1764

hop the perch 1: 1532
hore 10: 1100
horizontal 10: 1888
horn 2: 1893, 8: 1842
horn and spoon 8: 1842
horndoon 4: 1691 [2]
horn spoon, by the (great) 8: 1842
hors d'oeuvres 4: 1688 [2]
horse-breaker 10: 1861
hospitable 9: OE [1]
host 9: OE [1], 9: 1377 [1], 9:
    1382 [1]
hostel 9: 1377 [1], 9: 1384 [1], 9:
    1687 [2]
hostelar 9: 1424 [1]
hosteler-house 9: 1424 [1]
hostelry 9: 1377 [1], 9: 1386 [1], 9:
    1424 [1]
hostery/hostry 9: 1377 [1]
host-house 9: 1570 [1]
hot damn 8: 1929 [5]
hotel 9: 1687 [2], 9: 1925 [2]
hotel garni 9: 1744 [2]
house, common 5: 1596 [1]
house, handbag 14: 1991 [5]
house, lady of the 10: 1550
house, little 5: 1750 [1], 5: 1858 [2]
house, necessary 5: 1612 [1]
house, privy 5: 1463 [1]
house, sporting 9: 1615 [1]
House of Commons 5: 1961 [2]
house of ease 5: 1662 [1]
house of easement 5: 1508 [1]
House of Lords 5: 1961 [2]
house of office 5: 1405 [1]
how mischance 8: 1330
hreohful 12: eOE [2]
huddle-duddle 13: 1599 [2]
hulver(-head) 6: 1699
Humphry 6: 1599
Humpty-Dumpty 6: 1988
Hunt, Berkeley/Berkshire 6: 1929
hunt the fox 3: 1611
hunt the gowk 6: 1605
hurry-whore 10: 1630
hutu 11: 1820

idiot 6: 1577, 6: 1598
idleton 6: 1643
independent 14: 1990 [5]

old crow 13: 1925 [3]
old dear 7: 1230
older 13: 1450 [1]
old fog(e)y 13: 1848 [1]
Old Harry 8: 1693
old hen 13: 1958 [3]
oldie 13: 1799 [1]
old man 13: eOE [2]
old Mr Goree/Gory 11: 1699
Old Nick 6: 1673
old school/skool 14: 1987 [5], 14:
    1997 [5]
old sir(e) 13: 1557 [2]
oldster 13: 1846 [1]
old tad 13: 1877 [2]
old thing 7: 1625
old trout 13: 1897 [3]
old wife/wives' tale 13: eOE [3]
omadhaun 6: 1818
ontron 4: 1691 [2]
onyon 6: 1570
oof (-bird) 11: 1885
ooftish 11: 1885
oonchook 6: 1818
oragious 12: 1590 [2]
orbiter 15: 1958 [8]
oscar 11: 1917
other side, pass to the 1: 1340
oubaas 13: 1824 [2]
outhouse 5: 1819 [1]
overflown 3: 1579
overseen 3: 1500
overshot 3: 1931
oversparred 3: 1890
over the limit 3: 1966
owl, as drunk as a boiled 3: 1886
owl, drunk as an 3: 1613
owl-eyed 3: 1613, 3: 1886, 3: 1904

P 14: 1975 [5]
pacific 12: 1633 [1]
pack off 1: 1764
pack up 1: 1925
pagan 10: 1600
pagard 3: 1923
pagart 3: 1923
paid 3: 1638
paiker 10: 1555
palace car/hotel/steamer 9:
    1870 [2]

palatic 3: 1843
pantaloon 13: 1602 [2]
papa 13: 1844 [2]
Paphian 10: 1598
parador 9: 1845 [2]
paralytic 3: 1843
parbleu 8: 1696 [8]
parlatic 3: 1843
parlor girl/house/maid) 10: 1979
parrot, pissed as a 3: 1812
part 1: 1330
pass 1: 1340, 5: 1646 [1]
passage (-house) 5: 1646 [1]
pass away 1: 1400
pass from (this world) 1: OE
pass in 1: 1904
pass in one's checks/chips 1: 1869
pass in one's marble 1: 1904
pass on 1: 1805
pass out 1: 1867
pass over 1: 1340
pass over to the majority 1: 1687
pass to one's reward 1: 1703
patriarch 13: 1819 [2]
patriarchess 13: 1639 [3]
pavé, nymph of the 10: 1563, 10:
    1900
pavement, girl of the 10: 1900
pavement princess 10: 1976
pax 8: 1592 [4]
pay dirt/gravel 11: 1882
pay one's debt to nature 1: 1513
pay the cole 11: 1673
peace, part in 1: 1325
peaceable 12: 1425 [1]
peak 1: 1532, 6: 1500
pearl, my 7: 1920
peasecod 8: 1606 [4]
peck 1: 1532
pecuniary 11: 1604
pecuny 11: 1400
peg (it/peg out) 1: 1870
peloothered 3: 1805
pelt 13: 1757 [1]
pence, sum of 11: 1290
penny 11: 1275
people, gathered to one's 1: 1382
pepst 3: 1577
perch 1: 1886

Chronological index of people

Chronological index
of general topics